T0321810

Experience–Based Human–Computer Interactions:

Emerging Research and Opportunities

Petr Sosnin
Ulyanovsk State Technical University, Russia

A volume in the Advances in Human
and Social Aspects of Technology
(AHSAT) Book Series

Published in the United States of America by
    IGI Global
    Information Science Reference (an imprint of IGI Global)
    701 E. Chocolate Avenue
    Hershey PA, USA 17033
    Tel: 717-533-8845
    Fax: 717-533-8661
    E-mail: cust@igi-global.com
    Web site: http://www.igi-global.com

Library of Congress Cataloging-in-Publication Data

Names: Sosnin, P. I., author.
Title: Experience-based human-computer interactions : emerging research and
   opportunities / by Petr Sosnin.
Description: Hershey, PA : Information Science Reference, [2018]
Identifiers: LCCN 2017012051| ISBN 9781522529873 (hardcover) | ISBN
   9781522529880 (eISBN)
Subjects: LCSH: Human-computer interaction. | Computer
   software--Development--Technique. | Experiential learning. |
   Explanation-based learning.
Classification: LCC QA76.9.H85 S6375 2018 | DDC 004.01/9--dc23 LC record available at https://
lccn.loc.gov/2017012051

This book is published in the IGI Global book series Advances in Human and Social Aspects of Technology (AHSAT) (ISSN: 2328-1316; eISSN: 2328-1324)

British Cataloguing in Publication Data
A Cataloguing in Publication record for this book is available from the British Library.

All work contributed to this book is new, previously-unpublished material.
The views expressed in this book are those of the authors, but not necessarily of the publisher.

For electronic access to this publication, please contact: eresources@igi-global.com.

Advances in Human and Social Aspects of Technology (AHSAT) Book Series

ISSN:2328-1316
EISSN:2328-1324

Editor-in-Chief: Ashish Dwivedi, The University of Hull, UK

MISSION

In recent years, the societal impact of technology has been noted as we become increasingly more connected and are presented with more digital tools and devices. With the popularity of digital devices such as cell phones and tablets, it is crucial to consider the implications of our digital dependence and the presence of technology in our everyday lives.

The **Advances in Human and Social Aspects of Technology (AHSAT) Book Series** seeks to explore the ways in which society and human beings have been affected by technology and how the technological revolution has changed the way we conduct our lives as well as our behavior. The AHSAT book series aims to publish the most cutting-edge research on human behavior and interaction with technology and the ways in which the digital age is changing society.

COVERAGE

- ICTs and social change
- Gender and Technology
- End-User Computing
- Technoself
- Technology Dependence
- Public Access to ICTs
- Cyber Behavior
- Computer-mediated communication
- Digital Identity
- Activism and ICTs

IGI Global is currently accepting manuscripts for publication within this series. To submit a proposal for a volume in this series, please contact our Acquisition Editors at Acquisitions@igi-global.com or visit: http://www.igi-global.com/publish/.

Titles in this Series

For a list of additional titles in this series, please visit:
https://www.igi-global.com/book-series/advances-human-social-aspects-technology/37145

Optimizing Human-Computer Interaction With Emerging Technologies
Francisco Cipolla-Ficarra (Latin Association of Human-Computer Interaction, Spain & International Association of Interactive Communication, Italy)
Information Science Reference • ©2018 • 471pp • H/C (ISBN: 9781522526162) • US $345.00

Designing for Human-Machine Symbiosis Using the URANOS Model Emerging Research ...
Benjamin Hadorn (University of Fribourg, Switzerland)
Information Science Reference • ©2017 • 170pp • H/C (ISBN: 9781522518884) • US $125.00

Research Paradigms and Contemporary Perspectives on Human-Technology Interaction
Anabela Mesquita (School of Accounting and Administration of Porto, Polytechnic Institute of Porto, Portugal & Algorithm Research Centre, Minho University, Portugal)
Information Science Reference • ©2017 • 366pp • H/C (ISBN: 9781522518686) • US $195.00

Solutions for High-Touch Communications in a High-Tech World
Michael A. Brown Sr. (Florida International University, USA)
Information Science Reference • ©2017 • 217pp • H/C (ISBN: 9781522518976) • US $185.00

Design Solutions for User-Centric Information Systems
Saqib Saeed (Imam Abdulrahman Bin Faisal University, Saudi Arabia) Yasser A. Bamarouf (Imam Abdulrahman Bin Faisal University, Saudi Arabia) T. Ramayah (University Sains Malaysia, Malaysia) and Sardar Zafar Iqbal (Imam Abdulrahman Bin Faisal University, Saudi Arabia)
Information Science Reference • ©2017 • 422pp • H/C (ISBN: 9781522519447) • US $215.00

Identity, Sexuality, and Relationships among Emerging Adults in the Digital Age
Michelle F. Wright (Masaryk University, Czech Republic)
Information Science Reference • ©2017 • 343pp • H/C (ISBN: 9781522518563) • US $185.00

For an enitre list of titles in this series, please visit:
https://www.igi-global.com/book-series/advances-human-social-aspects-technology/37145

701 East Chocolate Avenue, Hershey, PA 17033, USA
Tel: 717-533-8845 x100 • Fax: 717-533-8661
E-Mail: cust@igi-global.com • www.igi-global.com

Table of Contents

Preface

Year to year the complexity of our computerized environments are increased, and it leads to problems as in professional activity so in daily life. On our deep believe the root of majority problems is caused by the essential difference between natural and artificial forms of our interactions with a surrounding area. Natural forms are a basic feature of human beings who intellectually process information entering from senses while computerized forms are based on interfaces that are programmed for definite goals. Moreover, when a human interacts with a computer, both kinds of interactions will be intertwined in any case and conditions of their differences.

This gap between the two forms of interaction is the source of negative manifestations of the human factor. Especially unpredictable these negatives influence on the success in the development of computerized environments that intensively use the software. Until now, the degree of successfulness of designing the software intensive systems (SISs) is extremely low. In designing these systems, the human factor is a source of costly mistakes and failures.

When I first learned about the reports of the Standish Group Corporation, whose statistics regularly recorded success for about a third of the projects, I was shocked. It was happened about 15 years ago and has led to the research, a part of which discloses in this book. In our research, we chose the way, in which we sequentially investigated reasons of the success and failures with the viewpoint of interactions of designers with natural experience and its models. In parallel, in our practice, we use analogies with conceptual solutions used in Rational Unified Process.

Thus, step by step, we came to the idea of increasing the naturalness of human-computer interactions that can be achieved when interactions with natural experience and its models will be similar. In the ground of the work with this idea, we laid our experience of the use of question-answering in conceptual designing, taking into account such subject areas as "Concept development and experimentation" and "Design Thinking."

The choice of the conceptual stage of designing was caused by our intention to investigate an intellectual side of interactions with units of experience and their models, beginning with initial states of their creating and steps of integrating into the ordered wholeness. From this viewpoint, we took into account the experience of the subject area "Software Engineering Methods and Theory" (SOMET) that came us to project theories of the substantially evolutionary type.

Especial attention was focused on an unpredictable appearance of a new task in the real time process of designing. Processing of any new task requires active use of natural experience in conditions of the intensive use computerized technology of designing. Similar technologies can be qualified as specialized software intensive systems, interactions in which can be served as patterns for interactions in SISs developed with these technologies. And so, improving HCI aimed at effective reactions on new tasks can be used for extending the experience of the subject area of HCI.

This book discloses our understanding of questions that are implicitly concerned above and results of our research and practice as answers these questions. Basic features of our solutions include realizing of HCI in conditions of unpredictable appearance of new tasks in the context of any computerized activity when a human have the possibility for automated mental imagination and conceptual experimenting for the search of tasks solutions and preparing them for future reuse. In this book, such extending of HCI is qualified as experience-based HCI.

This book is intended for practitioners and theoreticians, whose interests are bound with the search of innovations in the subject area of HCI, and also who investigate intellectual forms of interactions with the computerized world and try to embed means of Artificial Intelligence in designing socio-cyber physical systems. As I think, this book will be useful for students whose study computers, software engineering, and their applications.

Any book is ever really written in definite conditions. Therefore, I would like to thank my colleagues at the Computer Department of t the Ulyanovs state technical university who kindly read through an earlier *version* of the book. I am especially grateful to my students and postgraduates who helped me to test numerous attempts to program the solutions of tasks arising in the process of research presented in the book.

And finally, I would like to add thanks to my wife Olga and my children, Kate and Dmitry who were the first listeners and readers of the written text. They provided a comfortable home environment for my creative work.

Chapter 1
Introduction

ABSTRACT

This first chapter provides an overview of and an introduction to the book.

1. TOWARDS IMPROVING THE HUMAN-COMPUTER INTERACTIONS

An effective, ubiquitous computerization of all spheres of human activities can be achieved only in conditions of interactions of a human with computerized environments in forms which are similar to (natural) interactions of the human with a natural environment (with the physical world). In this case, both types of interactions (natural and artificial) will be intertwined enriching each other in an implemented work.

Now, existing forms of human-computer interactions are far from the naturalness, and such the state of affairs is a source of different problems one of which is an incredibly low level of the success (about 40%) in designing the systems with an intensive use of the software.

The extremely low degree of success in developments of such systems is an important reason for searching new approaches to the designing in this subject area. One of such approaches can be connected with taking into account not only software intensity but also the intensive use of knowledge and experience in conditions of human-intensive systems. Additional intensities are directly related to the designing of systems because, in such a work, the team of designers has to creatively use the workflows with complicated toolkits that also belong to this class of systems. The integral result of these

DOI: 10.4018/978-1-5225-2987-3.ch001

intensities is a high complexity of the environment with which the designer forced to interact.

There are many kinds of complexity definitions caused by numerous kinds of its manifestations but, in any case, the complexity characterizes a view on a system with numerous elements and numerous forms of relationships among the elements. In the general explaining, the complexity expresses a measure that estimates a difficulty for a human interacting with a presentation of a corresponding system or its part with definite objectives. One of the most important of these objectives is the achievement of necessary understanding.

The system or its any component is complex if the designer (interacting with the system) does not have sufficient resources for the achievement of the necessary level of understanding or achieving the other planned aims. In most general case, the complexity or simplicity is a function of three variables – time, accuracy (variety) and volume of information. The complex system is being produced more difficulty, than the simple system. The typical way to reduce the complexity is a division of a complicated system on parts taking into account a useful set of its architectural views. In this case, designers of the system usually try to achieve a satisfactory degree of the complexity at the conceptual stage of their work.

Among other approaches that facilitate reducing the indicated complexity, one can notice the use of mature technologies of software engineering and methods and means applied in science. Last seven years, combining of these approaches is the basic goal of research and development (R&D) in the subject area SEMAT (Software Engineering Methods and Theory).

In normative documents of SEMAT, a way of working used by a team of designers is marked as a very important essence. There "way-of-working" as a notion is defined as "the tailored set of practices and tools used by the team to guide and support their work." Similar sets of practices must include subsets of units oriented on an empirical maintenance of human activity.

The above leads to following assertions:

1. We need new ways of increasing the naturalness of human-computer interactions (HCI) that must be coordinated with effective, ubiquitous computerization of all spheres of human activities.
2. One of the perspective directions for searching the indicated ways can be bound with including the experiential abilities in Human-Computer Interactions.

These ways will positively develop the subject area of Human Computer Interactions. In particular, they will facilitate increasing the successfulness of designing the SIS of any nature.

In this book, we present results of our long-term research that concerns the real-time use of question-answer interactions (QA-interactions) of designers with accessible experience in developing the systems. Accessible experience is understood as combining the natural experience of the working team and models of experience created during the process of designing. For including the use of an integrated experience into the design process, we have developed a question-answer approach and precedent-oriented approach.

The basic idea of the first approach is creating the substantially evolutionary theory of the project at its conceptual stage (substantially $\to$ in the sense of informational content). The created theory is a visualized semantic net, nodes of which are questions and answers that are formulated during stepwise refinement of statements of solved project tasks. These nodes of the semantic net can have different types corresponding the reasons of questions and appointments of answers. Any node as a certain construct of the theory is verified with the use of thought experiments and an ontology of the project. The theory is a useful artifact, interaction with components of which are reusable and based on explicit and implicit access to the experience and its models. Therefore, they can be qualified as experience-based human-computer interactions The project theory combined with the corresponding ontology, conceptual experiments (automated thought experiments) and models open a new opportunity for the improvement of conceptual designing.

The essence of the precedent-oriented approach is defined by the use of models of tasks from the viewpoint of behavioral actions of the designer who solves project tasks. These models correspond to an experimentation with behavioral units provided the future reuse of solved tasks. Models of precedents are created with the use of a specialized framework that is adjusted on intellectual processing the solutions of the task. In such processing, the designer also uses thought experiments.

2. THE STRUCTURE OF THIS BOOK

The remainder of the book is structured as follows. We begin Chapter 2 with a description of a problem that is bound to the extremely low degree of the success in the developments of software intensive systems (SISs). For indicating the features of this problems, a set of regular reports of the company "Standish Groups International, Inc." are discussed. Analysis of these reports and other publications lead to understanding an especial role of human factors in their influence on positive and negative reasons for such state of affairs. In pour deep opinion, the root reason of negatives is a lack of the naturalness of Human-Computer Interactions when a human interacts with the physical world or with a cyber-world. The chapter focuses on an empirical side of the naturalness. After that, we describe features of human behavior in the physical world and underline the role of the reuse of behavioral actions in human activity. Then we analyze the theory and practice of human interactions with computerized environments. This analysis includes comparing both versions from the viewpoint of their naturalness.

At the beginning of Chapter 3, we focus the attention on the use of theories in software engineering and the becoming of the theories in designing the systems. As a result, we chose substantially evolutionary theories as a more appropriate class for its application in designing the system. Such type of theories is especially appropriate for conceptual designing that is impossible without research by designers of numerous and practically unpredictable situations of a task type. In such situations, the designer should behave as a researcher who uses the appropriate type of the research in which the personal and collective experience are applied in the real time. In these actions, the designer explicitly or implicitly builds and uses models representing the items of experience that reflect processes of experimenting or their results. We mark that, in such experimenting, the designers operate with definite conceptual objects. Then, we describe a number of typical conceptual objects used in designing. After that, we focus our attention on the subject area "Concept Development and Experimentation" and "Design Thinking" as the richest sources of prompts for our attempts to make a positive contribution to Human-Computer Interactions based on the real-time use of the experience. At the end of the chapter, we analyze the possibility of automating the experimental activity in conceptual designing.

At the end of Chapter 3, we describe our approach to the theorization of the project in the conceptual stage of the life cycle. The main feature of this approach is the use of question-answer analysis in applying the stepwise refinement to work with statements of project tasks. It was the reason to call the approach as "Question-Answer approach" or shortly QA-approach. The use of this approach leads to substantially evolutionary theory, which is visually observed in the form of a semantic net in the monitor screen. Such implementation of the approach is oriented on the use of the toolkit WIQA

(Working In Questions and Answers), that has been developed in our research. In an environment of this toolkit that includes a semantic memory of the question-answer type (QA-memory), designers can use thought experiments (conceptual experiments) for substantiating the constructs of the project theory.

In conceptual experimenting, designers use analogies with the work of scientists when conducting experiments. Moreover, they simulate such behavior with the help of conceptually algorithmic (pseudocode) programs that describe the plans for the experimentation. Thus, designers investigate the programmed plans of experiments that they prepare. They conduct and describe the results of experimenting with the use of understandable and checkable forms, for the future reuse.

The offered version of conceptual experimenting has following features:

1. Conceptual experiments are conducted by designers in the conceptual space (C-space) conceptual artifacts of which are accessible as visualized objects stored in the QAmemory.
2. The C-space unites conceptual models of components of the operational space, including models of designers, occupational tasks, ontology and units modeling the applied experience.
3. Such C-space is interpreted as the area of conceptual thinking that is aimed at the conceptual development of systems with the software. Developing of systems, designers create the C-space in the QA-memory, and they interact with this space for achieving the useful purposes.

In Chapter 4, we disclose the structure and features of a semantic memory that is embedded to the toolkit WIQA. This memory is intended for saving the constructs of our version of the project theory. Reifying the cells of the memory is fitted on the semantics of questions and answers that can have various types. A potential of the question-answer memory is sufficient for uploading the models of project tasks combined in a tree of the task of designed project. In this tree, any task is presented by its model of question answer type (QA-model), that registers question-answer reasoning in a form of a specialized protocol (QA-protocol), items of which correspond to constructs of the project theory (its principles, settings, requirements, restrictions, assertions, cautions, reasons, cause and effects, motives, aims and the other kinds of constructs). Items are combined and visualized in the form of the semantic net. At the end of the chapter, we describe the specialized algorithmic language of the pseudocode type that is specified above the QA-memory.

The content of Chapter 5 presents details question-answer approach to the conceptual design of software intensive systems. For describing the approach, the retrospective style is used. At first, the history of the conducted research is presented through its directions, some of which are finished while the others are active now. Each of stages is bound with basic obtained results. The chapter contains the description of first three stages. In the first stage, the following results were obtained:

1. The system of architectural views on the use of question-answer reasoning in conceptual designing of SISs.
2. The framework of a question-answer model of the task (QA-model).
3. The toolkit for the use of question-answering in the process of designing.
4. The way of question-answer modeling in solutions of project tasks.

At the second stage, the essence of its results defined the interpretation of the database (intended for the keeping of QA-models) as the semantic memory of the question-answer type (QA-memory). Obtained results include following items: constructive data view on QAmodels that has led to specifying the specialized type of data called QA-data; pseudocode language adjusted on programming the tasks with QA-objects; instrumental environment for conceptually algorithmic programming. The third stage focuses on reflections of basic artifacts of operational space of designing the family of SISs on the semantic memory. For each of such reflections, its description includes following positions: formalized specification, a way for its materialization for the corresponding artifact, necessary technological practices.

The chapter 6 begins with a description of our framework for models of precedents. This framework combines a number of components each of which opens the model from the definite view of the intellectual process in the solution of the corresponding task. The framework specifies textual, logical, analytical, graphical and algorithmic views. After that, the description includes following results: features of the stepwise refinement in creating the models of the precedents; the way (method) of the conceptual solutions of tasks; the life cycle of the precedent model; iterative creating the model of the definite precedent; the structure of the precedent-oriented Experience Base.

Any new precedent model accumulates a system of conceptual objects composition of which was absent before the (conceptual) solution of the definite project task.

In the C-space, its processes are managed by interactions with the experience, the typical units of which are models of precedents. Models of precedents obviously or implicitly reflect the regularities of the C-space or, by other words, "laws" of this space. These regularities reflect regularities of the operational space (regularities of the subject area of SISs, norms of the used technology, requirements and restrictions managed by developing of SISs).

The chapter_6 presents the second our approach that concerns the use for tasks their models providing the controlled reuse. For this, we reflect the work with tasks on their models as precedents built with the use of analogies with "intellectually processed conditioned reflexes." The use of conceptual experimenting suggests intellectual processing the solutions of tasks and their results. Conducted experiments are embedded into such activity. The important role in processing fulfills building the statements of tasks and real-time interaction of the designer with textual components of this statement. Such actions are impossible without the controlled use of a controlled vocabulary of the applied language. That is why a specialized subsystem for the real-time creation and use of project ontologies was embedded into the toolkit WIQA.

The creation and use of project ontologies are the content of Chapter 7. Any created ontology helps to achieve the following positive effects: reaching the coordinated understanding in collective actions; using the controlled vocabulary; extracting the questions from generated texts and reasoning; systematizing the methods and means used in an occupational activity; specifying the conceptualization; checking the semantics of the built text and applied reasoning; operating with machine-readable and machine-understandable content.

In QA-approach, the use of the ontology is oriented on all called effects and the systematization of models embedded into the Base of Experience. Also, it is planned to create such models with the use of conceptual experimenting when designers solve the project tasks in the real time. If it is important, the designer can use programmed forms of the access to the ontology in executed actions or, by the other words, the designer can use Programmable Human-Computer Interactions with Ontology.

Chapter 8 focuses on semantic modeling of a mental imagery caused by processing of a new project task in real-time designing when designers conduct necessary conceptual experiments. In such cases, for each experiment, the responsible designer should define and embody necessary conditions in the C-space where these conditions will be mentally perceived and provoke the phenomenon of the mental imagery in the mind of the designer.

In the toolkit WIQA, for an explicit expression of conditions, the designer can use textual and graphical means or their combination. In its last version, this toolkit supports figuratively semantic maintenance of the designer's activity in precedent-oriented solving the project tasks and, in parallel, conducting the necessary conceptual experiments. The base of this maintenance is the real-time use of a specialized graphical editor that provides creating the following versions of interrelated visual images:

1. Prolog-oriented versions of visual images in the form of the figuratively semantic schemes that are coordinated with their Prolog-like descriptions.
2. Pictured versions of visual images any of which can be drawn by the designer with the use of units of the chosen palette.
3. Conceptually algorithmic versions of images, examples of which express the programmatic point of view on the precedent sub-model PI.

Moreover, any visual image of any type can be transformed to the executed program, correction of which is reflected in the image. Indicated possibilities help to organize controlled intertwining of images for achieving the useful aims, first of all for achieving the necessary level of understanding.

Chapter 2

Lack of Naturalness in Human–Computer Interactions

ABSTRACT

There is a problematic difference between interactions of a human with natural and computer environments. The negatives of this difference are particularly painful in the design of software intensive systems, the success of which is unpredictable and extremely low. The root reason for such state of affairs is a very high complexity with which the designers have deals. What we name as "Complexity" is a characteristic of estimations that is discovered in interactions of a human or humans with perceived essences. Therefore, for example, designers need means that will help them in interactions with environments of their activity during real-time work. This chapter tries to show that one of the possible directions of mastering the complexity is bound with the possibility for designers to create conditions of interactions that are similar to conditions of natural interactions. In this case, both types of interactions will be intertwined in coordination in search of simplifying an arisen complexity.

1. PROBLEMS OF HUMAN-COMPUTER ACTIVITY

1.1. Features of Designing the Software Intensive Systems

The development and continuous improvement of Socio-Cyber-Physical reality (SCP-Reality) are useful to understand how artificial evolutionary process

DOI: 10.4018/978-1-5225-2987-3.ch002

that intertwines with the natural processes on Earth, including the processes of life. In this interlacement, artificial and natural processes influence each other so that this leads to important events {ei}, the estimations of which are useful for future.

Particularly, similar events correspond to situations of completing the work of designers on projects of software intensive system (SISs). The reality of indicated kind of designing and characteristics of its results have shown that exists a problem with achieving the predictable success in this kind of activity.

Before describing this problem, it needs to present this class of systems. Below, in the text, we will orient on the following definition "A software intensive system is a system where software represents a significant segment in any of the following points: system functionality, system cost, system development risk, development time" (Software Intensive systems, 2006).

In general, this definition admits that software intensive system may include social, physical and software components interacting with each other. Thus, we can assume that now and in the future, the software intensive systems (SIS) are and will be the main components of SCPRealty.

This book focuses on increasing the naturalness of HCI, the current state of which is most fully disclose the problems of designing the SISs. That is why, below, the text of the book will explicitly or implicitly concern this kind of systems. Furthermore, software systems we will qualify as a subclass of SISs, and this will allow us the use of the name "system" as for SISs so for software system when it is not principal.

More particularly, our choice of designing the SISs as a source of used artificial and natural processes and problems in their intertwining was caused by the following:

1.   Development of SISs requires the use of the rich experience of software engineering and the experience of different subject areas.
2.   The accumulated experience of designing includes a part that supports the continuous improvement of processes, workforces, and products.
3.   There is a richest statistics of the success and failures of the completed projects based on software.
4.   Numerous and varied developments of different SISs have also led to the creation of mature technologies, the workflows of which help to creatively solve the tasks of different types.
5.   In the life cycle processes, designers create and use varied forms of HCI that support personal and collaborative work of designers in the real-time.

Returning to the problems of achieving the success in designing the systems, it is useful to analyze the reports that regularly published by Standish Group (Reports, 2016). Each of these reports evaluates the definite set of completed projects regarding their successfulness. In the report, evaluated projects are distributed on three classes with the following characteristics: "success," "failure," and "challenged."

The first report that was called "Chaos Report" was published in the 1994 year. In the name of this report, its adjective "chaos" reflected an extremely low degree of the success in designing the software systems because only 16% of projects have been estimated as successful. Other reports register similarly unacceptable results that presented in Figure 1.

In all records up to 2012, their developers used following criteria for the distribution of classes: all promised requirements (onTarget) within the planned time (onTime) for the allocated budget (onBudjet).

It should be noted, this set of criteria (called the Iron Triangle) is understood and used as a classical base for estimation of the management processes in developments of systems. Thus, marked reports of the Standish Group reflected the success only with the side of the project management.

In its use, the word "success" is understood as a multifaceted concept, and such its feature should find the appropriate reflection in the developing the systems for measuring their success. Therefore, for an adequate evaluation of the success of the certain system, stakeholders should use the characteristics of the life cycle of this system.

That is why, there are many publications, authors of which suggest other versions of criteria' sets. It was caused by other versions of understanding and specifying the success and failure. For example, we mark following versions of specifications:

Figure 1. Retrospective of success estimations

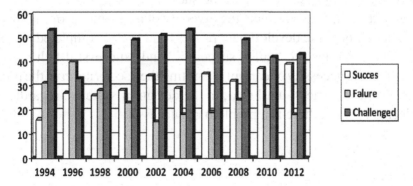

1. In paper (Wasmun 1993) that was published before the 1994 year, its authors interpreted the success as a multidimensional construct, integrating: System quality (measuring the developed system), information quality (measuring the system's output), user satisfaction, system use, individual impact (effect on behavior)and organizational impact user (effect of organizational performance).

2. In 2008, the authors of paper (El Emam and Koru, 2008) suggested a set of criteria, including three dimensions: Project management success (on-time, on-budget, sponsor satisfaction, steering group satisfaction, project team satisfaction, customer/user satisfaction, stakeholder satisfaction), technical success (customer/user satisfaction, stakeholder satisfaction, system implementation, met requirements, system quality, system use), and business success (business continuity, met business objectives, delivery benefits).

Also, some works, such as (Jørgensen and Moløkken, 2006) and (Glass 2005), criticized and evaluated the criteria used by Standish Group as not reflecting the reality of the system with software.

Given the criticism and improving the used approach, the Standish Group "has redefined project success as onTime, onBudget with a satisfactory result, that integrates subordinated criteria on-target (% requirements) and satisfied (very high to very low), value (very high to very low) and on strategic corporate goal (precise to distant)" (Chaos, 2014)

Widening the set of criteria leads to the change of the distribution picture on the classes indicated in Figure 1. Into this picture, the Standish Group included orthogonal measures that correspond to value-based view on characteristics of analyzed projects. Moreover, in (Haze, 2015) they presented comparing of statistics from the success driven and value driven views. For instance, Table 1 shows the part of this comparing where the first line emphases the different approach to estimations of the success.

Even part of this table reflects the diversity of assessments of the success from standpoints of the development process and use of completed projects. This diversity can lead to "failed successes" and "successful failures" that points out on the necessity of careful weighting the used criteria of the project evaluation. Nevertheless, until now, in the design of systems, regardless of the selected criteria, there is a problem of success.

Table 1. Comparing the orthogonal views on the success

SUCCESS VALUE COMPARISON		
Attribute	**Success Driven**	**Value Driven**
Measurement	Triple Constraints	Company Benefits
Scope Of Measurement	Individual Projects	Portfolio of Projects
Domain	It Management	Business Management
Company Culture	Avoiding Risk	Risk Tolerant
Managed	Project Managers	Product Owners
Supervision	PMO	Executive Sponsors
Project Stakeholders	Absent & Reluctant	Engaged & Inspired
Governance Process	Heavy	Light
Compliance Orientation	Reporting	Results
General Orientation	Process	People
Kill Switch	Recommended	Not Recommended
Budget Process	Per Project	Portfolio (Breadbasket)
Product Delivery	Slow	Rapid
PM Tool Usage	Heavy & Dependent	Light & Independent
Application Types	Static	Ground Breaking
	Clearly Defined	Vaguely Defined

1.2. Factors of Success and Failures

As told above, statistics accumulated in Base of the Standish Group are the important source of information for its use in the research aimed at the search of ways for increasing the degree of the success in designing the systems. The central place in this information occupies the detected factors of the success and failures. Each report does not only disclose the lists of these factors but also arranges them according to the degree of their influence in positives or negatives. Combining this information in tables for each criterion prompts possible directions for the research of the successfulness problem. One of these tables is Table 2 that shows success factors with ranks to ten.

Factors called in Table 2 present conditions of designing the violation of which can lead to failures. In reports, each of these success factors has a definition that helps to organize and realize the corresponding conditions for the fulfilled project. Reports also contain useful information about failure factors. So, both of such sources of information can be used by designers for the rational project management.

Table 2. CHAOS Report Success Factors by Rank

Factor	1994	1998	2000	2002	2006	2008	2010	2012
User Involvement	1	1	2	1	1	1	2	2
Executive Management Support	2	2	1	2	2	2	1	1
Clear Statement of Requirements	3	6	7					
Proper Planning	4	8						
Realistic Expectations	5							
Smaller Project Milestones	6	5						
Competent Staff	7	7		10	8	8	8	4
Ownership	8	9						
Clear Vision and Objectives	9	3	4	4	3	3	3	7
Hard-Working, Focused Staff	10							
Project Management		4	3	3	6	7	7	5
Minimized Scope			5	5				
Standard Tools and Infrastructure			6	7	10	10	10	10
Formal Methodology			8	8	9			
Reliable Estimates			9	9				
Agile Requirements Process					6	5	6	
Optimizing Scope/Optimization					4	5	5	3
Financial Management					7		4	4
Emotional Maturity						4		6
Execution						9	9	9
Other		10	10					

For the new set of criteria used in reports of the Standish Group after redefining (2012 year) the concept "success" and for other sets of criteria, it is also possible to build the corresponding tables that help to enumerate all kinds of success and failure factors called in reports and results of investigations. As told above, additionally to the other factors, these tables will include descriptions of conditions that will influence on achieving the satisfactions of stakeholders.

Thus, collections of revealed factors explicitly or implicitly point out on potential directions of the research that could lead to positives in achieving the success in designing the systems. One of such directions is the search of innovations in the subject area of HCI.

For example, the Table 2 includes the factor "User involvement" that is located there at top positions. In general, this factor reflects an activity of potential users who interact with designers and states of the designed system in chosen points of its life cycle. Effects of this activity essentially depend on how it is organized, what methods and means of interactions are used and from answers the other questions that can be additionally stated and investigated.

Factors "Clear Vision and Objectives" and "Competent Staff" are also implicitly related to CHI the innovations in which can facilitate to increasing the success in the development of systems. The first of these factors points out the achievement of the necessary understanding by the team of designers at early steps of them works with the conception of the project that should be developed. For example, in the master technology "Rational Unified Process," these works are conducted in the frame of interactive workflows "Business Modelling" that are led to the creation of a very important artifact "Vision." In this technology and the others, the competent staff must use interactive workflows accompanying the phase and steps of developing the systems.

As told above, evaluating the success, it needs to take into account the satisfaction of stakeholders of all categories (customers, users, members of the team, managers and the others). The greater part of these evaluations should be based on results of stakeholders' interactions of CHI-kinds with processes and products of works in the life cycle of systems.

Generalizing, we note that the domain of developing the systems has the rich potential for the HCI-research aimed at not only to increase the success in this subject area but also to increase the effectiveness of the human-computer activity. That is why, in this book, this domain was chosen for representing the SCP-Reality in the search of novelties in HCI.

2. PROBLEMS OF COMPLEXITY

2.1. Complexity and its Overcoming

The extremely low degree of success in developments of systems is an important reason for searching new approaches to the designing in this subject area. One of such approaches can be connected with taking into account not only software intensity but also the intensive use of knowledge and experience in conditions of human-intensive systems. Additional intensities are directly related to the designing of systems because, in such a work, the team of designers has to creatively use the workflows with complicated toolkits that also belong to the class of systems (SISs). The integral result of these intensities is a high complexity of the environment with which the designer forced to interact.

There are many kinds of complexity definitions caused by numerous kinds of its manifestations but, in any case, the complexity characterizes a view on a system with numerous elements and numerous forms of relationships among the elements. In the general explaining, the complexity expresses a measure that estimates a difficulty for a human interacting with a presentation of a corresponding system or its part with definite objectives. One of the most important of these objectives is the achievement of necessary understanding.

The system or its any component is complex if the designer (interacting with the system) does not have sufficient resources for the achievement of the necessary level of understanding or achieving the other planned aims. In most general case, the complexity or simplicity is a function of three variables – time, accuracy (variety) and volume of information. The complex system is being produced more difficulty, than the simple system.

Often enough various interpretations of Kolmogorov measure (Li M. and Vitanui, 2008) are applied for estimations of a degree of the system complexity. This measure is connected with "the minimal length of program P providing the construction of system S from its initial description D." Distinctions in interpretations are usually caused by features of system S, and also what contents are connected with constructs P and D and how these contents are defined.. In any interpretation, P-construct reflects an activity of creators who use appropriate technologies and toolkits in the development of the system. Thus, the process of developing the system corresponds P-program, which disclose this process (P-process) with the viewpoint of "programming."

In creating the system, the programs of the P-type are being built by step by step into the process of designing with using the certain "method of programming M." The reality of such a work demonstrates that the complexity of "P-program" no less than the complexity of the system in its any used state. Moreover, any use of M-programming that provides the construction of a P-program should be built on the basis of the same initial description D of the system S. It can be presented by the following chain $D \rightarrow M \rightarrow P \rightarrow S$.

Named relations between D, M, P can be used by designers for disuniting the process of designing on stages $[D(t_0) \rightarrow M_1 \rightarrow P_1 \rightarrow S(t_1)]$, $[D(t_1) \rightarrow M_2 \rightarrow P_2 \rightarrow S(t2)]$, ..., $[D(t_i) \rightarrow M_{i+1} \rightarrow P_{i+1} \rightarrow S(t_{i+1})]$, ..., $[D(t_{n-1}) \rightarrow M_n \rightarrow P_n \rightarrow S(t_n)]$ where a set $\{S(t_i)\}$ collects the states of creating system.

A division of a design process into stages is a typical decision in any modern technology that involves the creation of systems. In different technologies, such an approach is used in different forms for different aims among which is reducing the degree of the complexity. So, this approach helps to decrease the complexity of the interactions with the system in any of its state $S(t_i)$.

The division on stages, each of which leads to creating the corresponding state $S(t_i)$, can be detailed because the system in any state consists of related parts and so on till components $\{C_j(t_i)\}$ that correspond to the project tasks $\{Z_j(t_i)\}$ distributed among members of the team. By other words, the complexity of any component $C_j(t_i)$ is estimated (first of all) by the designer who is responsible for the solution of the corresponding task $Z_j(t_i)$. This case can be presented by the chain of reflections $DCj(ti-1) \rightarrow Mij \rightarrow Pij \rightarrow C(ti)$, 2-1 where $DCj(t_{i-1})$ is an initial description of the component $C_j(t_i)$. This chain is given only to show that the Kolmogorov approach to estimating the complexity is applicable not only to the whole system but also for its components at different levels of detail. Chains of reflections will be used below only in general reasoning.

Consequently, the Kolmogorov measure of the complexity can be applied to any stage and components of designing the system, including stages on which designers work with conceptual representations of systems. However, we note, that until now, the viewpoint of programming on the designer activity has not been supported instrumentally in the early design stages.

Returning to the meaning of the word <complexity>, in order to disclose the feature of its understanding, that will be used below, we give the following details of its content:

1. For a useful management of the complexity of designing the system, the question about of measured value of the complexity is not so essential. Suffice representation of the value, which helps to answer the question "How designers can reduce complexity?" When designers use Kolmogorov's measure, a division of M- and P-programs on parts is a way for decreasing the complexity.

2. The complexity of the system is an objective characteristic, the value of which depends largely on the complexity of the construction of the system represented by software models in a way that facilitates understanding, research, and modification. The main purpose of these programming models (such as P, P-models) - to master the complexity and try to reduce it without attempts to measure.

3. P–programs, which will be discussed below, are models (P-models) of a collective humancomputer activity, that aim at solutions of project tasks and their compositions in the process of conceptual designing the system. At this stage, due to the construction and execution of the corresponding P-programs, the team of designers creates the conceptual project of the system. The choice of the conceptual design stage is because without mastering the complexity at this stage by designers there is no reason to believe that the system development will be successful.

4. Mastering the complexity is based on the experience of the team of designers and used models, which should be presented in a way that facilitates the construction of the P-models and their use. In order to increase the effectiveness of conceptual designing in achieving the success, the collective experience and the system of its models (experience base) should be continuously improved. The current state of collective experience and its model will be called below as affordable or available experience.

5. Particularly important part of the available experience is associated with the technology of development of the system and its mastering by the team of designers. The use of the applied technology can be interpreted as an execution of appropriate technological programs (T-programs) supported the creation of the system. Any of such T-program has the definite structure that can be extracted from the technology guides that helps the designer to understand the technology at a level sufficient for its use. Note, the T-program built by designers for creating the definite system occupies the central place in the corresponding P-program.

6. The above reasoning about the complexity in designing the systems helps us to simply clarify our position on the process of designing with the programmatic point of view. By this view, P-programs include behavioral actions that correspond to normative instructions described in manuals on the technology and tools. These actions are fulfilled by designers in coordination with other actions of computerized workflows.

7. Algorithmic schemes of workflows (correspondent to T-programs) with their detailed tasks help to designers in mastering the complexity of some processes in designing the systems, but they do not reflect the complexity of the problem-solving in the subject areas of created systems. Schemes (models) of workflows are nothing more than sources of templates, copies of which are included in the actual processes of developing the systems, whose scheme is often significantly different from the stereotyped

8.   For the definite P-program, designers are usually forced to build "program" components for solutions of necessary tasks that reflect the domain of the corresponding system. Designers build such components in the real time of designing when they use and evolve accessible experience.

The system approach to the controlled division of the P-process on parts is not the only approach that helps to manage the complexity in conceptual designing the systems. Among other approaches we mark a view on the P-process from the position of the initiative SEMAT

(Software Engineering Methods and Theory), which was claimed in 2009 (Jacobson, 2009). Nowadays, this initiative has been got the normative grounds (Jacobson, 2012) that is reflected with the framework shown in Figure 2.

With the use of specialized concepts "Alphas" (Abstract-Level Progress Health Attributes), this framework discloses a related net of important aspects that must find their materialization in the development of software systems. Alphas are intended for coordinated evaluating the states of corresponding parts of areas of concerns that help, first of all, to separate from each other "Things to Work With".

In the general case, all of these things are formed in designing the system and their preliminary and controlled separation facilitates reducing the complexity for those persons who will participate in the process. Furthermore, in the SEMAT-approach, such process is implemented by the method (Way-

Figure 2. Framework of areas of concerns (inherited from (Jacobson, 2012))

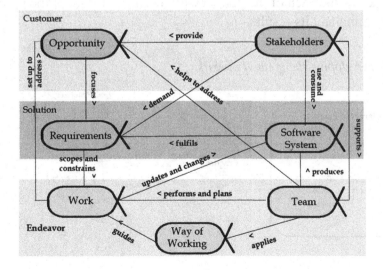

of-Working) that combines the SEMAT-kernel with best practices chosen by designers for realizing the definite endeavor (Figure 3). By definition (Jacobson et al 2012), Way-of-Working is "the tailored set of practices and tools used by a team to guide and support their work."

The SEMAT-approach not only defines the presented framework, but it also suggests the rich practice library that helps to organize and manage the activity aimed at the creation of the software system. Additionally, to Things to Work With, normative documents specify a set of "Things to Do," "Needed Skills" including competency, and "Support Materials." All of these resources are accessible and used in conditions where they can be added with the help of other necessary resources.

Let us note, initially; the SEMAT-approach has been developed for software engineering, but its basic ideas already have found their application in system engineering, for example in the version presented in Figure 4.

The possibility of inheritance is caused by a similarity of human activities when developers create complex systems. Moreover, for the team applying the SEMAT-approach in developing the software part of the system, the possibility becomes the expedient necessity.

Returning to the SEMAT-approach, we note the following:

1. At present, this approach is at the stage of professional becoming and its achieved state can be used for practical applications that, in its turn, can serve as useful sources for the approach improvement.
2. Alphas of the kernel and relations among them clearly indicate the need for effective interactions as among persons involved in the processes of works so and each of the person with the current state of the process of designing and its results.

Figure 3. Developing the method of work

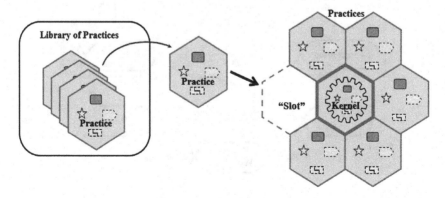

Figure 4. Framework for system engineering

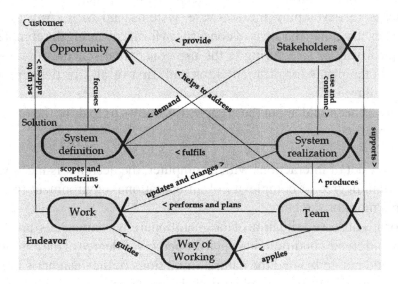

3. Becoming of the SEMAT-approach is a vivid example of the need for rethinking not only the foundations of software engineering but grounds of human-computer activity including HCI also.

Thus, in this book, we reference on SEMAT because it is one of the last attempts to find more rational ways of professional activity in the software developments that correspond the essence of human activity. It so happened, that in its current state, the SEMAT-approach only partially cover the following aspects:

- Theoretical foundations of the proposed approach (in SEMAT-glossary the word "theory" is absent);
- Dynamics of activity and its "engine" taking into account iterative process and its multitasking;
- The creatively intellectual behavior of persons who use an accessible experience when they participate in the development processes.

Therefore, marked aspects (and not only in the context of the SEMAT-approach) point out important directions for improving the human-computer activity. These directions lead to the need for innovations in designing the SISs.

It should be additionally noted, except SEMAT, there are many other approaches to developing the software systems and SISs. Any of these approaches structures the areas of concerns in forms reducing the complexity. The typical way of structuring is the use conceptual schemes that can be applied as templates for different aims and, first of all, for the support of understanding.

What has been said about the complexity, allows us to draw the following conclusions:

1. In any act of interactions with a computer, the designer is faced with a certain degree of complexity of an operational environment reflected on a monitor screen.
2. For any observed situation of the operational environment, its developers should create conditions in which the perceived degree of the complexity should not go beyond the natural limitations of the designer's mind.
3. In cases, where the complexity of the perceived conditions is beyond natural limits of the mind, it would be useful to provide the operational environment by reducing the complexity.

2.2. Technological Aspects of Human-Computer Interactions

As told above, the rational management of the degree of the complexity positively influences on an effectiveness of human interactions with the computer. The typical version of such management is a division of an observable complex (structure) on parts. In designing the systems, designers interact with different kinds of complexes that are better to classify, and this work can be fulfilled with the use of different viewpoints. On the strategic level, frameworks described in the previous subsection are useful sources for the choice of appropriate viewpoints and structuring.

One of the basic principal of the SEMAT-approach is appropriate extensions of the kernel by appropriate practices. Such extension leads not only to ontological details but also to the extension of lexis that finds their controlled usage in reasoning, requirements and restrictions, documents and other artifacts including items of HCI.

That is why and only hypothetically, we disclose a number of entities that correspond such areas of concerns as "Solution" and "Endeavor." In disclosing the details, we start with references on the technology Rational

Unified Process (RUP). Our choice RUP is due to its accepted estimate how rich, well thought-out and implemented a system of the best technological practices. In detailing, we will use terms of the RUP-glossary without specifying their strict definitions.

The interesting attempt to present the RUP in the SEMAT-notations is described in (GonzálezPérez et al., 2014) where authors applied the kernel RUP that was combined with its ground practices shown in Figure 5. Furthermore, these practices were distributed by authors between areas "Solution" (Manage requirements, Use component-based architecture, Visual model software, Verify Software Quality) and "Endeavor" (Develop software iteratively, Control changes to software.

By the SEMAT-glossary (http://semat.org/documents/20181/27952/conceptual_glossary.pdf/741a889f-332c-48fe-9af0-62334eeaf767), any practice is "a repeatable approach to doing something with a specific objective in mind. A practice describes how to handle a specific aspect of a software engineering endeavor, including the descriptions of all relevant elements necessary to express the desired work guidance that is required to achieve the purpose of the practice. A practice can be defined as a composition of other practices." This definition leads to the second version of separating the RUP on practices shown in Figure 6.

Figure 5. Emulation of RUP at the level of principles

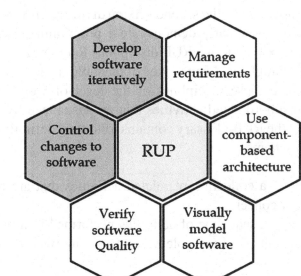

Figure 6. Emulation of RUP

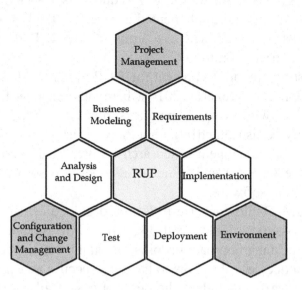

In the second version, the RUP is a composition of the six disciplines (workflows, Business Modeling, Requirements, Analysis and Design, Implementation, Test, Deployment) and three support disciplines (Project Management, Configuration and Change Management, Environment) that are cross-catting among four phases (Inception, Elaboration, Construction and Transition) of works and their iterations. It should be noted, that actions of the first composition are intertwined among phases in a very complicated manner while components of the second version divide workflows on classes and parts that are more clearly demonstrate a programmatic approach to reducing the complexity. For two RUP-disciplines Requirements 7 (only for demonstating the complicated complexes of technological works).

Schemes disclose these disciplines at the level of workflows (RWX and PMWY) and subordinated activities that are visualized by pentagonal icons. Let us note; the RUP-glossary contains following definitions of terms corresponding in schemes:

1. "A discipline is a collection of related activities that are related to a major" area of concern."
2. "A workflow is a sequence of activities performed in a business that produces a result of observable value to an individual actor of the business."

Figure 7. Emulation of RUP at the level of workflows

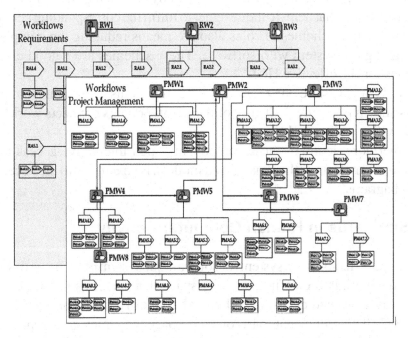

3. "A workflow detail is a grouping of activities which are performed in close collaboration to accomplish some result. The activities are typically performed either in parallel or iteratively, with the output from one activity serving as the input to another activity. Workflow details are used to group activities to provide a higher level of abstraction and to improve the comprehensibility of workflows."

4. "Activity is a unit of work that provides a meaningful result in the context of the project. It has a clear purpose, which usually involves creating or updating artifacts. Every activity is assigned to a specific role. Activities may be repeated several times, especially when executed in different iterations."

One can note, all indicated definitions include the term "activity" underlining that the corresponding unit of the work is fulfilled by the designer who plays the definite role. In its general understanding, "a role defines the behavior and responsibilities of an individual, or a set of individuals working together as a team, within the context of a software development organization. A role is responsible for one or more artifacts and performs a set of activities" (Borges, Machado and Ribeiro, 2012).

The RUP supports the use of a set of roles any of which leads to the definite interactive model that helps to the designer to fulfill the corresponding behavior. Thus, interactive schemes of roles also are means reducing the complexity of designing the system with software. These schemes are a good class of examples for the effective HCI.

In RUP, artifacts are one more class of components of visualized models. As it is shown in Figure 8, the use of these components connects workflows and activities inside workflows.

Furthermore, icons of these components open interactive access to the templates of artifacts or their visualized models, for example, to the necessary UML-diagrams.

2.3. Standards in Human Computer Activity

In developing the software system (or software subsystem of SIS), the designer fulfills the work in the definite activity space that specifies in the SEMAT-glossary as "a placeholder for something to be done in the software engineering endeavor." The important part of this space occupies a computerized environment with which designers interact using an appropriate experience with definite aims when fulfilling the work in the real time. In any item of interaction, the designer perceives the definite view on the chosen state of the

Figure 8. Relations among artifacts in RUP

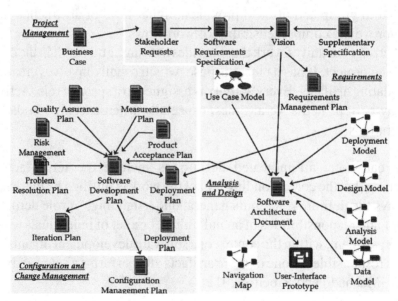

computerized environment. In the general case, the chosen state combines the states of the system being developed and the used part of way-of-working.

The first of these states reflects the future system that will be exploited in the definite subject domain D. The development of any of such systems is impossible without the use of experience E^D that corresponds to the domain D. Usually, developers of the system acquire the needed volume of E^D in the process of developing. On this base, they must express the acceptable degree of complexity in adequate requirements to computerized interfaces embedded into the system. Such requirements must reflect the comfortable access to the necessary experience and its real-time usage by future users. This experience will include not only experience E^D but also the technological experience E^T_1 that will be necessary for the use of way-of-working embedded to the system by its developers.

The second of indicated states corresponds to the applied technology and toolkits, creators of which should ensure an acceptable degree of complexity in any points of potential interactions of developers with the used way-of-working. Usually, best practices and corresponding instrumental means are developed as independent from potential domains of their applications, but these components of the activity space also reflect corresponding technological experience E^T_2 that must be easy mastered and comfortably used by developers of the future system.

Thus, in providing the acceptable degree of complexity for developers who will interact with computerized components of the activity space, it needs to create conditions, where they will effectively master and use marked above kinds of experience (E^D, E^T_1 and E^T_2). By other words, in conditions of human-computer interactions, developers of the system should be provided by means that support access and use of the necessary experience in the real-time. This recommendation, which is best understood as a requirement, is extended to the creators of systems such as way-of-working. Let us remind, in accordance with the SEMAT approach; necessary way-of-working is better to build by developers of the definite system during the process of their work.

In any version of developing the technology and corresponding toolkit, its creators should use appropriate sources of experience E^T, among which we can mark standards.

For conceptual stage of designing, the important place occupies standards accumulating the experience of architectural solutions. There are two well-known standards provided developing a system architecture −IEEE-1471 and ISO 42010. The main idea of both of these standards is developing an architecture as an appropriate set of architectural views, any of which discloses the system with a certain viewpoint. More strictly, fin accordance with the standard ISO 42010, the normative structure of the architecture is shown in Figure 9.

Explicit construction and use of architecture in the development of systems have repeatedly demonstrated significant positive effects. In more detail, the architecture:

1. Contributes to extracting of requirements and combining them in the system;
2. Clearly shows a set of early design decisions;
3. Prescribes the organizational structure of the system (well-structured systems are full of samples);
4. Plays the role of a common architectural basis for software product lines;
5. Makes it possible to consider, negotiate and predict the quality characteristics, including the results of its research;
6. Provides information on the distribution of work and calendar plans;
7. Makes it possible to more accurately assess the cost and schedule of work;
8. Reduce the risks;
9. Is the first form of existence of the system, which can be verified (tested) as a whole;

Figure 9. Framework of system architecture (inherited from IEEE-1471)

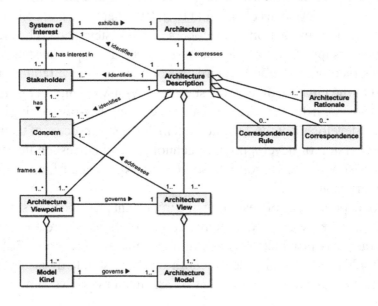

10. Provides the ability to transfer or reuse of architectural styles and skeletons;
11. Brings the benefit in limiting the project alternatives or parts thereof;
12. Helps in the evolutionary prototyping;
13. Draws up the conceptual integrity of the AU and its development process;
14. Supports understanding and mutual understanding in the individual and collective work;
15. Supports expressing the ideas and arguments in the communication of persons involved in the development of the systems;
16. Provides an opportunity of reasoning about the potential changes in the course of the development of the AU, and contribute to the management of such changes;
17. Can be the basis for the study of the system.

The above list is impressive, but what is especially important, the architecture reduces the complexity by separating the possible designer's interactions with the system and the process of its development on domains in accordance with a set of useful viewpoints. For each viewpoint, the architecture opens access for potential users to corresponding block-and-line scheme with normative semantics.

In this book as related to its interests, we also mark the standard called Capability Maturity Model Integration for Development (or shortly CMMI, http://resources.sei.cmu.edu/library/assetview.cfm?assetid=9661). This standard divides the technological processes applied in developing the systems on levels in accordance with their professional maturity that can be measured by experts. By other words, any used process can be compared with the normative scheme of the maturity that is generally presented in Figure 10.

This scheme reflects not only goals of combining the best practices, but also the expedience of continuous improving as processes of developing so libraries of best practices including their units. The use of the indicated model leads to many positive effects, one of which is reducing the complexity of ways-of-working.

Let us notice, similar models oriented on five levels have been developed for different collections of best practices. Among these models, we mark following of them:

1. People Capability Maturity Model that specifies a professional maturity of a development team and each member of the team;

Figure 10. Model of Professional Maturity f Processes

Level	Focus	Process Areas	Result
5 Optimizing	*Continuous process improvement*	Organizational Innovation & Deployment Causal Analysis and Resolution	Productivity & Quality
4 Quantitatively Managed	*Quantitative management*	Organizational Process Performance Quantitative Project Management	
3 Defined	*Process standardization*	Requirements Development Technical Solution Product Integration Verification Validation Organizational Process Focus Organizational Process Definition Organizational Training Integrated Project Management Risk Management Decision Analysis and Resolution	
2 Managed	*Basic project management*	Requirements Management Project Planning Project Monitoring & Control Supplier Agreement Management Measurement and Analysis Process & Product Quality Assurance Configuration Management	
1 Initial	*Competent people and heroics*		

2. Organizational Project Management Maturity Model pointing out on ways to improve the project management;
3. Business Process Maturity Model that corresponds the form and means of improving business processes without relations to the development of SIS;
4. Business Intelligence Maturity Model that focuses its attention on achieving perfection from the point of intellectualization of activities;
5. Enterprise Architecture Maturity Model that includes lists of practices to establish enterprise architecture and recommendations for their improvement.

3. FEATURES OF HUMAN ACTIVITY IN PHYSICAL WORLD AND COMPUTERIZED ENVIRONMENT

3.1. Empirical Nature of Human Activity in Physical World

The main difference of a human being from other creatures is the use of controlled natural interactions (N-interactions) with an environment. Moreover, when necessary, a person can simulate the interactions for situational planning in order to achieve the necessary or beneficial effects.

This difference is the result of the life evolution on the Earth due to the use of the various forms of experimentation in the evolutionary process. In evolution, Nature has not only experimented but also coded the results of experimentation for their reuse by living beings, by other words, coded the experience of beings.

For coding the experience of living beings, Nature has "invented" the following ways:

- The genetic way that uses coding of the experience in chromosomal memory for the reuse of tested forms of life;
- Reuse based on conditioned reflexes that are coded in neuron structures.

To support life through their experience, living beings use certain sense organs that allow supplying them with informational flows about environment conditions. After any perception act, entered information is uploaded into the neural memory where it is processed for achieving a number of useful effects.

Among those effects, no more than in the simplified version of indicating their features and without explanations, we mark the following basic kinds of effects:

1. Sense organs provide the real-time monitoring the environment conditions some of which as sources of certain stimulus initiate innate, typically fixed patterns of instinct reactions, coded in the genetic experience of a living being.
2. In monitoring, information processing shows that the perceived state of environment corresponds to the definite conditioned reflex in accordance with which living being activates the corresponding reaction the usefulness of which has been detected by this living being in previous perceptions of similar conditions of the surrounding world.

The first effect is based on the genetic experience, codes of which are formed in genetic structures during very long-term processing of perceived conditions by mechanisms of adaptation, which is possessed any kind of living beings. In this case, corresponding instinctive reactions are caused by innate biological factors.

Conditioned reflexes have opened a possibility of a positive influence of an additional adaptability on the natural selection when changing the life conditions of beings who have acquired similar reflexes. This mechanism fulfills its selective function at the level of generations of living creatures without the managed possibility of a transference of acquired conditioned reflexes among living beings and generations.

At a certain living being, units of experience based on conditioned reflexes are formed in neuron structures that fulfill a function of memory with learning. This feature of conditioned reflexes finds its applying in the theory and practice of artificial neuron nets, basic applications of which are bound with the subject areas of "Image Recognition" and "Scene Analysis" where simulating the conditioned reflex CR_i corresponds to the following logic expression: if <certain conditions C_i>, then <corresponding reaction R_i>.

For a set of { CR_i }, a certain kind of living beings must have not only mechanisms for forming { CR_i } but also mechanisms for the access to the units of this set. A cardinality of the set and features of both of these mechanisms essentially depend on biological restrictions of the kind. That is why the evolution of life on the Earth tried to find the necessity of increasing the cardinality of the set { CR_i } and improving the indicated mechanisms.

At the next step of evolution of life based on experience, Nature "has invented" an intelligent form of the natural experience E^N, units { ΔEiN } of which are created by human beings with the use of intellectual processing of conditioned reflexes. The basis of this processing is a natural language LN, which has led to an inclusion of means of the second signal system into interactions of a human being with the surrounding world.

In its general sense, the language LN is a system of signs any of which provides the reference on the corresponding object when it is necessary or useful for the human. The main in such references that they can use as secondary signals about a presence of corresponding objects in the perceived scene (situation). That is why I. Pavlov specified language LN as the second signal system.

Thus, objects in the environment can be perceived by human senses in the process that additionally uses appropriate signs of LN. Such inclusion leads, for example, to the following useful effects:

3. Chosen signs can be used for a correct perception of the scene due to following actions:
    a. Focusing of an attention of the human on corresponding objects;
    b. Extending the information perceived be senses by the use of meaning of used signs;
    c. Mutual correcting the informational flows coming from the primary (senses) and secondary signal systems.

4. Perceived signs or their compositions allow simulating the processes of sensing for following aims:
   a. Imagining of situations that are not accessible for perceiving by senses due to various reasons;
   b. Imitating the other kind of senses due to the use of measurement devices of physical quantities, which are not perceived by the human senses.

And yet, the main purpose of the language L^N is a principal extension and improvement of a set of mental mechanisms that provide creating the units $\{\Delta Ei N\}$ in forms of modified conditioned reflexes. Including this language in the process of creating the human experience has led to the formation of the system of intellectual abilities supporting, for example, the following intellectual activities:

- Abstraction as a mental extraction of essential characteristics from their set specifying the certain object or their class;
- Analysis as a process of breaking a complex topic or substance into smaller parts in order to gain a better understanding of it;
- Generalization as a transfer at more higher level of an abstraction by revealing common attributes of objects in a certain area of concerns;
- Creative imagination as an invention of the useful images;
- Empathizing as creative imagination and understanding someone's feelings and thoughts in a rational way;
- Evaluation of an expression of value or amount by numbers or other ways;
- Ideation as forming an idea or concept;
- Prediction as declaration or estimation that will happen in the future or will be a consequence of something;
- Conscious motivation of creating the necessary unit [INSERT FIGURE 002];
- Goal setting in forms allowing an assessment of their achievement;
- Understanding of a human as an adequate estimating the certain perception or imagination at the level of the scheme (situation, system or process) from the viewpoint of its wholeness.

It needs to distinguish, where and how intellectual activities are implemented. In any case, they occur in the mental space or with the transference of certain parts of the intellectual processes beyond the brain structures or not. Indicated intellectual activities and their other kinds are continually improved. The base of improving is discovering their natural essences. Nowadays there exist richest collections of the best practices providing the use of automated intellectual activities and even their automatic simulations for applying in human life.

Attempts to discover the essence of intellectual activities and their use in creating the new units of human experience have a long history. These attempts have led to understanding the principal role of experiments and logics in mastering the experience E^N, acquiring of its new units and their continuous improvement.

When humans interact with surrounding world, they implicitly or explicitly use accessible experience E^N and language L^N and such reality creates the preconditions for experimentation. In such preconditions, if interactions support the person's activity that can lead to creation of the new unit $\Delta Ei N_{th}^{en}$ such activity can be interpreted as conducting the corresponding experiment. It is caused by presence of information flows coming from the senses, the transformation of these flows in the primary data that are intellectually processed for getting the necessary results in accordance with the objective of activity.

Thus, even in undeliberate mental activity that leads to the new unit, this activity can be qualified as implicit mental experimentation. Explicit and intentional use of language and affordable experience EN primarily provides managing of the process of mental experimentation. Additionally, they facilitate improvement of intellectual abilities involved in conducting of mental experiment that leaves "traces" of internal intellectual process outside of the brain. These traces not only reflect information about used intellectual activities, but they can be applied for controlled influence on the process of mental experimentation.

There was a time when people have understood that experimentation should be distinguished as an independent subject area, especially in the science. After that, mankind has invented, developed, mastered, continuously used and apply now the rich collection of experimentation practices. That is why experience EN of experimenting will apply and be continuously improved for its intensively use in the human-computer activity. It should be noted; experimentation is the creative kind of activity and, therefore, it always includes actions inside of brain that is intertwined with actions beyond the brain. Therefore, any experiment can be understood as a mental experiment, conducting of which is supported by actions outside of the brain.

As told above, the logic also occupies the important role in creating and using the units. In this area, the logics open the following basic possibilities for intellectual processing of information:

1. Reflection at the conceptual level of abstractions where a human can effectively model and simulate objects and processes that are placed or happened as beyond brain so in a mental space.
2. Implementation of inference, proof, and argumentation for substantiation of the prediction or confirmation of the hypotheses or theorems.
3. Implementation of reasoning with controlled use of language and artificial languages.
4. Management of intellectual processing.
5. Programming as natural programming (N-programming) in the language L^N so programming in artificial algorithmic languages (programming is applied logics).

For trustworthy use of logics, reflections of concerned components of activity space must provide the necessary degree of adequacy, which is expressed by the value of truth. Furthermore, in inverse reflections from the language description to the reality, results of logical processing must be checked by conducting the experiments in the corresponding activity space.

Additionally, to supporting and improving the mechanisms of creating the units, the use of language L^N almost remove restrictions on the cardinality of a set of experience units, primarily due to the systematization of this set and improving the mechanisms of the access to its elements. In this responsibility of L^N, it is necessary to distinguish implicit and explicit intellectual mechanisms of ordering and searching based on the language potential.

The essence of implicit ordering and searching is due to the system nature of language L^N and associative relations among elements of the system, primarily associative relations in the lexis and its use. These features of L^N provide functioning such phenomenon of human memory as "remembering."

Developments of explicit systematizations of the language L^N and the use of them in controlled mechanisms of ordering and searching lead to the essential improving the implicit interactions of a human with experience.

In both kinds of interactions of a human with natural experience, any act of interactions begins with an attempt of an automatic access to the experience E^N in the certain preconditions. At this step of any interaction, appropriate preconditions are converted into a list of keys (expressed in the language L^N), an assignment of which is similar to the request to the database.

For increasing the adequacy of the request, the list of keys can be transformed to the appropriate question Q as a construct in language L^N. Among possible answers this question there are two strictly contradictory versions - experience E^N includes the unit corresponding to the request or not. If the request is valid, then the cause of a negative response is the lack of the needed unit $\Delta E i N_t$ hat can be due to the existence of a gap that, in different cases, can have different nature.

3.2. Features of Human Activity in Computerized Environment

What was said in the previous subsection is true when a person is involved in the humancomputer activity, which combines actions of the person with computer processes, for example, in fulfilling the certain work. This activity can be interpreted as a collaboration of the person and computer in the fulfillment of the common work, effectiveness and other characteristics of which are essentially depends on how this collaboration is organized and implemented. In this case, an objectification of this collaboration is a responsibility of human-computer interactions that must be developed, programmed and embedded into the common process.

That is why, in famous ACM SIGCHI Curricula for Human-Computer Interaction (Hewett et al., 1992), HCI is formally defined as "a discipline concerned with the design, evaluation, and implementation of interactive computing systems for human use and with the study of major phenomena surrounding them." Ibid, the use and context of HCI are connected with the system of HCI learning that includes following courses

1. **Nature:** The Nature of HCI (N1. (Meta-) Models of HCI).
2. **Use:** Use and Context of Computers (U1. Human Social Organization and Work; U2. Application Areas; U3. Human-Machine Fit and Adaptation).
3. **Human:** Human Characteristics (H1. Human Information Processing; H2. Language, Communication and Interaction; H3. Ergonomics).
4. **Computer:** Computer System and Interface Architecture (C1. Input and Output Devices; C2. Dialogue Techniques, C3. Dialogue Genre; C4. Computer Graphics; C5. Dialogue Architecture).
5. **Development:** Development Process (D1. Design Approaches; D2. Implementation Techniques; D3. Evaluation Techniques; D4. Example Systems and Case).

6. **Project:** Project Presentations and Examinations.

The presented structure of HCI learning reflects a diversity of the knowledge and experience that are related to the corresponding subject area, and this diversity points out on its interdisciplinary character.

In this manuscript, our interests concern the area of HCI only from the viewpoint of using the affordable experience by the designer who solves the task in the frame of human-computer activity. That is why, below in the text, we shall open and specify the known details of the HCI area only in fragmentary manner, and only when it will be needed for reasoning or solutions. In this subsection of the text, it is needed for comparing the N-interactions with interactions of the HCI-kind.

Moreover, when comparing, and in the text below, we will only consider the visual interaction of the human with a computerized environment. This limitation is chosen by due to the presence of a vast experience in the use of visualization in a variety of its applications in humancomputer activity. Therefore, the use of this diversity is sufficient for a representative comparison of N-interactions with human-computer interactions.

One of the sources of systematizing the information on the monitor screen is the periodic table of visualization (Lengler and Eppler, 2007) which interactively demonstrates one hundred methods. Authors of the table define a method as "a systematic, rule-based, external, permanent, and graphic representation that depicts information in a way that is conducive to acquiring insights, developing an elaborate understanding, or communicating experiences." In general, Figure 11 discloses the structure of the table, any cell of which presents the corresponding method.

In the table, methods are distributed on groups (1-6) and in accordance with a period into any group. Used groups indicate the following areas of applications:

1. Data Visualization that combines methods for visual representations of quantitative data in the schematic form.
2. Information Visualization, for example, semantic networks or tree maps that are intended for visual representations of data to amplify cognition
3. Concept Visualization graphically helps to reflect qualitative concepts, ideas, and results of their analysis.
4. Metaphor Visualization as templates that convey complex metaphoric insights.

Figure 11. Structure of periodic table

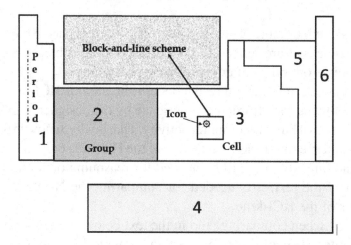

5. Strategy Visualization "as the systematic use of complementary visual representations to improve the analysis, development, formulation, communication, and implementation of strategies in organizations."
6. Compound Visualization corresponds to the use of several methods that are chosen from groups defined above.

The dimension "period" reflects the complexity of visualization that is expressed in any cell of the table by "the number of rules applied for the use and/or the number of interdependences of the elements to be visualized" (Lengler and Eppler, 2007).

Additionally, any cell includes the certain icon, attributes of which indicate following features of methods (Lengler and Eppler, 2007).

Point of View [when?]: Detail (highlighting individual Items), Overview (big picture), Detail and Overview (both at the same time).

1. **Type of Thinking Aid [Why?]:** Convergent (reducing complexity) vs. Divergent (adding complexity).
2. **Type of Representation [What?]:** Process (stepwise cyclical in time and/ or continuous sequential), Structure (i.e., hierarchy or causal networks).

Authors of the periodic table have created it for learning aims, and, therefore, the table partially reflects the experience of computer visualization. For practice use, this experience distributes for a set of standards among which we mark the family of standards IDEF (Integration DEFinition) and the standard

Unified Modeling Language (UML, latest Version 2.5). The family IDEF and UML are developed for aims of visual modeling in the field of system and software engineering. Therefore, standards are deeply thought-out and have the strict semantics.

Any standard of the family IDEF helps to the designer to create a block-and-line scheme for their certain applications. For example, the standard IDEF5 supports visual modeling in developing and maintaining the usable, accurate, domain ontologies. As a method, this standard includes a graphical language to support conceptual ontology analysis, a structured text language for detailed ontology characterization, and a systematic procedure that provides guidelines for effective ontology capture. It is supposed, that the designer creates necessary diagrams, controlling them by mind eyes in the process of visual modeling. This language as other languages of the family IDEF is not executable automatically. The typical instrumental support of IDEF versions of visual modeling is the use of specialized graphical editors.

UML was originally aimed at the visual modeling in software engineering from the perspective of translating the UML diagrams in the executed code of corresponding parts of the designed program. This target remains, but till now the automatic translation of the certain complex of UML diagrams in corresponding executed code is not already achieved. Ways of translations are developed and tested for some UML diagrams but not for all diversity of their types. Therefore, graphical editors are also basic means for diagrammatic reasoning based on UML.

Analyzing the visual interactions of a human with a computer, it needs to consider interactions with integrated instrumental environments, the rich source of which is the instrumental means embedded into Microsoft Office in any its versions. These means open the access to variety kinds of visual scenes any of which reflects a set of situations for potential actions. Figure 12 presents the fragment of one of these scenes used in Microsoft Word 2013.

As it can be seen; the shown scene is far from habitual situations arisen in front of a human outside of the computer. It is also far from visualized images of these situations. Any observed scene consists of a map of areas labeled by words or used for input informing, icons with their names or not. The greater part of observed components supports the choice of actions, some of which only fulfill the role of informational help.

Thus similar scenes are intended for the use of their components in technological aims in conditions when these components reflect the surface content of actions and their groups and usually at the level of their names.

Figure 12. Instrumental environment of artificial interactions

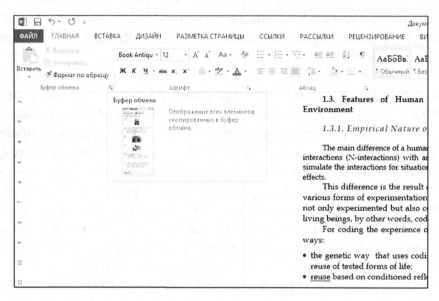

3.3. Human-Computer Interactions from the Viewpoint of Complexity

In reality of developing the system, any designer interacts with the computerized environment when natural and artificial interactions are intertwined in the real-time work in conditions that are schematically shown in Figure 13.

Figure 13. Conditions of human-computer interactions

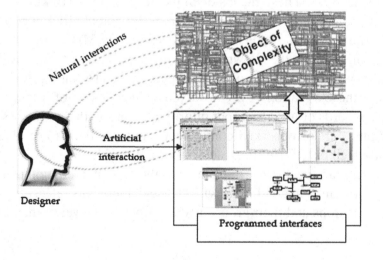

The scheme points out a part of natural interactions that implicitly focuses on a certain object of complexity while their second part implicitly perceive the programmed interfaces. In parallel, the designer is involved in explicit artificial interactions with programmed interfaces that reflect the object of complexity with a technologically predefined side.

Thus, a predefined feature of artificial interactions brings to limitations in reflecting the object of complexity. Furthermore, they one-sidedly activate natural interactions that find implicitly objectified expression only in their second part. The first part of natural interactions remains without an automation support while this part has considerably greater useful potential that is not comparable with the opportunities provided by the second part.

If in the context of designing the systems, implicit natural interactions will be automated by the useful way then such automation will help to reduce the complexity not only in predefined situations of human-computer interactions. In our deep opinion, automating the interactions with natural experience is the perspective way for real-time reducing the complexity in unpredictable situations and decreasing the negative influence of human factors in designing the systems

4. SOME NOTES TO THE CHAPTER 2

1. Developing the software intensive systems is considered one of the most problematic activities, the degree of success of which is still unacceptably low.
2. In developments of SISs, the extremely low degree of success is because this kind of human activity has not yet reached the level of the guaranteed predictability of its results.
3. In software engineering, there are many various specifications of the concept "success," and a lot of different approaches to its evaluating that takes into account numerous factors of the success and failures, among which the central place occupies human factors.
4. In designing the systems, negative influences of human factors are basically caused with the phenomenon "complexity."
5. The success of the creation of any SIS to a large extent depends on what tools are used by designers for managed mastering the complexity.
6. The complexity can manifest in interactions of designers with a design process (or fragments thereof), or with states of a system (or their parts) during the lifecycle of the system.

7. System or any of its component is complex if a designer does not have enough resources (mainly informational resources) for its effective perception. The same is true for a process or component.

8. If designers do not master the complexity of their activities at the conceptual design stage of the SIS, the consequences of this will influence on the subsequent stages, and, therefore, the development of SIS is unlikely to end successfully.

9. In assessing the degree of the complexity of constructing the systems, the scientists and practitioners most commonly use different interpretations of Kolmogorov' measure, which corresponds to a "minimum length of the program of building the system S P from its initial description given D." Differences in interpretations are due to the features of the system S, and as well in the content that is embedded in the constructs of the P and D and how this content is expressed.

10. Mastering the complexity is based on the experience of the team of designers and used models, which should be presented in a way that facilitates the construction of the P-models and their use. In order to increase the effectiveness of conceptual designing in achieving the success, the collective experience and the system of its models (experience base) should be continuously improved. The current state of collective experience and its model will be called below as affordable or available experience.

11. Particularly important part of the available experience is associated with the technology of development of the system and its mastering by the team of designers. The use of the applied technology can be interpreted as an execution of appropriate technological programs (T-programs) supported the creation of the system. Any of such T-program has the definite structure that can be extracted from the technology guides that helps the designer to understand the technology at a level sufficient for its use. Note, the T-program built by designers for creating the definite system occupies the central place in the corresponding P-program.

12. The above reasoning about the complexity in designing the systems helps us to simply clarify our position on the process of designing with the programmatic point of view. By this view, P-programs include behavioral actions that correspond to normative instructions described in manuals on the technology and tools. These actions are fulfilled by designers in coordination with other actions of computerized workflows.

13. Algorithmic schemes of workflows (correspondent to T-programs "written" by developers of the technology in "Technological language of programming" or shortly in "T-language") with their detailed tasks help to designers in mastering the complexity of some processes in designing the systems, but they do not reflect the complexity of the problem-solving in the subject areas of created systems. Schemes (models) of workflows are nothing more than sources of templates, copies of which are included in the actual processes of developing the systems, whose scheme is often significantly different from the stereotyped.

14. For the definite P-program, designers are usually forced to build "program" components for solutions of necessary tasks that reflect the domain of the corresponding system. Designers build such components in the real time of designing when they use and evolve accessible experience.

15. Thus, it needs to differentiate two sources of resources that help to reduce the complexity. The first kind of resources is purposely created and embedded into the technology and related means. The second source is a natural experience that is activated in situations, in which the use of only resources of the first kind doesn't make sufficient.

16. The first kind of resources (artificial resources) includes well-thought technologies, toolkits, standards, approaches (for example, SEMAT-approach), frameworks, models and others means oriented on their use in the computerized world. Humancomputer interactions with this world are reified on the base of visualized interfaces that are programmed for certain goals.

17. The second kind of resources (natural resources) is based on empirical nature of human activity with the physical world. Components of these resources are units of natural experience and intellectual activities providing the creation and use of these units and their compositions.

18. To reduce the perceived complexity, the designer participates in interactions with the source of complexity, applying interactions with artificial and natural appropriate resources. In general case, all of these interactions are explicitly or implicitly intertwined.

19. The maturity level of the design process - is the extent to which a particular process is defined, managed, measured, controlled and effective.

20. For the modern technologies of developing the systems (especially the conceptual stage) are characteristically the simplification of the complexity of the use of Unified Modeling Language and figuratively semantic schemes of other types.

REFERENCES

Borges, P., Machado, R. J., & Ribeiro, P. (2012). Mapping RUP Roles to Small Software Development Teams. *Proc. of International Conference on Software and System Process*, 190-199. doi:10.1007/978-3-642-27213-4_5

El Emam, K., & Koru, A. G. (2008). A Replicated Survey of IT Software Project Failures. *IEEE Software*, 25(5), 84–90. doi:10.1109/MS.2008.107

Glass, R. L. (2006). The Standish Report: Does it really describe a software crisis? *Communications of the ACM*, 49(8), 15–16. doi:10.1145/1145287.1145301

González, M., Zapata, C., & González, L. (2013). Toward a standardized representation of RUP best practices of project management in the SEMAT kernel. In *Software engineering: Methods, modeling and teaching* (vol. 3, pp. 47-52). Universidad Nacional de Colombia.

Haze - The Standish Group. (2015). Available at https://www.standishgroup.com/sample_research_files/ Haze4.pdf

Hewett, T., Baecker, R., Card, S., Carey, T., Gasen, J., Mantei, M., … Verplank, W. (2002). *ACM SIGCHI Curricula for Human-Computer Interaction*. ACM Technical Report.

IBM Rational Unified Process (RUP). (n.d.). Retrieved from http://www-01.ibm.com/software/rational/rup/

Jacobson, I., Meyer, B., & Soley, R. (2009). *The SEMAT Initiative: A Call for Action*. Retrieved from http://www.drdobbs.com/architecture-and-design/the-semat-initiative-a-call-for-action/

Jacobson, I., Ng, P.-W., McMahon, P., Spence, I., & Lidman, S. (2012). The essence of software engineering: The SEMAT kernel. *Queue*, 10(10), 1–12.

Jørgensen, M., & Moløkken-Østvold, K. (2006). How large are software cost overruns? A review of the 1994 CHAOS report. *Information and Software Technology*, 48(4), 297–301. doi:10.1016/j.infsof.2005.07.002

Lengler, R., Martin, J., & Eppler, M. J. (2007). Towards A Periodic Table of Visualization Methods for Management. In *Proceedings of the IASTED International Conference on Graphics and Visualization in Engineering (GVE '07)*. ACTA Press.

Li, M., & Vitanui, P. M. B. (2008). *An Introduction to Kolmogorov Complexity and Its Applications, Series: Text in Computer Science* (3rd ed.). Springer. doi:10.1007/978-0-387-49820-1

Reports of Standish Group. (2016). Available at www.standishgroup.com/outline

Software Intensive systems in the future. (2006). *Final Report//ITEA 2 Symposium.* Retrieved from http://symposium.itea2.org/ symposium2006/ main/publications/ TNO_IDATE_study_ ITEA_SIS_ in_the_future_Final_ Report.pdf

Windholz, G. (1990). The Second Signal System As Conceived By Pavlov And His Disciples. *The Pavlovian Journal of Biological Science, 25*(4), 163–173. PMID:2075026

ADDITIONAL READING

Card, S. K., Thomas, T. P., & Newell, A. (1983). *The Psychology of Human-Computer Interaction.* London: Lawrence Erbaum Associates.

Cule, P., Schmidt, R., Lyytinen, K., & Keil, M. (2000). Strategies for heading off IS project failure. *Information Systems Management, 17*(2), 65–73. doi: 10.1201/1078/43191.17.2.20000301/31229.8

Eveleens, J. L., & Verhoef, C. (2010). The rise and fall of the CHAOS Report figures. *IEEE Software, 27*(1), 30–36. doi:10.1109/MS.2009.154

Ewusi-Mensah, K. (2003). *Software Development Failures: Anatomy of Abandoned Projects.* Cambridge, MA: The MIT Press.

Glass, R. L. (2005). IT failure rate - 70% or 1015%? *IEEE Software, 22*(3), 110–111. doi:10.1109/MS.2005.66

Hartmann, D. (2006). Interview: Jim Johnson of the Standish Group. Retrieved June 30, 2010, from InfoQ: http://www.infoq.com/ news/Interview-Johnson-Standish-CHAOS

Harwardt, M. (2016). Criteria of Successful IT Projects from Management's Perspective/ Open Journal of Information Systems (OJIS),Vol. 3, Issue 1, pp. 29-54.

Humphrey, W. S. (2005). Why big software projects fail: The 12 key questions. ross Talk: The Journal of Defense Software Engineering, pp. 1-8.

Johnson, J. (2006). Reader Comments - Re: Two questions to Jim Johnson of the Standish Group. Retrieved June 30, 2008, from InfoQ: http://www.infoq.com/news/ Interview-Johnson-Standish-CHAOS.

Johnson, P., & Ralph, P. Goedicke, M. Ng P.-W., Stol K.-J., Smolander, K., Exman, J. and Perry D.E. (2013). Report on the Second SEMAT Workshop on General Theory of Software Engineering (GTSE 2013). SIGSOFT Softw. Eng. (Notes 38, 5, pp. 47-50).

Jørgensen, M., & Moløkken-Østvold, K. (2006). How large are software cost overruns? A review of the 1994 CHAOS report. *Information and Software Technology*, *48*(4), 297–301. doi:10.1016/j.infsof.2005.07.002

F. Karray, M. Alemzadeh, J. A. Saleh,& Arab, M. N. (2008). Human-Computer Interaction: Overview on State of the Art Smart sensing and intelligent systems. vol. 1(1), 2008, pp. 138-159).

The Standish Group. (1995). *The CHAOS Report*. Boston, MA: The Standish Group International, Inc.

The Standish Group. (1998). *CHAOS: A Recipe for Success*. Boston, MA: The Standish Group International, Inc.

The Standish Group. (2009). *CHAOS Summary 2009: The 10 Laws of Chaos*. Boston, MA: The Standish Group International, Inc.

Chapter 3
Experimental Actions With Conceptual Objects

ABSTRACT

In the previous Chapter, we described the direction of decreasing the differences between interactions of a human with natural and computer environments. The basic feature of this direction is to create appropriate conditions for the real-time intertwining of both types of interactions in designer's activity. In this Chapter, we pay our attention to such kind of designer's activity as solving the project tasks at the conceptual stage of designing. We consider these tasks as a dynamic system described as a project theory of a substantially evolutionary type. Such position leads to useful inheritances from the scientific practice. The basic inheritances are the becoming of the theory of the project and applying the thought experiments. The becoming of the theory is coordinated with the use of the stepwise refinement (based on question-answer analysis) and design thinking in their applications to the solving the project tasks. Conceptual experiments are considered as means for verifying the theory constructs.

DOI: 10.4018/978-1-5225-2987-3.ch003

1. SUBSTANTIALLY EVOLUTIONARY APPROACH TO DESIGNING THE SYSTEMS

1.1. Theorization in Designing the Systems

In its initial settings, and even in the title, the SEMAT-approach stresses the need for theorizing the foundations of software engineering. In the same time, the normative document "Kernel and Language for Software Engineering Methods, Version 1.1" does not include constructive answers about the creation and use of appropriate theories in the development of software systems.

Even with the coordination of positions on the initiative SEMAT and in the early stages of evolution in SEMAT, A. Cocburn criticized this aspect of the approach (Cockburn, 2010). In recent years, there were a numerous attempts to offer versions of theorization. Some of these attempts and their results were presented in four workshops on General Theory of Software Engineering (GTSE 2011-2015) and 5th International Workshop on Theory-Oriented Software Engineering (2016). At the same time, it can be stated that the satisfactory general theory is absent till now.

Typically, after workshop its results have been generalized, and, for example, such report for the second workshop indicated that the theory should "explain and predict software engineering phenomena at multiple levels, including social processes and technical artifacts, should synthesize existing theories from software engineering and reference disciplines, should be developed iteratively, should avoid common misconceptions and atheoretical concepts, and should respect the complexity of software engineering phenomena" (Johnson, 2013).

Reports of the next workshop extended features that must find their embodiment in content and responsibility of a GTSE, for example, the report on results of the third workshop marked papers of following authors:

Ralph (Ralph, 2014) who "distinguished between variance theories (which predict a dependent variable regarding independent variables) and process theories (which explain how a phenomenon occurs)."

Ng (Ng, 2014) who "proposed a software engineering approach informed by Essence. It posits

that every software project is unique and sensitive to its context."

Very often, researchers, which were participated in attempts to build the general theory have referenced on the paper (Sjoberg, 2006) that includes an analysis of assignments of theories and a way for creating the useful theories oriented on their applications in software engineering.

In their research, authors of this paper referenced on the following classification that was specified in (Sjoberg, 2006):

1. **Analysis:** Theories of this type include descriptions and conceptualizations of "what is." Also included are taxonomies, classifications, and ontologies.
2. **Explanation:** Theories of this type explicitly explain. What constitutes an explanation is a nontrivial issue. However, a common view is that an explanation answers to a question of *why* something is – or happens (rather than *what* happens).
3. **Prediction:** These theories are geared towards predicting what will happen, without explaining why.
4. **Explanation and Prediction:** Theories of this type combine the traits of II and III and correspond to what many consider a "standard" conception of empirically-based theories.
5. **Design and Action:** These theories describe "how to do" things, that is, they are prescriptive.

Additionally, the paper (Sjoberg, 2006) analyzed following steps that help to build the certain theory:

1. Defining the Constructs of the Theory.
2. Defining the Propositions of the Theory.
3. Providing Explanations to Justify the Theory.
4. Determining the Scope of the Theory.
5. Testing the Theory Through Empirical Research.

Then, in An Initial Theory for UML-Based Development in Large Projects, for demonstrating this way, these steps have been applied for building "An Initial Theory for UML-Based Development in Large Projects." The developed theory was evaluated by authors with the use of following characteristics:

*   Testability as the degree to which theory is constructed such that empirical refutation is possible.
*   Empirical support as the degree to which theory is supported by empirical studies that confirm its validity.
*   Explanatory power as the degree to which a theory accounts for and predicts all known observations within its scope is simple in that it

has few ad hoc assumption, and relates to that which is already well understood.

- Parsimony as the degree to which theory is economically constructed with a minimum of concepts and propositions.
- Generality as the breadth of the scope of a theory and the degree to which the theory is independent of specific settings.
- Utility as the degree to which a theory supports the relevant areas of the software industry.

For our reasoning that will be lower, we note one more paper (Perry, 2015), which was called "Theories, Theories Everywhere," and where its author claimed that a general theory of software engineering must have "two logical parts: design and evaluation, D and E, each of which as a theory T." On the base of an analysis of this position, the author "delineate a rich variety of theories related to D and E and consider these to be sub-theories critical to understanding the relationships between the theories in D and E."

In specifications of analysis results, it is used such construct as model M the essence of which clarifies the following assertion « a theory T (a more or less abstract entity) is reified, represented, satisfied, etc., by a model M (a concrete entity).» In the paper (Perry, 2015), the important place occupies dividing the theories that correspond D and E on sub-theories among which, for example, we mark following sets of them: Theories of Behavior and Constraints, Theories of Model Structure, Theories of Interface Usability, Theories of Usefulness, Theories about Evaluating Models and Theories about Evaluating Theories.

1.2. Becoming a Theory

The concept of "theory" in the modeling of scientific activity corresponds the knowledge system combining the set of common ideas, aimed at streamlining the facts and supporting the processes of explaining or understanding in a certain domain of reality.

The specific theory of their sets may have other properties, for example, have the ability to evaluate states of affairs or generate predictions, and it leads to distinguish between different kinds of theories from a descriptive to deductive-axiomatic types. That is why, depending on the level of theory, it provides an opportunity to support the appropriate type of processes in human-computer environments: formal, semi-formalized or heuristic, non-formalized. In each process, a certain load falls from the theory on the computer components or a human.

The theory brings the order and coherence in the reflected world. This order has a logical character. The theory is useless without its interpretation in the subject area. Many problems associated with the construction and use of the theory, solves by its language. In this regard, with the use of the theory, it is associated a methodology of sign versions of modeling the investigated subjects. One of the features of the theory manifests itself in the fact that it provides a system of concepts for their using by the researcher who will formulate questions and plan of experiments in the human-computer environment. The theory, forming some conceptual system, determines what should and what should not be classified as a fact. It stimulates a meaningful search.

The theory never appears in its final form without previous attempts of its descriptions. Unfinished, imperfect theory is not at all uncommon. The process of creating the theory, as well as the process of its checking, never ends and requires creativity and imagination. It is better to stick to the theory that has weaknesses than remain without theory.

In our research and practice of a certain subject area W, we use the scheme of becoming the theory Th(t) that is shown in Figure 1 where dynamics of Th(t) combines processes and theory extensions occurring in a number of theory phases.

Figure 1. Developing the phase structure of the theory

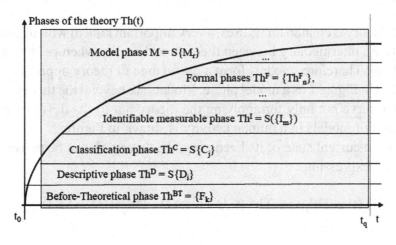

1. Before-theoretical phase involves the collection of facts $F(t) = \{F_k\}$, relevant to the corresponding subject area, but rather to the properties of its components $\{B_p\}$ and the relations between them.

2. In the descriptive phase, registered facts are used for constructing the texts of $T(t) = \{Ti\}$ linking the facts in the description of essences distinguished in the subject area, and these constructs already brings a certain ordering in the set of facts.

3. In building the theory, a special attention focuses on a vocabulary and especially on developing its part that presents a system of concepts $S(\{N_p\})$, semantic value and order of which defines a certain set of classifications $C(t) = \{Km\}$. Developing the system $S(\{Np\})$ on the base of $\{Km\}$ is a very important phase of becoming the theory. In Figure 1, this part of the theory marked as the classification phase.

4. In becoming the theory and its use, the identifiably measuring phase introduces the possibility of (empirical) interpreting the theoretical constructs, in particular, the ability to control the adequacy of any concept (notion) in its use in a chosen fragment of a description or fact. The typical approach to the identification is a pattern recognition with the use of appropriate means that lead to names of classes. The measurement helps to defines values of attributes for recognized essences of the theorized reality.

5. Formal phase is usually expressed by one or a number of formal theories $ThF(t) = \{ThFk\}$ systematizing material of prior phases and transferring the solution of the task from the level of manipulations with entities $\{Ur\}$ of the subject area POs to the level of manipulations with symbolic constructs of the theory. Such transition opens the possibility to use an inference for a prediction and apply a proof to verify the prediction.

Any theory is created for its uses, a very important kind of which is models. Models are intermediary between theories and reality when people interact with them. Therefore, models form a useful area of theory applications that indicated in Figure 1 as a model phase. Models are beyond the theory frames, and they serve not only for applying the theory but for its developing also. The place of models in a human activity is shown in Figure 2.

Thus, in current state of its becoming, the theory Th can be presented by following expression

$$Th(t) = [D_s(t) \cup Th^T_s(t) \cup Th^K_s(t) \cup Th^I_s(t) \cup \{Th^F_{sk}(t)\}] \leftrightarrow M_{sq}(t), \qquad (1)$$

Figure 2. Developing the phase structure of the theory

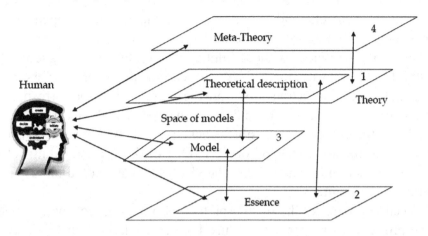

Figure 3. Interpretation of theory constructs

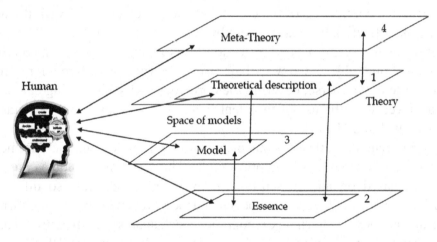

where symbol "↔" points out on relation between the theory and models which the theory helped to build.

Additionally, it needs to mark, the transition from phase to phase can lead to the necessity to define useful abstractions for already existing theoretical constructs, systematizing of which helps to build appropriate meta-theory that is also shown in Figure 3. In this case, the theory includes meta-theoretical components that are a specific contribution in developing Th and its systematization.

In the methodology of science, the term "meta-theory" is understood as the theory of logicalsemiotic properties of the reflected theory. In scientifical practices, meta-theories help to study: the property of the logical consistency of the theory, syntactic and semantic completeness; logical dependence or independence of the proposals and other theoretical features.

The theory is useless without implicit or explicit interpretations of its constructs when they use for achieving the certain aim. In any its version, the interpretation suggests a transition from the construct C to the corresponding essence in reality, for example, to the certain object Ob of the certain subject area. Such transitions are possible when, previously, between constructs of theory (or meta-theory) and objects {Ob} of the corresponding subject area was defined the adequate reflection R. Similar state of affairs is shown figuratively in Figure 3.

It needs to note, results of interpretations, for example (the attribution of the properties $\{g_c\}$ for constituting $\{B_v\}$ and relationship $\{r_d\}$ between them) find their expression in forms of predications used in textual constructs $\{C_r\}$ and $\{C^M_r\}$ of the theory and meta-theory correspondingly. Of course, ensuring the correctness of the certain attribution can only be with the use of the identification or measurement by suitable means $\{I_m\}$ and $\{I^M_m\}$.

It needs to note, typically, reflection finds its expression in predicative forms that bind objects Ob with their properties {gc} or with relations {rd} among them. Of course, ensuring the correctness of such binding can only be achieved with the use of the identification or measurement by suitable means {Im} and {IMm}.

In different situations, various means of identification and measurement provide an effectuation of the predication. These means include as human abilities based on natural senses (for example, mind eyes) so different artificial devices and practices. Specialized tools (various sensors, measuring instruments, devices and image recognition mechanisms) significantly expand the potential of predicative attributions in creating the theories and their using.

To the place to note, that the adequacy of predication, its accuracy, and quality fundamentally depend on the means of identification and measurement, as well as from the actions and methods for their use. One of the most useful ways of the predication is "experiment." In principle, one can assume that each act of predication is the result of the conducted experiment, mature of which is defined by the scheme of implemented actions.

Among different kinds of experiments, the central place occupies the scientific experiments that have a long history, in the course of which, their schemes are constantly improved. Note again that the experiments are the means of the identification and measurement.

If for the construct Cr of the theory Th(t), the necessary experiment aimed at testing the predication was conducted, by other words, was confirmed the correspondence

$$Cr \overset{\pi}{\leftrightarrow} Bsv \tag{2}$$

then this result (where π indicate a predicative relation) can repeatedly be used under appropriate conditions when it will be needed.

In the general case, the result of predication for the construct C_r can be obtained with the help of a number of different experiments, and this feature allows qualifying the correspondence

$$\{Cr\} \overset{\pi}{\leftrightarrow} \{Bsv\} \tag{3}$$

as a multi-valued reflection of constructs $\{B_{sv}\}$ onto constructs $\{Cr\}$ of the theory.

Let's move on to the details of reflections that register the correspondence between constructs of the subject area, its theories Th(t) and meta-theory ThM (t) for Th (t). In general, a set of constructs in the subject area includes objects (natural and artificial), connected set of objects in certain conditions, processes, and their combinations, as well as acted persons involved in the process.

As told above, the predicative reflection of any object Obt onto the theory Th(t) lies in its specification as the theoretical construct Cr, that is, in the description of its properties and relationships with other components of the subject area. In the theory, basic units of any description (based on predication) are the following two types of simple sentences (SS) expressed with the use of Backus–Naur Forms (BNF)

$SS^g ::= g (<Ob>) <AS>$

$$SS^r ::= <r>(< Ob_1>,< Ob_2>)<AS>, \tag{4}$$

where predicates g denote property of the object Ob in the first sentence, r presents relation between Ob_1 and Ob_2 (the second sentence), AS expresses association component that corresponds to a context of the predication.

Using these basic units of predications, predicative representation of an object Ob can be represented by the expression

$$C_r = \pi(Ob) = S(\{SS^g_{ti}\}, \{SS^r_{tj}\}, t),$$ (5)

In which the S captures the integration of simple predicates in a single unit C_r, and the time t reflects the dynamics of becoming the construct Cr. These expansions allow describing any component in the domain of the theory as a decomposition in the basis of simple predicates.

The expression (2-5) shows that in the π-interpretation should be distinguished simple and compound predicative representations, which consist of simple predicates united into a whole so that they are successfully applied in solving the tasks of the corresponding subject area.

1.3. SUBSTANTIALLY EVOLUTIONARY APPROACH TO BECOMING A THEORY

Creating the project P(t) of any SIS is implemented in the process of solving a set of diverse and different but connected tasks that form a certain subject area SA^{SIS} for a collaborative professional activity.

Recently, for creating the SIS, developers most commonly use an iterative design process, during which they develop a version for the version of the project, each of which increases the level of detail and finds its description in a system of normative documents a project documentation $P^D(t)$). In the early stages of the design, the documentation has a textual form S ({Ti},

Figure 4, Becoming of the project documentation

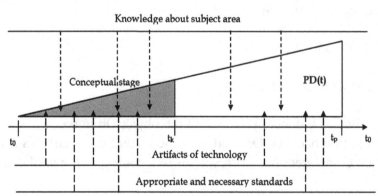

t) that additionally includes graphical units (usually in the block-and-line view) and tables. S ($\{T_i\}$, t). At the subsequent stages, the program codes and technological artifacts are included in the project documents. The general scheme of becoming the project documentation is shown in Figure 4.

Becoming is a dynamic process during of which the documentation $P^D(t)$ expands by the inclusion of informational units inherited from the following sources:

- Required knowledge from the subject area;
- Artifacts of technologies (for example, normative textual templates and diagrams);
- Appropriate and necessary standards.

In the development of the documentation, especial attention focuses on systemizing of the texts S($\{Ti\}$, t), achieving of which is regulated by a huge number of professional standards. So nothing prevents for binding each project P(t) with its theory $Th^P(t)$. It should be noted that the development of present-day SISs and especially their families are knowledge-intensive activity including scientific component. Additionally, it needs to note, when a new SIS is developing, and the theory of its project is absent, it is expedient to orient on the becoming of the theory that is shown in Figure 1.

In the most general sense, any theory is a system of sentences combined in textual units, relations among which define the structure of the theory. For uses of the theory, it is typical to combine its theoretical constructs with constructs of corresponding meta-theory, appropriate graphical units, and tables. A similar combination is built in the conceptual stage of designing the SIS and corresponding states of the $P^D(t)$ that can be understood as combining $Th^P(t)$, its meta-theory $Th^{PM}(t)$, textual models (used textual templates and tables) and graphical models. In the current state of $P^D(t)$, combining is provided by the use of naturally professional language $L^P(t)$ of the project and this language is also evolved during the design.

There is a question "What is define and provide developing the $P^D(t)$ in its dynamics?" By the SEMAT-approach, any system is a result of a work implemented by a team of developers interacting with stakeholders. In its turn, the work is specified as a system of activities, an implementation of each of which leads to a corresponding "product of work." In project management and programming, such activities are usually called as tasks.

As naturally artificial essences, tasks have following features:

1. They are oriented on achieving the definite goals that must be confirmed by obtained results and their checks.
2. In the general sense, a life cycle of a task includes creative actions that help to overcome definite gaps as in problems. In these cases task should be solved, usually for the future reuse.
3. The task description that provides the task reuse can be interpreted as the model of the corresponding precedent that simulates the unit of experience.

What has been said about the tasks enables to answer the above question by the following assertion, solutions of planned and situational tasks provide dynamics of developing as the SIS so the $P^D(t)$. Below we will often use term "task" in a sense defined above.

Thus, any solved task Z_i leaves textual and other traces in $P^D(t)$ and its component $Th^P(t)$ as the system $S(\{T_i\}, t)$. Let us assume, that textual part T_i of traces included in $S(\{T_i\}, t_j)$ as its increment $\Delta S(Z_i, t_j)$ in the moment of time t_j. Then, this system of texts can be expressed in a form

$$S(\{T_i\}, t_j) = S(T_0, t_0) \cup (\bigcup_i \Delta S(Zi, tj)), \tag{6}$$

where T_0 is a textual description with which designers start their work with the project $P(t)$ in the moment of time t_0, $\{Z_i\}$ is a set of solved tasks and t_j indicates on the current moment of time.

Because the expression correspond the textual structure of the theory $Th^P(t)$, it can be presented in the form

$$Th^P(t_j) = Th^P(t_0) \cup (\bigcup_i \Delta Th P^{Z_i}i, tj)), \tag{7}$$

where Zi can be interpreted as the certain rule in theory $ThP(t)$. Theory $ThP(tj)$ is evolved by the use of the set of rules $\{Zi\}$, and any of these rules and each of these rules should not make any contradictions in the theory.

The absence of contradictions is possible when for any $\Delta Th^R(Zi, tj)$ its inclusion in the theory does not change the previous structure and content of the theory $ThP(tj_{-1})$. If it is so, then, by typology of theories, the theory $ThP(t)$ can be qualified as the theory of substantially evolutionary type.

Any theory of this type is evolved in correspondence with the principle of additivity as a system $s(\{T\}, t)$ of texts T each of which embeds into $s(\{T\}, t)$, beginning with initial state $s(T_0, t_0)$, only if there are sufficient justifications for embedding.

The principle of additive expresses the relevant consecution in its application to the creation of the theory Th(t). Reifying this principle corresponds to the method of stepwise refinement that is widely used in programming and practice of designing the SISs. It should be noted, clarifying the theoretical construct C_r is possible by the use of following rules of checking:

1. Clarify some component of the construct C_r by specifying the structure of this component or modifying its structure, so that has not changed the functional essence of the component (clarifying in "depth");
2. Add a new construct C_p or to change the old version of the construct C_r by the way that saves specifications of the previous state of the theory (clarifying in "width").

Thus, before embedding of any increment $\Delta Th^P Zi, t)j$ into the current state of the theory ThP^t), the increment is need to check on its correspondence to the principle of additivity. In practice of designing the systems, there are cases, when checking of $\Delta Th P^{Z}i, tj)$ indicates on the violation of this principle, but the solution of the correspondence task Z should include in the project. Similar cases are usually processed by the specialized workflows "Management of Changing". After processing the documentation, the corresponding theory will be without contradictions.

In concluding this sub-section, it should be noted, the phase structure of becoming the theory is expedient to use for creating the substantially evolutionary theory of ThP^t), or, that the same, the theory of conceptual designing the system. The central place in this theory occupies the description phase evolved on the base of the before-theoretical phase. The potential of ThP^t)) can be essentially increased if others phase of becoming the theory will be additionally developed

2. EXPERIMENTING IN HUMAN ACTIVITY

2.1. Features of Experimental Activity

At the end of point 3.1.1, we referenced on the paper (Perry, 2014) where its author underlined the necessity of building the theories D and E reflecting the development of the system and the evaluation as a process of developing so its results. In software engineering, there is the rich experience of evaluations that must also be rethought as and ways of theorization. The perspective direction of such rethinking is an orientation on ways of evaluations in science, especially ways of scientific experimentation adapted to the features of human-computer activity.

Implicit experiments of the everyday life of people are roots of scientific experimentation. Typical reasons for such type of experimenting are to predict results of conceived actions or to define, which action or complex of actions can lead to conceived results.

The history of scientific experimentation begun from the position of Francis Bacon (1561– 1626) who claimed that the theoretical deductive statements must necessarily be checked in practice. In the centuries that followed and till now, scientific experiments were and are indispensable means for the progress of science and practice.

In its general understanding, a scientific experiment is a method of empirical research in which a scientist affects on the object under study by a special material resources (experimental set up and devices) in order to obtain the necessary information about the properties and characteristics of these objects or phenomena.

Let us present some definitions of experiments:

1. Dictianary.com, http://www.dictionary.com/browse/experiment:
   a. A test, trial, or tentative procedure; an act or operation for the purpose of discovering something unknown or of testing a principle, supposition, etc.
   b. A test or investigation, esp one planned to provide evidence for or against a hypothesis: a scientific experiment.
   c. The act of conducting such an investigation or test.
2. Businessdictionary http://www.businessdictionary.com/definition/experiment.html.Research method for testing different assumptions (hypotheses) by trial and error under conditions constructed and controlled by the researcher. During the experiment, one or more conditions (called independent variables) are allowed to change in an organized manner, and the effects of these changes on associated conditions (called dependent variables) are measured, recorded, validated, and analyzed for arriving at a conclusion.
3. Oxford Dictioary, https://en.oxforddictionaries.com/definition/experiment. A scientific procedure undertaken to make a discovery, test a hypothesis or demonstrate a known fact.
4. Free Dictionary, http://www.thefreedictionary.com/experiment. A test under controlled conditions that is made to demonstrate a known

truth, examine the validity of a hypothesis, or determine the efficacy of something previously untried

5. Merriam-Webster, https://www.merriam-webster.com/dictionary/experiment. An operation or procedure carried out under controlled conditions in order to discover an unknown effect or law, to test or establish a hypothesis, or to illustrate a known law.

Presented definitions prompt that experiments are appropriate means for evaluating the theories of D-type. That is why in this section, we disclose such kind of a human activity more detail.

Any experimentation has a goal, in accordance with which, scientists distinguish the following types of experiments:

1. Converting (creative) experiment requires active changes in the structure and function of the object being studied, for example, in accordance with the claimed hypothesis. This kind of experiments can be aimed at the formation of new connections and relationships between the components of the object or between the object under study, and other objects. In accordance with the opened trends of development of the research object, researcher intentionally creates conditions that must contribute to the formation of new properties and qualities of the object.

2. Ascertaining (declaring) experiment is used for checking any initial assumption. In the course of this experiment, the researcher ascertains the existence of some relationship between exposure to the object of research and the results confirming the existence of certain facts

3. Controlling experiment solves the problem of providing control over the object under study, management of the object using the influencing factors while studying changes its state depending on the exposure.

4. The searching experiment is conducted in the event if the classification of factors influencing the phenomenon under study due to lack of sufficient preliminary (a priori) of data is difficult. As a result, the searching experiment establishes the importance of factors, and nonessential factors are excluded. Often it is only the initial step in a series of experimental studies

5. The decisive experiment tests the validity of the main provisions of the fundamental theories in the case where two or more hypotheses is equally consistent with a number of phenomena. This consistency leads to difficulty, which is regarded as the correct hypothesis. The

decisive experiment reveals the facts, which are consistent with one of the hypotheses and contrary to the other.

Dedicated goals are typical for designing the system so that experiments of indicated kinds can be useful not only for evaluating the theoretical constructs but for solving the project tasks also.

Any experiment beginning with a question, answer on which must be obtained in the process of experimentation that will be conducted with the use of an experimental set up in the certain conditions. Therefore, in designing the system, the conceived experiment should also be developed for its effective conducting. Thus, intention to conduct any useful experiment will previously include:

1. Conceiving (inventing) the experiment with choosing its kind;
2. Wording the task of experimenting and conceptually solving this task;
3. Developing the appropriate set up with taking into account conditions of experimenting;
4. Developing the plan and technics of experimenting.

Any of these works essentially depends on objects with which the experiment will be conducted. In designing the SIS, the space of experimenting is a computerized environment with which the designers interact, solving the appointed tasks or tasks that appear situationally.

The difference among the objects used in experimenting allows distinguishing the mental and computerized experiments. Objects of mental (thought) experiments are mental models of the objects or phenomena (sensory images, figurative and symbolic models, symbolic models). Sometimes, one can use the term to refer to a thought experiment: an idealized or imaginary experiment. A thought experiment is a form of mental activity of the knowing subject, in the course of which is reproduced in the imagination of the real structure of the experiment.

In computerized experiments, designers work with objects that are programmed models of the computerized environment. The main difference between the computerized experiment and the mental that this experiment is a form of objective connection of consciousness with the outside world, while the thought experiment is a specific form of theoretical activity of the subject.

It should be noted, the current state of Artificial Intelligence is the richest source of means and methods for modeling the mental essences and mechanisms, and this source opens the possibility for a controlled automation of mental experimenting.

After preparing the experiment, it can be conducted in accordance with the developed plan by using the set up and technics of experimenting. This part of the experiment process includes following steps:

1. Determine results and assess their validity.
2. Determine if results support or refute claimed hypothesis.
3. Describe the conducted experiment in the form that helps its reuse any designer of the team developing the system.
4. Go over from an empirical study to logical generalization, analysis and theoretical processing of the resulting factual material.

Finalizing this subsection, we note, if in parallel with creating the theory $Th^P(t)$, designers build the corresponding theory E of experimenting, then this work leads to expanding the theory $Th^P(t)$ on the level of the identifiably measuring phase.

2.2. Concept Development and Experimentation

In this book, among directions, that focus their interests on the experimentation with conceptual objects we mark the study and practices that concern the subject area "Concept Development and Experimentation (CD&E)."

The main ideas contained in the CD & E direction are disclosed in such publications of its founders David S. Alberts and Richard E. Hayes as "Campaigns of Experimentation" and "Understanding Command and Control" (both books are available at http://www.dodccrp.org/html4/books_downloads. html). It also needs to mark the normative document "Military decision on MC-0056 (2010): "NATO Concept Development & Experimentation (CD&E) process. Secretary General, NATO" (available at http://www.act.nato.int/ images/stories/events/2011/cde/rr_mcm0056.pdf).

The substance of CD&E discloses the following definitions:

1. The term "Concept Development and Experimentation" designates a method which allows us to predict, by way of experimentation, whether certain concepts, theoretical constructs, sub-systems or systems are apt to meet the requirements imposed by the transformation process and can be constructively integrated into an overarching system." www.baainbw. de/portal/a/baain/start/project/cde.

2. CD&E is a science-oriented procedural model, designed to optimize the capabilities of armed forces across all levels of military actions and missions, especially against the background of the security-political challenges in the 21st Century. CD&E uses a variety of different scientific procedures, methods, and instruments. CD&E helps armed forces to determine, analyze and close capability gaps fast and in a mission-oriented manner. This concerns, among other aspects, the conceptual design, material, training, mission planning or the command structure (http://www.iabg.de/en/business-fields/defencesecurity/services-solutions/capability-management/concept-developmentexperimentation/).

3. CD&E "is the application of the structure and methods of experimental science to the challenge of developing the future military capability. CD&E is a forward-looking process for developing and evaluating new concepts, before committing extensive resources. CD?E is a process to identify the best solution not only from a technical perspective, but also for possible solutions for challenges involving doctrine, organization, training, and material to achieve significant advances in future operations. CD&E is a way of thinking your way through the future before spending money" (https://en.wikipedia.org/wiki/Concept_development_and_experimentation).

4. CD&E is "{a method which allows us to explore and predict, by way of experimentation, whether new concepts that may impact people, organization, process and systems will contribute to transformation objectives and will fit in a larger context".

In CD&E, term "concept" corresponds to "a general proposed solution that encompasses an overarching and firm idea of how a problem can be solved or of how advantage can be taken of an opportunity, with the aim of fulfilling a capability requirement in a given context. A concept according to this definition includes a description of the issue to be addressed (a problem or opportunity), why it is to be addressed (a capability requirement) and how it is to be addressed (the essential idea)" (http://blogg.forsvarsmakten.se/utvecklingsbloggen/files/2012/06/CDE_Method_Description_I-1_0_INT.pdf).

In the schematic form, the essence of CD&E clarifies Figure 5 that is inherited from the book (Alberts and Hayes, 2005).

Figure 5. Essence of CD&E

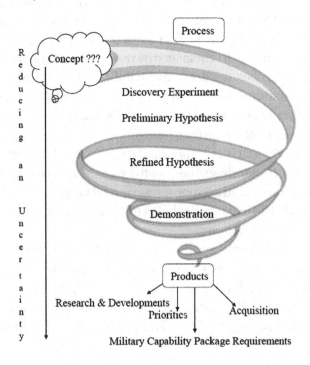

Figure 6. Iterative process

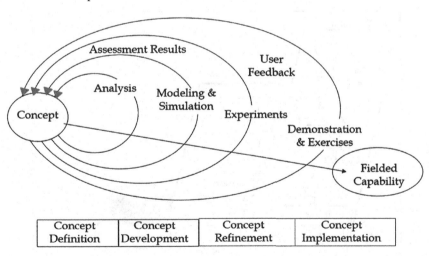

Any implementation of CD&E leads to the certain project, an implementation of which must provide iterative intertwining the concept development and experimentation. The scheme of such work is shown in the Figure 6.

Iterative intertwining that is managed by results of experiments and feedback continues until it reaches the desired capability. Thus, in this process, each step of experimentation is followed by the step in which the concept is further completed, adjusted and refined on all of the selected lines of development.

Any used experiment has an own lifecycle, the typical structure of which is shown in Figure 7, which is also inherited from the book (Alberts and Hayes, 2005). This scheme underlines that, on the base of the used knowledge, it is necessary to choose or build an appropriate model because the CD&E process is model-oriented. The used model helps to create an executed prototype that will be tested in experimenting.

Let us note that terms used in block-and-line schemes on Figures 5 – 7 clarify the essence as CD&E processes and the place and role of experiments in concept developments. Schemes help to understand applying the experimentation in the conceptual space in any applications including the domain of developing the SISs. These schemes will help to understand

Figure 7. Life cycle of experiment

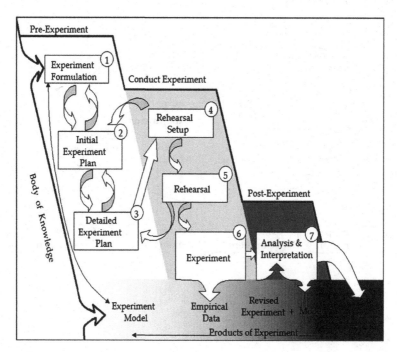

our versions of an experimentation that we suggest below for their use in conceptual designing the systems.

In practice, any implemented process consists of workflows, each of which combines a number of technics. Any used composition of the process can be estimated from the viewpoint of its maturity. There is developed a framework (Wiel et al., 2010) that helps to evaluate the maturity level by the use of following metrics:

1. **First Level - Initiation:** Principle idea is formulated.
2. **Second Level - Operational Validity:** Customer expresses the need and states requirements for the development of the principle idea.
3. **Third Level - Applicability:** Positive identification of a concept void and research on the applicability of the concept within the operational environment.
4. **Forth Level - Identification:** Component conceptual solution likely to fulfill stated requirements
5. **Fifth Level - Feasibility:** Analytical proof that conceptual solution is acting as required in a simulated environment.
6. **Sixth Level - Prototyping:** Proof-of-Principle building of integrated concept solutions.
7. **Seventh Level - 7 Prototype Validation:** Solutions are operable in a laboratory environment.
8. **Eights Level - Solution Validation:** Solutions are operable in the operational environment and validated through military assessment.
9. **Ninth Level - Solution Integration:** Developed block-solution integrated into full solution fulfilling requirements over DOTMLPFI spectrum.
10. **Tenth Level - Demonstration:** Full implementation in all DOTMLPFI areas.

To ensure that a CD&E project can close and that the resulting products can be approved – at which ever level – the only need for the project is to ensure that a certain maturity level is reached. The project can even declare beforehand which level they are targeting for.

It should be noted that we have conducted an analysis of reports(https://www.tno.nl/en/abouttno/more-about-our-work/annual-reports/), prepared in the Netherlands Organisation for Applied Scientific Research (2011-2014 years, one of the CD & E application development leaders). Research presented in the reports are guided by well-established practice of CD & E. Thus, noted in the preceding paragraphs of scientific novelty extends to a comparison with the results of research and the organization, as well as the following organizations: Defence Research and Development Canada (Canada, http://www.drdc-rddc.gc.ca/en/index.page, http://pubs.drdc-rddc.gc.ca/pubdocs/pcow1_e.html) and The Swedish Defence Research Agency (Sweden? https://www.foi.se/en.html), reports of which were examined as well.

2.3. Design Thinking

One more subject area of R&D that focuses its interests on the experimentation with conceptual objects is "Design Thinking." This domain has many faces, features of which one can disclose by the following set of definitions:

1. "What's special about Design Thinking is that designers' work processes can help us systematically extract, teach, learn and apply these human-centered techniques to solve problems in a creative and innovative way — in our designs, in our businesses, in our countries, in our lives." https://www.interaction-design.org/literature/topics/designthinking
2. "Design thinking is a human-centered approach to innovation that draws from the designer's toolkit to integrate the needs of people, the possibilities of technology, and the requirements for business success." http://www.ideou.com/pages/design-thinking 3. "Design thinking can be described as a discipline that uses the designer's sensibility and methods to match people's needs with what is technologically feasible and what a viable business strategy can convert into customer value and market opportunity." http://www.ideou.com/pages/design-thinking
4. Design thinking uses a process-based approach to solving problems, and like any process, it involves a series of steps that are carried out in a particular order to achieve a goal. In this case, the goal is to identify a solution that is capable of succeeding, can be carried out in a timely manner and is likely to be accepted by all stakeholders. http://whatis.techtarget.com/definition/design-thinking
5. Design thinking is an iterative approach to problem-solving that intentionally seeks out people with different perspectives, knowledge, skills and experience and has them work together to create a practical solution to a real-world problem. http://whatis.techtarget.com/definition/design-thinking
6. Design thinking is a human-centered, iterative problem-solving process of discovery, ideation, and experimentation that employs various design-based techniques to gain insight and yield innovative

solutions for virtually any type of organizational or business challenge. This method combines both analytical and creative approaches to generating solutions. http://flevy.com/browse/business-document/design-thinking-1980

7. Design thinking is the discipline of re-imagining and creating sustainable processes, systems, structures and business models through an empathetic and anticipatory humanistic approach using today's brilliant technologies and cross-disciplinary thinking which addresses unmet, desired and unanticipated needs of all affected stakeholders.

8. Design thinking is an approach to innovation that can be applied to all areas of human activity. Design thinking does not refer to a formal step-by-step process, but to a framework and a mindset. It is focused on a bias towards action, a human-centered viewpoint and a mode of continual experimentation. The core idea is that by deeply understanding customer needs, opportunities for innovation will emerge. These ideas can be further refined through rapid prototypes and iterations to result in breakthrough outcomes. http://www.managementexchange.com/story/reweaving-corporate-dna-building-culturedesign-thinking.

Thus, more generally, Design Thinking is a methodology for the solution of engineering, business, and other tasks, based on creative, rather than analytical approach. As opposed to the analytical thinking, the design thinking is a creative process in which sometimes the most unexpected ideas lead to better address a revealed problem.

In this process, a designer uses thinking that combines following its sides: Logical and Figurative; Rational and Emotional; Intuitive and Constructive; Analytical and Synthetic. The bipolar orientation of the design thinking has a number of inherent properties:

1. Intuitive and creative insight into the subject of design and integrity of the vision.
2. Ability to work with the details without losing sight of the whole.
3. Ability to work with the undeveloped and unconscious problems, as well as with nonprogrammable data that require an intuitive "grasp" and not a logical construction.
4. Coherence and unity of analytical and synthetic components lead to the act of synthesis

5. The ability to predict.
6. Correlation of creative imagination with reality.
7. The ability to visualize abstract concepts and ideas.
8. Ability to work in a team.

The process of design thinking is shown schematically in the Figure 8.

This scheme presents the typical division of the process on five steps that correspond to following actions:

1. Empathize that focuses on revealing and understanding explicit and implicit needs that have potential customers or users of innovative design solutions.
2. Define that specifies new opportunities by looking at things differently from viewpoints of users' needs and insights.
3. Ideate that is aimed at generating and exploring the ideas and solutions taking into account different perspectives in a short amount of time.
4. Prototype that provides a visual representation of one or more of chosen ideas to show to others
5. Test the main goals of which are to evaluate found a solution and to understand how user understand and use the appropriate ideas.

All of these actions are intertwined in a step-by-step process that is repeated over multiple iterations with using feedbacks. This process is managed by questions and tested answers on their correspondence to the targeted needs.

Figure 8. Process of design thinking

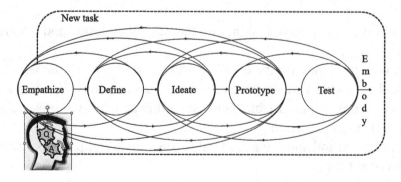

2.4. Features of Thought Experimentation

The real experiment usually has a limited scope. Sometimes it is not feasible for economic reasons or because of its complexity. Often material experiment does not give the desired result because its scope is limited by a level of development of knowledge and technology. Just a thought experiment, in which logical thinking and creative imagination of the researcher combined with the experimental and theoretical material, allows to push off from reality and go further - to understand and explore what previously seemed an unsolvable mystery. In all cases, when for knowing of the most profound essence is needed the experiment, the researcher try to conduct the thought experiment especially for a high degree of abstraction from the actual conditions.

Thought experiments are not invented quite arbitrarily. They are mental operations that meet certain requirements and principles of proven scientific theory. As in any other theoretical construction, in a thought experiment, all operations should be subject to some rules deriving from the knowledge of the objective laws of science. This requirement ensures a high degree of reliability of the knowledge gained during the study

The thought experiment is an experiment in the field of consciousness in which the leading role belongs to thinking. This determines by its subjective nature. However, the fact that the thought experiment is implemented on the level of consciousness says that its content is objective. In practice, some parts of the mental experiment are conducted beyond consciousness that can be presented by the scheme shown in the Figure 9.

In this scheme, the designer helps to mental operations of the thought experiment by reflecting the objects of the subject area on working area where

Figure 9. Conditions of thought experimenting

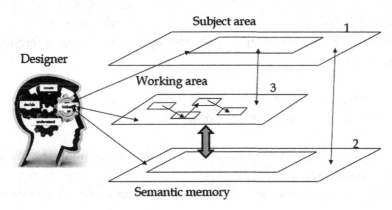

objects are used as conceptual models with descriptions in an appropriate semantic area.

Assessing the thought experiment, it is impossible to treat it as a finished knowledge; in this case, it acts as a simple illustration. Also, its content cannot be reduced only to the thinking about planning the material experiment (although it is always preceded to the material experiment). The thought experiment is rather a continuation and generalization, schematization of the latter, rather than the other way around.

The value of thought experiment, first, is that it allows investigating the situation is practically unfeasible, though possible in principle. Second, in some cases, it allows creating the knowledge and producing the verification of its truth, without resorting to material experimentation. However, a thought experiment is both direct and model and these its sides ultimately requires a practical verification of the results. If in the material experiment, its process already serves as confirmation of the truth of premises, the same can not be said about the mental experiment: a final assessment of a thought experiment can be only got in the process of validation of the results in practice.

Summarizing, we can describe the thought experiment as a heuristic operation with the following features:

1. It is a cognitive process that takes the structure of a real experiment;
2. The whole chain of reasoning is implemented on the basis of visual images;
3. Mental experimentation associates with the process of idealization;
4. By its logical structure, mental experiment is a hypothetical-deductive construction;
5. Thought experiment is usually caused by the task that is solved in the research;
6. Mental experimentation is based on the development of the scheme of mental action aimed at processing the initial information;
7. Thought experiment combines the strength of the formal inference with the experimental reliability

As it is generalized in (Sjøberg, 2008), regarding their practical application, thought experiments are created in order to:

1. Extrapolate beyond (or interpolate within) the boundaries of already established fact;
2. Predict and forecast the (otherwise) indefinite and unknowable future;

3. Explain the past;
4. The retrodiction, postdiction, and hindcasting of the (otherwise) indefinite and unknowable past;
5. Facilitate decision making, choice, and strategy selection;
6. Solve problems, and generate ideas;
7. Move current (often insoluble) problems into another, more helpful and more productive problem space (e.g., see functional fixedness);
8. Attribute causation, preventability, blame and responsibility for specific outcomes;
9. Assess culpability and compensatory damages in social and legal contexts;
10. Ensure the repeat of past success; or
11. Examine the extent to which past events might have occurred differently.
12. Ensure the (future) avoidance of past failures.

Thus, the thought experiment - a form of thinking objectively arisen as a result of the active human impact on nature. The specificity of this form is that the abstract and the concrete, rational, conceptual and sensory-visual make it dialectical unity. Thought experiment has an effective means of obtaining new knowledge about the world.

3. QUESTION-ANSWER APPROACH TO DEVELOPING THE THEORY OF THE PROJECT

3.1. Question-Answer Analysis of Project Tasks

At the point 3.1.3, we clarified the role of objects of task-type as in developing the project documentation and the project theory so in developing the project of the certain SIS. The meaning of such objects allows interpreting the project as a whole from the viewpoint of the certain task also. In this book, such interpretation of the project we will call '' the main task Z^* of the project.'' It will simplify both as our reasoning so used symbolic designations.

It should be noted, from this 'point' of the text, we begin reasoning that will present our approach to the use of the affordable experience in developing the systems (software systems or software intensive systems). Let us remind that our interests focus only at the conceptual stage of designing.

As told above, the becoming of the project documentation $S(T_0, t_0)$ begins with the text T_0, the content of which will also defines the first construct of the theory $Th^P(t_0)$. Because of we are deeply convinced that tasks are reasons of developing the $Th^P(t)$ then it can be assumed that the main task $Z*$ of the project initiates recording the text T_0 that will be used as an initial ground of the $Th^P(t)$. Moreover, this text must express the initial statement $St(Z*, t_0)$ of the task $Z*$. By other words, the text T_0 is produced outside the theory $Th^P(t_0)$, but this text should be used as the initial (informational) ground of $Th^P(t_0)$, from which the theory begins its becoming by the use of stepwise refinement (see sub-section 3.1.3). Let us assume, that text T_0 is produced by the designer who used steps Empathize, Define and Ideate of the design thinking approach.

This informational ground must satisfy to the following requirements:

1. **The Short Text:** The statement must be perceived as the understandable wholeness when attention is focused on it. As the "area" focusing is limited by the human possibilities, the text $S(Z*, t_0)$ should be as short as possible.

2. **Most Abstractly:** The statement $St(Z*, t_0)$ is the initial version of the dynamic construction $St(Z*, t)$ that will be evolved step by step (or state $S(Z*, t_k)$ by state $S(Z*_j, t_{k+1})$)) during the lifecycle of the task $Z*$. Any step decreases the definite "volume" of uncertainty $\nabla U(Z*, tk)$ existed in $S(Z*, t_k)$ by the inclusion of it the next increment $\Delta S(Z*, t_k)$. The sequence of increments and their contents reflects the sequence of decision-making acts and their results each of which can lead to restrictions on future acts. Accordingly, at the initial state $S(Z*, t_0)$ of the statement, the uncertainty $\nabla U(Z*, t_0)$ must be so indeterminate as possible. Therefore, the text $S(Z*, t_0)$ must be formulated as abstract as possible.

3. **The Level of Abstraction in Sufficient Measure:** In accordance with the previous point the text $S(Z*, t_0)$ with its corresponding uncertainty $\nabla U(Z*, t_0)$ are the initial source for generating the sequence of increments $\Delta S(Z*, t_1), \Delta S(Z*, t_2), ..., \Delta S(Z*, t_{K-1})$ that evolve the initial text till the necessary state $S(Z*, t_K)$. For such generating, the text can be interpreted as a source of initial axioms that are included in this text. These axioms must be sufficiently for inferring the state $S(Z*, t_K)$.

In the described version of the developing the $St(Z*, t)$, indicated requirements had led us to the pattern of the initial state $St(Z*, t_0)$, the text of which combines following three sentences:

1. The first sentence reflects the orientation of its content to a goal of a task Z*. This offer includes pointers not only to the goal but also on the ability to achieve it. An accompanied uncertainty can be hidden or registered by appropriate signs.
2. The second sentence prompts a feature of an idea which can help to solve this task. The feature implicitly indicates the way of achieving the goal.
3. The third sentence concerns an environment (with its restrictions), in which the team of designers will work with the task Z*.

Thus, the life cycle of the theory $Th^P(t)$ begins with the state $Th^P(t_0)$ which consists of the three sentences of the text $S(Z^*, t_0)$, each of which has the certain function. This text corresponds to the initial statement $S(Z^*, t_0)$ of the task Z*, the work with will be aimed at designing the corresponding system.

There is a way for extending the statement $S(Z^*, t_0)$ by its analysis on the base of accessible experience. The meaning of this way is figuratively shown in the Figure 10.

This figure demonstrates controlled reducing the uncertainty $VU(Z^*, t_0)$ of the statement $S(Z^*, t_0)$ by the use of question-answering in an actual division of its sentences. In interactions with the text, actual division as a communicative mechanism breaks up any sentence on two part – theme and rheme, where "theme" is the predictable starting point of the communicative interesting, and "rheme" indicates a new information that should receive an additional value in answering to the corresponding question. Thus, the result of the transition from the state $S(Z^*, t_0)$ to state $S(Z^*, t_1)$ can be presented by the construction shown in the Figure 11.

Figure 10. Process of question-answer analysis

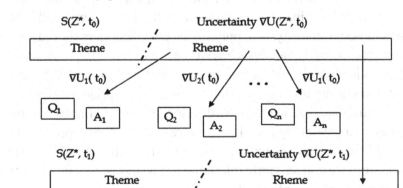

Figure 11. Transition between reflections

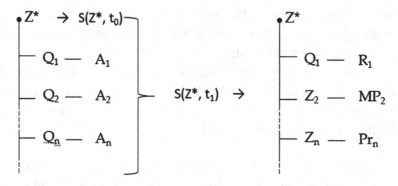

In communicative practice constructs Q_x and A_x can have different types and purposes, for example:

1. If answer A_x on question Q_x exists and the person should extract the value of the answer from the corresponding ontology of database or other informational sources, the question Q_x can be qualified as "Query" with symbolic designation "Q"
2. If answer A_x is absent and can be obtained only after solving the certain task then the question Q_x can be qualified as "Task."
3. If constructing the answer A_x has led to the certain requirement, then this type of answers can be called "Requirement".

To point out on the diversity types of question and answer, in Figure 11 nodes of the graph that shows results of question-answer analysis of $S(Z^*, t_0)$ are reassigned, where R_1- requirement, Z_2 and Z_n present tasks, MP – model of precedent and Pr – prototype.

In accordance with the stepwise refinement, this way of reducing the uncertainty can be continued for each node of the graph generated with the use of question-answer analysis. Applying the way, designers should take into account that the use of this analysis has similarity for any task. Consequently, step by step, it is possible to develop the graphical structures of the question-answer analysis, reducing the uncertainty till its appropriate degree.

In our research and practice, we have developed a question-answer approach (QA-approach) to designing the SISs []. More detailly, QA-approach and the toolkit WIQA for its realizing will be described in fourth and fifth chapters. In this sub-section, we concern only relations of this approach with our version of theorizing the projects of systems.

Figure 12. Typical result of question-answer analysis

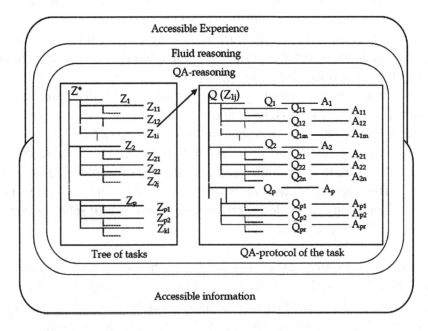

The kernel of the approach is the question-answer analysis (QA-analysis) some features of which were presented above. In implementing the QA-approach to tasks of the project, results of QA-analysis are registered in graph structures that are schematically shown in Figure 12.

The scheme underlines that these question-answer structures (QA-structures) are generated on the base natural reasoning (fluid reasoning) of designers when they constructively apply question-answer reasoning (QA-reasoning) during solving the project tasks. In this work designers operatively use affordable experience and appropriate information.

Let us clarify the essence of indicated QA-structures. For the certain project P, they present its tree of tasks $TT(Z^*,t)$ in a current moment of time t. By other words the artifact $TT(Z^*,t)$ reflects the real-time state of the project P from the viewpoint of its task structure. This artifact has the following features:

1. The artifact is placed in the semantic memory of the toolkit WIQA.
2. For any task from $TT(Z^*,t)$, the reflection includes a question-answer protocol (QAprotocol, QA(t)) that codes QA-reasoning used in solving this task.
3. All nodes of $TT(Z^*,t)$ are visually accessible for designers.

4. Cells of this memory help to adequately express the semantics of any project task and any component of its QA-protocol.
5. The important place among attributes of any cell occupies the field that is intended for a verbal description of an uploaded unit (description for any type of question or answer).
6. Designers have the possibility for binding a group of nodes in the structure of TT(Z*,t) by a necessary relation.
7. There are two basic viewpoints on the artifact TT(Z*,t):
    ◦   In accordance with the first view, the artifact has a hierarchical structure that is coordinated with the use of stepwise refinement.
    ◦   The second viewpoint reflects a net structure of TT(Z*,t) in conditions when designers have set some useful relations among nodes of the artifact.

Thus, in step-by-step conceptual designing, the tree of tasks accumulates built and used descriptions of questions and answers of any types. Moreover, designers have the possibility for checking, correcting, processing, modifying and using any of these descriptions if it will be necessary or useful.

One of the useful applications of this informational source is developing the project documentation where it is typical to place the reusable textual units in predefined positions of documents in their system.

In section 3.1.3, we described the system $P^D(t)$ in its relations with the project theory $Th^P(t)$. Any project documents and their system should be built as models of the theory $Th^P(t)$. And therefore, the artifact TT(Z*, t) can be also used as the informational source for creating the theory of the project. Moreover, constructs of the theory should be extracted from TT(Z*, t) and after that they need to include in the current state of $Th^P(t)$. Only after that, designers can use such constructs in corresponding documents. This sequence corresponds to the following chain of implications

$$TT(Z^*, t) \rightarrow Th^P(t) \rightarrow P^D(t). \tag{8}$$

In this chain, the first transition suggests that verbal components of TT(Z*, t) that will be included to the theory $Th^P(t)$ must be carefully processed to correspond the requirements the theory. Any of these components and its useful combinations with other constructs of the theory must be correspond to the current state of its phases (descriptive, classification and identifiable measurable phases).

Figure 13. Theory of the project in conceptual designing

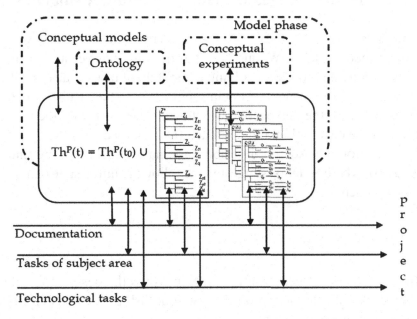

Such processing is implicitly shown in Figure 13, the scheme of which uncovers that in conditions of becoming the theory $Th^P(t)$ it is better to use an ontology (realizing the classification phase) and means for conducting the conceptual experiments (supporting the work of designers at the level of the identifiably measurable phase).

The scheme also demonstrates that through conceptual models (model phase) the theory can be used by designers for interacting with the documentation (tasks of documentation) and with tasks of the subject area and used technology.

One of the positive effects from the use of theory $Th^P(t)$ was shown above. It is controlled management of uncertainty in step-by-step solving the project tasks. This type of managing positively evolves the potential of project management. Uniting the theory with the ontology that is evolving in parallel and coordination with the theory opens the opportunity for the use of controlled lexis in specifications, documentation, communication and reasoning of designers. The theory is also capable of making a positive contribution to the re-use of solved tasks.

3.2. Coordination of Design Thinking and QA-Analysis

As told in subsection 3.1.3, the work with project tasks is a source of developing the project theory $Th^P(t)$. When using the question-answer approach, this theory is built in the process of solving the system of tasks, starting with the root task Z^*, solving of which is being registered in the artifact $TT(Z^*, t)$. In this case, one of the perspective way to start the work with the root task is the use of the design thinking approach (DT-approach).

This assertion is based on describing the nature of design presented in (Dorst, 2010) where K. Dorst suggested the following initial state of applying the DT-approach:

$$??U \overset{???W}{\rightarrow} ?V \tag{9}$$

This expression reflects a situation S, in which the designer decided to start the work with the new project (new root task Z^*). Let us clarify our understanding this expression:

1. There is a goal G to achieve a certain value for potential customers, and in the current moment of time, this value V expressed with some uncertainty (?V).
2. Conditions U, in which the goal can be achieved, are vague perceived, and they can be expressed with essential uncertainty ??U for reducing of which conditions can be constructed and reconstructed during designing the SIS.
3. The construct ??W is unknown, and it cannot be qualified as a problem gap between ??U and taking into account their uncertainties.
4. Having the goal G expressed by ?V opens the possibility for interpreting the situation S as an indicator of the task Z^* that should be solved.
5. For reducing the uncertainties in the expression (1), it should apply design thinking based on question-answer reasoning.

This position led us to combine the design thinking approach with question-answer approach that can be expressed by the following implication:

$$?^U U\left(Z^*\right) \overset{?^W W(Z^*)}{\rightarrow} ?^V V\left(Z^*\right), \tag{10}$$

where symbols $?^U?^V$ and $?^W$ indicates applying of QA- approach to the components of U, V and W of the the task Z^*. In the described case, this approach is implemented after formulating the initial statement of the task Z_i and with coordination with the process of design thinking.

Furthermore, the use of QA-approach for the task Z^* will generate the subordinated tasks as nodes of the tree $TT(t)$, and for any new task Z_i, all that told above for the task Z^* is also applied.

Thus, at the conceptual stage of designing the SIS, solving the root task Z^* of the project will continue until the moment of time t_k when solving all subordinated tasks will be finished. So, before this point in time, the statement of the task Z^* and a statement of any subordinated task could be changed. Therefore, in reality, designers will know which task Z^* they conceptually solved only at the end of the conceptual stage. Thus, the tree of tasks $TT(t)$ is a useful artifact that adequately reflects the process of conceptual designing the SIS

3.3. Question-Answer Structure of the Project Theory

In the previous subsection, we presented and uncovered some details of the idea of theorizing the project on its conceptual stage. The idea has the following basic features:

1. The project theory $Th^P(t)$ should be created as the theory of the substantially evolutionary kind.
2. Becoming of the theory should begin with its initial ground in the form of a textual description, which is as short as possible and as abstract as possible, but the essence of the theory must be expressed in the sufficient measure.
3. The basic goal of developing the theory is to reduce the uncertainty in conceptual solving the project tasks by using the stepwise refinement in coordination with QA-analysis in its application to statements of tasks.
4. Designers develop the theory when they interact with the accessible experience and use appropriate information in the real-time of conceptual designing, when, in addition to traditional forms of Human-Computer Interaction they are forced to use the experiencebased forms of HCI.

As told above, in its application, the theory is a source of a number of positive effects that influence on components of the design process and their results. It is achieved when the described approach to developments of such theories is reified. In our study and practice, this approach has been reified and got the name "Question-and-answer approach to conceptual design." Materialization of this approach has led to the development of the toolkit WIQA in a number of versions that support conceptual designing the systems.

In the development of this toolkit, its central tasks were aimed at reifying the typical constructs of the theory That is why, the set of a basic attribute can be extended by the designer with the use of the mechanism of "Additional attributes," and their compositions, taking into account the reflection on the reality.

The toolkit has been realized so that the class of typical constructs includes questions and answers of different types. In its turn, types were divided into two sub-classes – basic types and types specified by designers. In assigning the attributes for the basic types, we used the essence of their referents.

We understand such essence as "question" as a naturally artificial phenomenon that appears in mind of the certain person who implicitly or implicitly try to apply natural experience. To control the access to the experience, the person expresses this phenomenon by the use of appropriate signs of the natural language. Thus, verbal expression of the "question" is no more than its sign model.

Therefore, in the specification of such construct as question Q, we use a set of basic attributes that includes following items:

1. Symbolic expression of "question" registered in the language of the project.
2. Creator of the sign expression
3. Time of creation or last modification of the expression.
4. An identifier is corresponding the type of question.
5. Identifier of the construct defining its place in the theory.
6. Address of the construct defining its place in a semantic memory of the toolkit.
7. Attribute defining the subordination between related questions.
8. Reference on the necessary graphical scheme or image.
9. Reference on corresponding material in before-theoretical phase.

Taking into account mutual complementarity of the question and the corresponding answer, the answer as a construct of the theory has the same basic attributes. However, any answer expresses the reaction on the corresponding question, and this reaction can correlate with any type of answers. That is why the set of a basic attribute can be extended by the designer with the use of the mechanism of "Additional attributes." For example, if an answer corresponds to the certain action, then basic attributes are extended by characteristics of this action.

During registering any question or answer or later when it will be necessary, the designer has the possibility to assign this construct of the adequate type that corresponds to the construct function. For example, the certain question Q can be qualified as task Z after evaluating the possibility of answering. In this case, the question Q will have two points of its placing in theory – the first in the place of initial registering and the second in the corresponding point of the task tree. For linking of these places, both Q and corresponding Z are marked by the unique additional attribute.

The important components of any theory are propositions the typical forms of which are sentences (clauses) in the language of the theory. It should be noted, in theory, $Th^P(t)$, the sign model of any question or answer has the textual form including one or more sentences. For example, a question can include its preconditions, but even the question consist of one one sentence, its expression includes a part of the possible answer.

However, in theory, we can qualify as a typical proposition a pair of mutual complementary question and answer. Such proposition we can understand as a simple question-answer construct (QA-construct) of the theory $Th^P(t)$. Complicated QA-constructs consist of the necessary composition of simple QA-constructs.

When the theory $Th^P(t)$ is applied, its construct of any type becomes the object that uses in the certain application. Thus, in applications of the theory, designers can use and process Qobjects, A-objects and QA-objects of any type in different composition and even with objects that are beyond the theory $Th^P(t)$. In applications, the objects from the theory can be used as models. Among such models, important place occupies QA-protocols reflecting the conceptual solutions of corresponding tasks. Therefore, such types of models we called "QA-model of the task."

One more important application of the theory $Th^P(t)$ is the development of the corresponding ontology. Moreover, this application as the classification phase is included in $Th^P(t)$. That is why the ontology is created on the base of the same types of constructs as the descriptive phase of the theory $Th^P(t)$. In the ontology, any concept (term, notion) can be considered as an implicit (convolutional) sentence or their group.

At the same time, the ontology has useful and important applications not only in theory but also beyond its scope. For example, the ontology can be applied in extracting the answers from the studied sentences. The absence of the used words of the sentence in the ontology can be interpreted as reasons for questions about functions or values of these words in the verbal unit of the before-theoretical phase.

The ontology is also useful in experimental checking the sign models of questions and answers. In this case, if designer conducts the thought experiment, a part of which is implemented with models of concepts beyond the brain, then interactions with the ontology can improve any step of the experimenting, beginning with the stage of its preparing.

3.4. Conceptual Experimenting in the Conceptual Space

Designing the systems in the conditions of development and use of theory $Th^P(t)$ opens the possibility for targeted mental experimentation. First of all, any construct C_r of the theory must be verified on its preliminarily understandability. Then a creator of the construct should establish reasons and effects which were caused by the inclusion of the construct into the theory. Thereafter, the inclusion of the construct should be expressed at the level of causeeffect relation. And, that is obligatory, the inclusion of the construct into the theory must be tested for compliance with the principle of additivity.

As told above in the section 2.2.3, thought experiments have a more wide area of responsibility that can find their applications in various versions in the model phase of the theory.

In accordance with QA-approach, typical constructs of the theory are questions and answers expressed in textual forms. In designing the system, a correspondence of any question Q and answer A, and this correspondence can be interpreted as the following cause-and-effect relation

$$Q \rightarrow A, \tag{11}$$

which must satisfy to the logical principle of sufficiency. In the simplest case, this relation should accompany a sufficient number of arguments $\{Arg_i\}$. Thus, the verification of the relation can be achieved by the use of adequate thought experiment, after which the approved relation will have view

$$Q_i \rightarrow (\{Arg_k\} \rightarrow A_j). \tag{12}$$

In its turn, there are some mental works that must be fulfilled for wording the answer A. These works consist of following items:

1. Initial wording the answer A;
2. Controlling the lexis of the textual expression of A;
3. Controlling the predicates used in the answer;
4. Previously understanding the textual expression of the answer;
5. Controlling the lexis of A after understanding;
6. Revealing the arguments;
7. Controlling the sufficiency of the argumentation;
8. Controlling the understandability of the answer in its current wording.

If one compares these works with the list of applications of thought experiments that was described in the subsection 2.2.3, then one can view that the thought experiment can be applied for any of these works.

It should be noted, in the correspondence task, the answer A can fulfill the certain role, for example, it can be a requirement for the corresponding task or certain restriction. In designing the system, the answer can express a principle, setting, principle, motive, goal, factor, condition, consequence, effect, argument or any other role. So, for increasing the quality of the argued answer A, the enumerated works are applied to any argument of the implication $(\{Arg_k\} \rightarrow Ai)$.

In accordance with QA-approach, the textual expression of any answer A is a source of uncertainties that must be reduced by the use of QA-analysis. Such reducing the uncertainty suggests generating the set of questions $\{Q_{ij}\}$ that, in the general case, requires fulfilling the following works:

1. Discovering the question;
2. Identifying the question;
3. Wording the question.

Goals of discovering and identifying the question can be achieved when the designer fulfills the wording of the answer A_i, first of all during following works:

1. Controlling the lexis of the textual expression of A;
2. Controlling the predicates used in the answer;
3. Previously understanding the textual expression of the answer;
4. Controlling the lexis of A after understanding;
5. Revealing the arguments;
6. Controlling the understandability of the answer in its current wording.

The wording of any question is similar to the wording of the answer. So, all works that provide the wording of the answer are also applied to the wording of the question, and all kinds of thought experiments that support the wording of the answer can be useful in wording the question.

Thus thought experiments have numerous and various applications in the becoming of the theory Th(t) and its applications also. In any case such experimenting, any designer conducts any thought experiment in a conceptual environment that is schematically shown in the Figure 14.

This scheme demonstrates that certain components of experimenting are placed beyond of brain. The external conceptual environment includes following components:

1. Experimental set up, functions of which are fulfilled by the reusable complex of actions distributed between the designer and computer.
2. The object of experimenting that can be a construct of the theory or a certain model of the theory application.
3. Conditions of experimenting that point out on the conceptual surrounding of conducting the experiment.
4. Conceptual environment, in which external components involved in the thought experiment exist in computerized forms.

Figure 14. Thought experiment in conceptual environment

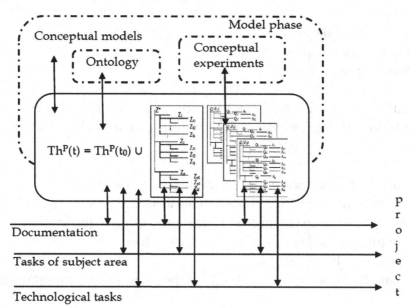

5.   The designer who is an active force of experimenting, who interacts with the conceptual environment and its components as with means that help to mental processes used in the conceptual experiment. Moreover, the designer participates in external actions and manages their effective execution.

Thus, in the question-answer approach, the process of thought experimenting is partially automated, that was a reason for us to call such version of mental experimenting as "conceptual experimenting" (Sosnin, 2015).

The main feature of conceptual experiments is the necessity of real-time interactions of the designer with the accessible experience. These interactions are based on natural questionanswer reasoning that is intertwined with question-answering beyond brain structures. Described specificity of human interactions with the computerized environment can be qualified as experience-based Human-Computer Interaction.

Additionally, specific features of conceptual experimenting are the use of reflections of essences involved in any conceptual experiment onto a semantic memory of a question-answer type and pseudocode programming of actions of the designer who executes them as intellectual processor (Sosnin, 2013). These features and their reifying will be clarified in chapter 4.

3.5. Theoretically Experimental View on the Project

Above we tried to substantiate expediency of using the project theorization on the base the question-answer approach. Our reasoning led us to the becoming of theory $Th^P(t)$, the phase structure of which is presented in the Figure 15.

The scheme points out that the phase structure combines the artifact $Th^P(t)$ with the corresponding ontology and a theorization of a set of conceptual experiments that have been conducted for substantiating the correctness of constructs of the $Th^P(t)$.

Constructs of the theory are visually observable into their system S {QA(t), t} that includes the tree of tasks and QA protocols for these tasks. Visually, this system is a composition of nets, a typical node of which is shown in the Figure 16.

By the fourth law of classical logics, any answer included into the theory structure should be sufficiently substantiated. In the Figure 16, the left composition of nodes reflects the case when substantiation of the answer A_i provides by the use of a list of arguments $\{Arg_{ik}\}$. The right composition

Figure 15. Phase stricter of the project theory

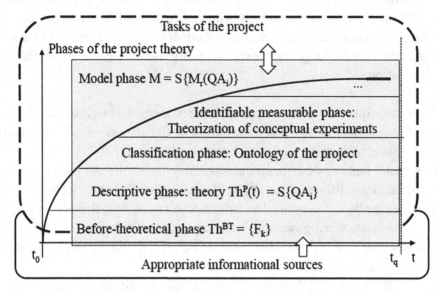

Figure 16. Typical compositions of nodes

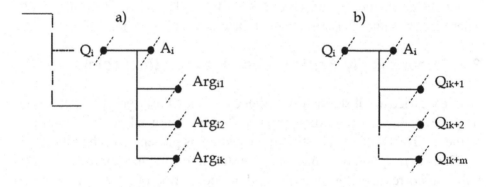

corresponds to the case when, additionally to argumentation, the answer was a source of more detail questioning.

As told above in the subsection, the answer can have a type of the following open list {a principle, assertion, setting, requirement, restriction, motive, goal, factor, condition, consequence, effect, argument, caution, advice, remark .....}. Furthermore, any node in these system has not only hierarchical relation with its context but other types of system relations caused by example the used ontology. Therefore, artifacts $Th^P(t)$ is visually accessible as a semantic net that explicitly and implicitly (through intermediaries) is bond with theory models applied in solving the project tasks.

Theory Th^P(t) combined with the corresponding ontology, conceptual experiments and models open a new opportunity for the improvement of conceptual designing. These opportunities are caused by the use of experience-based human-computer interactions, the main feature of which is question-answering with structures and conditions described above.

As it has been observed, questions are the naturally artificial phenomena that occur in certain conditions and provoke definite reactions. Therefore, any question should be discovered, identified, registered, described, specified, checked and applied. Applying the question is to build the adequate answer. This work can be implemented by the designer in one of three words – an artificial or artificially natural worlds or in the natural world. This side of questions is schematically shown in the Figure 17.

In the process of designing the certain system, tasks that stand behind questions help to create the theory Th^P(t) by appropriate answers each of which should be built. Among these answer we mark those that have a behavioral character or by other words answers in the form of behavioral actions. Such answers have two conceptual versions of their registering in the project. The first version is a description of the construct of the theory Th^P(t) while the second version is a guide for building the answer. The second version can be interpreted as a certain rule (in theory Th^P(t)) that specify an inference of the answer to the corresponding question. The second interpretation of the guide for generating the answer is its model (model of the corresponding construct

Figure 17. Types of questions

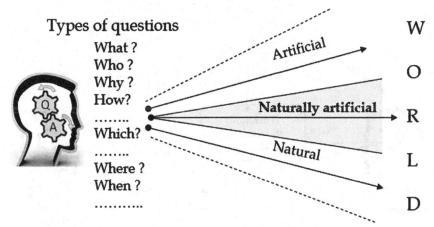

of Th^P(t)) which designers can repeatedly use in designing. In conceptual experiments, such guides fulfill the tole of set up for experimenting.

The similar reasoning we can conduct for an answer of any type that correlates with the corresponding question of a certain type. This reasoning leads to the additionality <ESSENCE – its VALUE >, which corresponds to an implicit question about the value of the essence. In practice, for example, for variables in physics, the explicit transition to the value corresponds to operational definitions of corresponding variables. In programming, the additionality is disclosed through "program variable and its value."

It should be noted, in designing the system, the necessity question-answering in conceptual forms arises in different cases. That is why, conceptual experimenting can be useful not only for creating the theory Th^P(t). Conceptual experiments are especially important for developing and testing the behavioral actions of designers, for example when they solve project tasks taking into account their reuse. These applications of conceptual experiments will be described below.

3.6. Interactions Based on Experience

To reifying the QA-approach, we have developed the specialized instrumentally technological environment WIQA (Working in Questions And Answers), the use of which is supported by workflows "Interactions with experience." In conceptual designing the systems, any designer applies these workflows

Figure 18. Conditions of interactions

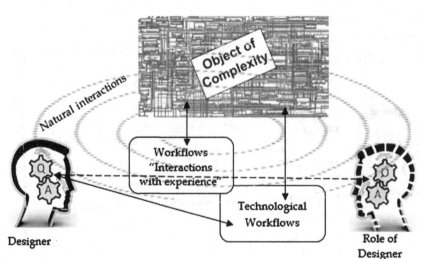

in combination with other technological workflows in conditions that are schematically shown in Figure 18.

This scheme figuratively discloses our idea of automating the natural interaction in reducing the complexity, about which we told at the end of section 2. There we underlined the necessity to find such way of automating the natural interactions with the object of complexity and programmed interfaces that can be used in unpredictable situations.

The meaning of our idea of automating includes follows:

1. In any time of implicit interactions with the object of complexity and implicitly or explicitly perceiving the state of programmed interfaces, the designer can break the technological process if designer's mind signalizes about appearing a question.
2. Let us suppose that discovered question Q corresponds to the theory and the designer mentally decides to react on it.
3. This decision will be a reason to activate the workflows "Interactions with Experience" that has own programmed interfaces that are developed for automating the natural interactions with natural experience.
4. In QA-approach, in the current state of its realization, these interfaces provoke controlled influences on dialogical structuring the verbal reflections in consciousness, mental imagination and thought experimentation conceived by the designer.
5. The indicated influences we interpret as controlled artificial interactions of the designer with the same designer who fulfills the specialized role (intellectual processor, I-processor).
6. This kind of artificial interactions is intertwined with corresponding natural interactions, and such integral process we define as "experience-based human-co0mputer interactions" that, in turn, can be combined with HCI of other kinds.

4. SOME REMARKS TO THE CHAPTER 3

1. In its initial settings and even in the title, SEMAT-initiative stresses the need for theorizing the foundations of software engineering. That is why the creation of a Ground Theory of software engineering was claimed as one of the most important goals of this approach.
2. How to the initial declaring the SEMAT initiative so during the becoming of corresponding domain, there were many attempts to build the ground

theory, but as it can be stated the satisfactory general theory is not built till now.

3. Attempts aimed at finding the adequate Ground Theory show that a potential of this theory should provide solving the tasks of analysis explanation, prediction, design, and action or, by another word, theorizing the software engineering should have an integral character.

4. For creating any theory, its developer or developers should define its constructs and propositions, provide explanations to justify the theory, determine its scope and test the theory through empirical research.

5. In accordance with the paper (Perri, 2014), a general theory of software engineering must have "two logical parts: design and evaluation, D and E, each of which as a theory T." Moreover, "delineate a rich variety of theories related to D and E and consider these to be sub-theories critical to understanding the relationships between the theories in D and E."

6. In science, the researchers create and use various types of theories, among which we mark the kind of substantially evolutionary theories, the becoming of which are similar to the step-by-step developing the applications of software engineering. In this book, among different applications of software engineering, we chose the development of the SISs and focus the especial attention on the conceptual stage of designing, with the theorization of which we bind the creation and use of the substantially evolutionary theory of project $Th^P(t)$.

7. The becoming of any theory $Th^P(t)$ of this kind begins with an initial state, the brief description of which reflects the essence of the theory and evolves by increments in a stepby-step process. The theory has a phase structure (before-theoretical, descriptive, classification, identifiable, measurable, formal and model phases), components of which are developed in parallel. Any new increment is tested on its conformity to the principle of additionality and adequacy of reality.

8. In the phase structure, the descriptive phase occupies the central place because this phase expresses the substance of the theory in the form of linked constructs each of which has sufficient substantiation. That is why this phase is a kernel of the theory. For the kernel, other phases fulfil subordinated roles. For example, the model phase reflects applications of the theory at the level of its constructs.

9. In terms of dividing the theory into two logical parts D and E, the identifiable, measurable phase of the theory $Th^P(t)$ corresponds to the logical part E. In science, the operational side

of the logical part E finds its expressions in scientific experiments that have the rich history, various types and numerous kinds of implementations.

10. In applications of software engineering can appear the necessity to conduct any type of experiments (converting, ascertaining, controlling, searching and decisive experiment), for any of which will need to prepare it, to conduct and process the obtained results. Experimenting is essential important at the conceptual stage of designing when designers creatively work with conceptual objects that find their reifying in verbal and graphical forms, values of which are expressed with the use of semantics.

11. This book focuses its interests on experiments with conceptual objects that are constructs of the theory $Th^P(t)$ or their compositions that are applied as models of the theory in solving the project tasks.

12. For our interests, one of the related subject areas (for an inheritance of useful decisions) is "Concept development and experimentation," in which typical approach to experiments is bound with model-driven prototyping. In this domain, the central place occupies conceptions that have an innovative character for important (originally military) projects. 13. One more related subject area that was chosen as the informational source is "Design Thinking" where investigated activities concern mental processes, for example, such for emphasizing and ideating.

14. More generally, Design Thinking is a methodology for the solution of engineering, business, and other tasks, based on creative, rather than analytical approach. As opposed to the analytical thinking, the design thinking is a creative process in which sometimes the most unexpected ideas lead to better address a revealed problem.

15. This subject area uses prototypes to build visual representations for one or more of chosen ideas for their comparing in processes of decision-making.

16. Among means that support an evaluation of the concepts in science and practice, one can mark thought experimenting, which are similar with prototyping on the level of works with concepts. A thought experiment is a form of thinking objectively arisen as a result of the active human impact on nature. The specificity of this form is that the abstract and the concrete, rational, conceptual and sensory-visual make it dialectical unity. Thought experiment has an effective means of obtaining new knowledge about the world.

17. One of the basic features of conceptual experimenting is a reflection of an investigated object on a semantic memory that must find its reifying in automating the thought experiments.

18. Our choice of the described type of the project theory with the orientation on thought experimenting has led us to develop the QA-approach for building the applied theories of the $Th(t)$-type.

19. QA-approach is intended for building the applied theories of projects by the use of question-answer analysis that, for any theory $Th^P(t)$, is conducted by the use of stepwise refinement, beginning with the initial state of the theory $Th^P(t_0)$. Refined results of this analysis, registered in the specialized QA-protocol as constructs of the theory, and these constructs are visually accessible for designers as nodes of the semantic net.

20. In the becoming of the theory, questions are understood as naturally artificial phenomena that appear in mind of the certain person who implicitly or implicitly tried to apply the natural experience. Any of such phenomenon should be discovered, identified, checked and processed.

21. Designing systems in the conditions of development and use of theory $Th^P(t)$ opens the possibility for targeted mental experimentation. First of all, any construct C_r of the theory must be verified on its previously understandability. Then a creator of the construct should establish reasons and effects which were caused by the inclusion of the construct into the theory.

22. In theory $Th^P(t)$, the typical version of cause-effect regularities is a relation between the question Q and corresponding answer A that are registered in the theory in textual forms. Verifying this relation can be achieved by the use of adequate thought experiment.

23. Thought experiments have numerous and various applications in the becoming of the theory $Th(t)$ and its applications also. In any case such experimenting, any designer conducts any thought experiment in a conceptual environment (conceptual space, C-space).

REFERENCES

Alberts, D. S., & Hayes, R. E. (2005). *Campaigns of Experimentation.* Washington, DC: CCRP.

Alberts, D. S., & Hayes, R. E. (2006). *Understanding Command and Control.* Washington, DC: CCRP.

Boehm, B. (2015). General Theories of Software Engineering (GTSE): Key Criteria and an Example. *Proc. of the Fourth SEMAT Workshop on General Theory of Software Engineering*, 1-2. doi:10.1109/GTSE.2015.18

Brown, T. (2009). *Change by Design: How Design Thinking Transforms Organizations and Inspires Innovation.* HarperBusiness.

Cockburn A Detailed Critique of the SEMAT Initiative. (2017). Available at http://alistair.cockburn.us/A+Detailed+Critique+of+the+SEMAT+Initiative

Dorst, K. (2010). The Nature of Design Thinking. *Proc. of DTRS8 Interpreting Design Thinking: Design Thinking Research Symposium*, 131–139.

Leifer, L., & Meinel, C. (2015). Manifesto: Design thinking becomes foundational. Design Thinking Research: Making Design Thinking Foundational, 1-4.

MCM-0056-2010. (2010). *NATO Concept Development and Experimentation (CD&E) Process.* Brussels: NATO HQ.

Ng, P.-W. (2014). Theory based software engineering with the SEMAT kernel: preliminary investigation and experiences. *Proceedings of the 3rd SEMAT Workshop on General Theories of Software Engineering*, 13-20. doi:10.1145/2593752.2593756

Perry, D. E. (2016). Theories, theories everywhere. *Proc. of the 5th International Workshop on Theory-Oriented Software Engineering*, 8-14. doi:10.1145/2897134.2897138

Ralph, P., Iaakov Exman, J., Ng, P.-W., Johnson, P., Goedicke, M., Kocata, A. K., & Liu Yan, K. (2014). How to Develop a General Theory of Software Engineering: Report on the GTSE 2014 Workshop. *SIGSOFT Softw. Eng. Notes*, *39*(6), 23–25.

Sosnin, P. (2012). Question-Answer Approach to Human-Computer Interaction in Collaborative Designing. In Cognitively Informed Intelligent Interfaces: Systems Design and Development. IGI Global. doi:10.4018/978-1-4666-1628-8.ch010

Sosnin, P. (2016). *Conceptual Experiments in Automated Designing.* In R. Zuanon (Ed.), *Projective Processes and Neuroscience in Art and Design* (pp. 155–181). IG-Global.

Wiel, W. M., Hasberg, M. P., Weima, I., & Huiskamp, W. (2010). Concept Maturity Levels Bringing structure to the CD&E process. *Proc. of Interservice industry training, simulation and education conference*, 2547-2555.

ADDITIONAL READING

Brooks, F. P. (2010). *The design of design: essays from a computer scientist.* Upper Saddle River, NJ: Addison–Wesley.

Cares, C., Franch, X., & Mayol, E. (2006). Perspectives about paradigms in software engineering, in *Proc. 2nd International workshop on Philisophiocal Foundations on Information Systems Engineering*, pp. 737-744.

Hirschman, L., & Gaizauskas, R. (2001). Natural Language Ques-tion Answering: The View from Here. *Natural Language Engineering*, 7(04), 67–87. doi:10.1017/S1351324901002807

Jeffery, D. R., & Scott, L. (2002). Has Twenty-five Years of Empirical Software Engineering Made a Difference, in *Proc. 2nd Asia-Pacific Software Engineering Conference*, pp.539-549. doi:10.1109/APSEC.2002.1183076

Jeffery, D. R., & Scott, L. (2002). Has Twenty-five Years of Empirical Software Engineering Made a Difference, in *Proc. of 2nd Asia-Pacific Software Engineering Conference*, pp.539-549. doi:10.1109/APSEC.2002.1183076

Johnson, P., & Ralph, P. Goedicke, M. Ng P.-W., Stol K.-J., Smolander, K., Exman, J. & Perry D.E. (2013). Report on the Second SEMAT Workshop on General Theory of Software Engineering (GTSE 2013). SIGSOFT Softw. Eng. (Notes 38, 5, pp. 47-50).

Sosnin, P. (2012). Experiential Human-Computer Interaction in Collaborative Designing of Software Intensive Systems, In *Proc. of 11th International conference on Software Methodology and Techniques*, pp. 180-197.

Sosnin, P. (2013). Role Intellectual Processor in Conceptual Designing Of Software Intensive Systems. In proc. of the 11-th International Conference on Computational Science and Applications, Part III, LNCS 7973 Springer, Heidelberg, pp. 1-16. doi:10.1007/978-3-642-39646-5_1

Southekal, H., & Levin, G. (2011). Formulation and Empirical Validation of a GQM Based Measurement Framework, In *Proc. 11th International Symposium on Empirical Software Engineering and Measurement*, pp. 404-413. doi:10.1109/ESEM.2011.59

Webber, B., & Webb, N. (2010). Question Answering, in: Clark, Fox and Lappin (eds.): Handbook of Computational Linguistics and Natural Language Processing. Blackwells. doi:10.1002/9781444324044.ch22

Xu, S., & Rajlich, V. (2005). Dialog-Based Protocol: An Empirical Research Method for Cognitive Activity in Software Engineering. In *Proceedings of the 2005 ACM/IEEE International Symposium on Empirical Software Engineering*, pp. 397-406.

Yang, F., Shen, R., & Han, P. (2003). Adaptive Question and Answering Engine Base on Case Based and Rea-soning Technology. *Journal of Computer Engineering*, 29(1), 27–28.

Chapter 4
Semantic Memory of Question–Answer Type

ABSTRACT

In this chapter, we represent the grounds of the question-answer approach to conceptual designing the SISs. Basic features of this approach are real-time interacting of designers with natural experience and its models, analytical thinking in the conceptual work with project tasks, generating the constructs of the project theory of the substantially evolutionary type, and the use of conceptual experimenting when it is necessary. In indicated actions, designers process conceptual objects in the conceptual space in the frame of design thinking. For providing such activity, we have developed the toolkit WIQA, the kernel of which is a semantic memory be described in this Chapter. The memory is intended for uploading the conceptual constructs, any of which integrates a corresponding composition of interactive objects of "question" and "answer" types. For interactions with the memory, designers can use a set of commands in manual mode or programs written on the specialized pseudocode language.

1. LOGICAL MODEL OF THE SEMANTIC MEMORY

1.1. Semantic Memory

As told above, realizing the question-answer approach has led to developing the toolkit WIQA in a number of versions as for team of designers so for the

DOI: 10.4018/978-1-5225-2987-3.ch004

personal use (Sosnin, 16). There are differences among versions, but in any version, the central place occupies its kernel that provides a reflection of a project on the corresponding tree of tasks and a set of QA-models of tasks. The very simplified scheme of the toolkit is shown in Figure 1.

In the use of the toolkit, the designer has a direct visual access to the content of question-answer base (QA-base) that is intended for uploading the QA-objects of any type. Such objects are created by designers in interactive mode when they solve appointed tasks. One of the important kinds of QA-objects are constructs of the theory $Th^P(t)$.

The scheme of WIQA includes a number of plug-ins, any of which can be qualified as the certain application of the kernel because this application interacts with QA-base. Moreover, plug-ins use data that are also uploaded in QA-base. For example, a model of an organizational structure of the team developing the project is similar QA-model of the task (Sosnin, 12).

Therefore, one can interpret QA-base of the toolkit as a semantic memory, cells of which allow uploading sets and systems of QA-objects. The Figure 2 demonstrates this view on QA-base, in depth of which are used structures of the used Data Base Management System.

Figure 1. Functional structure of WIQA

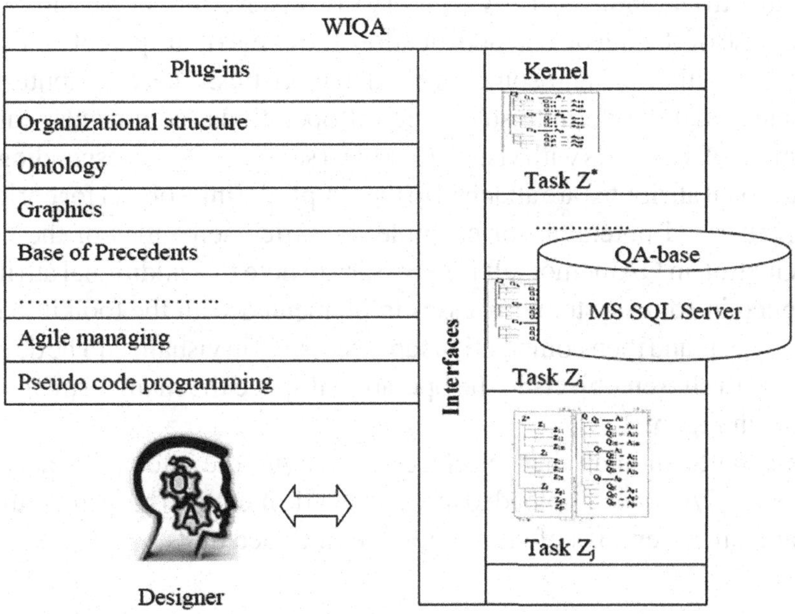

Figure 2. Interpretation of semantic memory

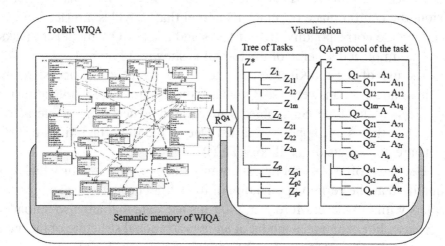

QA-memory with its cells is intended for registering the conceptual content of reflected units with taking into account the semantics of their textual descriptions. The necessary semantics is fixed in basic attributes of the cell and in additional attributes that can be added by the designer if it will be useful for a simple object stored in the cell. The potential structure of a simple object is presented in Figure 3.

A set of basic attributes of the cell helps to register for the stored object its unique identifier (address in QA-memory), type, description, the name of the creator, time of storing or last modification, the name of the parent object, the quantity of "children" and some other characteristics. These attributes with their values and the definite subsystem of operations (commands) support interactions of designers with visualized object stored in the corresponding cell.

Additional attributes are attached to the simple definite object for enriching its computerized potential, for example, to enrich semantics of the object representation in QAmemory. It is necessary to note that additional attributes are applied in some system processes implemented with the toolkit WIQA.

QA-objects and their compositions are accessible in visualized The designer interact with chosen objects in the operational space the main form of which is shown in Figure 4.

The main form and other interfaces (providing the interactive access of designers to QA-objects uploaded in the semantic memory) have instrumental strips and other versions of combining the interface units.

Figure 3. Specification of the interactive object

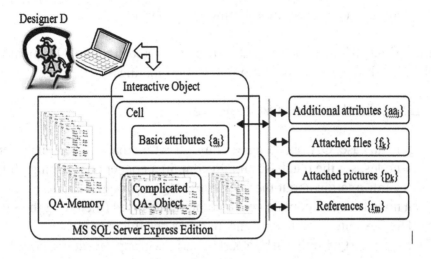

Figure 4. Visualization of the interactive object

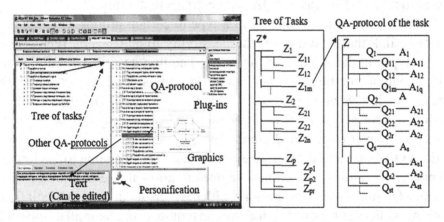

Below, for specifications of QA-objects in the QA-memory, a formal grammar GR^{QA} with extended BNF-notations will be used. For example, structures of created QA-objects should correspond to the following rules of GR^{QA}:

QA-Memory = {QA-object};
QA-object = Question, "←", Answer;
Question = Q | (Q,"↓",{Q});
(1) *Answer = A | (A, "↓", {A});*

Q = ({a}, {[aa]}, {[f]}, {[p]} {[r]}); A = ({a}, {[aa]}, {[f]}) {[p]} {[r]}; a
    = (address, type, description, time, the others),

where "Q" and "A" are typical visualized objects stored in cells of QA-memory, symbol "↓" designates an operation of "subordinating."

1.2. Specifications of QA-objects

In the general case, QA-object has a graph structure that can contain several types of nodes, so, the database should contain a concept describing all the necessary information about the node type – QA-unit type.

Each node type can contain certain other node types (including the same type). The QAunite type group concept describes this fact.

Each type of a QA-unit can be a part of various groups because a node type tree can have a very complicated node division logic. A type group contains several different types, and the link between these concepts is described as "many to many." The link is "QA-type belongs to a group."

This link covers the belonging of a type to certain groups. One requires one more link that would cover the possibility to add several type groups (all the types in the groups) to the types. The link describes the following rule: a node of a certain type can contain sub-units of all types from all the groups which have any links to the node type. So, each QA-type can have this link to several types. There is one more many-to-many link between the concepts – "Subgroups and QA-unit types."

Each QA-unit has a certain state (term "state" is an analog to the term of the previous version). Sometimes we need to know the reason for a certain state of a QA-unit, which can be done with the help of only one QA-unit field. Working with the corporate version, we can require classifying all the possible reasons. To describe them we need one more concept – QAunit state reason.

QA-units are parts of one project – QA-project. The QA-project is the root of the tree. A certain QA-node is connected to each project. This link is a one-to-one link. QA-project is additional information, which the QA-unit concept does not include. This link is "Project information about the node."

QA-unit (QA-node) is a concept describing one node of a solution tree and a description tree. Each node has several (sub-units). One node has only one "parent" that is why there are a one-to-many link "Sub-QA-units." Each node has only one state at a time; so, there is a one-to-many link between the concepts "QA-unit state" and "QA-unit" – "QA-unit state." One node has only one state, and the state has only one reason (the reason can be described in detail). So, there is a one-to-many link between the concepts "QA-unite state reason" and "QAunit state" – "QA-unit state reason." As mentioned above, each unit has a certain type, so, there should be a one-two-many link between these concepts which we call "QA-unit type." The following Figure 5 demonstrates all the links between the concepts described above.

When some challenge is met, it is necessary to use some means of fixing the results and solution steps. Different tools are used for these purposes: from a simple piece of paper to very powerful tools (e.g. Microsoft Excel). It is possible to highlight two very important steps from the task solution:

1. The process of describing the task. This process includes different steps, depending on the task. One of these steps is a decomposition of the task, i.e. the step of decomposition of a complex task into simpler subtasks.
2. The process of describing the solution. This process includes a description of all elementary subtask solutions and methods of its linking to solve the specific general task.

Also during the task solution, it is necessary to monitor the status of each of the subtasks, select the right methods and ways of solution, to analyze different methods and solutions for more detailed study of the task.

Often a situation arises when it is necessary to solve the task twice (in the framework of more complex tasks). Therefore, during the task solution and its fixing, there should be a very important function of the accumulation

Figure 5. Framework for QA-unit

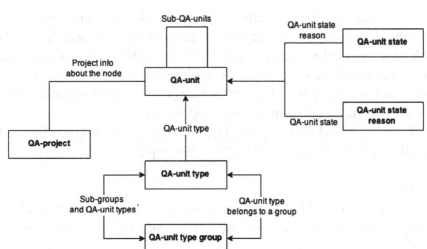

of experience in solving the tasks, and rapid reproduction of the results of their solutions.

Thus, "QA-protocol" component can be used for the following purposes:

1. Description and decomposition of tasks.
2. Description of the methods of task solution.
3. Control of the process of task solution.
4. The accumulation of experience and solutions to various tasks.

There exists a number of methods of describing a task. WIQA application applies its approach. This approach is that decision, or task-describing elements can be divided into four abstract types:

1. **Project:** This type is designed to describe the very initial stage of the task. That is the very task to be solved or to determine the possibility of its solution.
2. **Task:** In order to carry out the process of decomposition of the task and the task, description tasks are used. Each task can also be divided into subtasks and so on.
3. **Question:** Along with the task solution, there is a need for additional questions that can lead to a solution or part of the solution. Like the task, the question can be divided into simpler questions.
4. **Answer:** Each question always requires an answer. Every question in the WIQA application has only one answer. However, if the answer is complex, it can be divided into simpler answers.

This separation is not restrictive. We can say that it is just the category types, which are used for specific ways of task solution and description. The WIQA structure of the description and solution of the task is a tree. Every tree node has a specific type. In its turn, type belongs to one of the categories above. Tree nodes are called QA-units, which describe some specific element of the solution (task, question, answer, and so on).

As was mentioned above, every QA-unit has a certain **type**. In WIQA application type is characterized by the following fields:

1. Type name.
2. Short type name. This name is necessary for the text representation of the unit type in the tree. For example, "Question" type can be called «Q.»

3. System type name.
4. Whether the type belongs to the task description types. If the answer is "yes," then this type will only be used for the description and decomposition of tasks. If not, then the type will be used for solving the task.
5. Whether the type belongs to the question types. If so, the type will be interpreted as a question type, if not, then this type will be interpreted as an answer type. This type must not belong to the task description types.
6. Type description. This field can be used to describe the specifics of the selected type.

Since every node has a specific type, it is necessary to define a list of types that this unit can contain in child ones. For this purpose groups of the types are used, which are characterized by the following fields, and additional data:

1. Group name.
2. Group description. This field can be used to describe the properties of QA-unit types
3. List of the types that belong to the group.

Thus, after determining groups of the types, it is necessary to specify which of these groups of the types may be included in each specific type. To do this, each type of QA-units is matched with the type groups list. These groups of the types define a finite set of types.

Each element of the task description or solution might be in different states. For example, it may happen that the task has no solution. Of course, it can be deleted in this case. However, it is better to mark it with a specific state. The application states are characterized by the following fields:

1. State name. This field characterizes the state itself. For example, the state may be called "Lock-up"
2. System state name.
3. Whether the state is final: This field indicates that if the unit has this state, it will no longer be changed, or at least it should not.

In order to start solution of the task, it is necessary to create a project that will be identified with it. The application project is characterized by the following fields:

1. Project Name: This field can be used for the brief formulation of the task, or header that allows understanding the essence of the project.
2. Start date.
3. End date.
4. Project Description: This field can be used for the more detailed formulation of the task, which describes the project.

Every project is associated with the root node of the tree. There starts the process of describing and solving the task. Every QA-unit (tree node) is characterized by the following fields:

1. **Title:** This field can be used for the brief formulation of the task, raising the question or the formulation of the answer.
2. **Textual Description:** This field can be used for quick notes about the unit.
3. **Formatted Description:** This field can be used to produce articles about the unit. For example, formatted text answer to the question.
4. **System Index:** The value of this field is filled in automatically. Nodes of the project start with unique ID and a point in the end. For example, the first project will have the following index: «1.». Child nodes add to the parent index unique number among its child ones. E.g. «1.2.2.2.4.» means a path starting from the root (of the project) with the number «1.», in its child – node «1.2.», in its child – node «1.2.2.», and so forth to the node number «1.2.2.2.4».
5. **System Name:** The value of this field is filled in automatically. This field has the following format: "Short name of the node type" + System node index. For example, if the question type unit has «1.2.2.2.4» index, the system name will be «Q1.2.2.2.4». Also, if this question has an answer node, it will have «A1.2.2.2.4» index. I.e. the system name of questions and their answers differ only in the short name of the answer, and the indices coincide.
6. **Unit State:** This field has one of the user-created values of QA-unit states, which describes the state of the unit.
7. **The Reason for the Unit State:** During the transferring the unit from one state to another, it might be required to specify the reason for this translation.

1.3. Additional Attributes

In order to create composite types, one must develop some basic (primitive) types for them. To get the opportunity of creating enumerated types, one requires one more kind of types – enumerated one. While using attributes it is sometimes necessary to refer to system objects (for example, to a QA-unit), so there is another type – references to a WIQA object. To get the opportunity of working with collections, it is necessary to have a type of a collection. With the help of these basic types, one can create composite types. Let us call them meta types.

In order to describe a particular type, one requires a special concept "Attribute type." Each attribute type belongs only to one meta type.

Depending on the metal type, its type may have additional data. Composite objects have properties for which there is a concept "attribute type property." Each type may have several properties, but each property may belong to only one type. Therefore, between the concepts, there is a one-to-many link, which is called "Type property." Each property can have a value of a certain type. The property value may have one type, but each specific type may be the type of different property values. Therefore, between the concepts, there is another one-to-many link, which is called "Property value type."

Enumerated types have a finite set of values, therefore, to store information about these values one requires another concept "Enumerated type value." Each value may belong to only one type, and the type may contain a set of values. Therefore, between the concepts

"Attribute type" and "Enumerated type value" there is a one-to-many link, which is called "Value belongs to a type."

In order to combine the types of attributes in sets, there is another concept "Attribute type group." Each group may contain a list of subgroups. Therefore, between the groups, there is a one-to-many link (one group can have several subgroups but only one parent group), which is called "Group subgroup." The group may contain several types, and each type may belong to only one group. Thus, between the concepts "Attribute type" and "Attribute type group" there is an another one-to-many link, which is called "Type belongs to a group." The Figure 6 shows concepts and links between them described above.

After creating a system of types, one must create an attribute for the types. Another concept "Object attribute" is required. Each attribute can have only value type, but there can be several attributes of the same type, therefore, between these concepts, there is a one-to-many link, which is called "Object

Figure 6. Framework for additional attribute

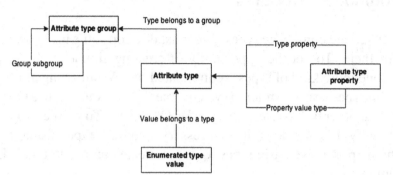

attribute type." Each attribute is assigned to a specific record (or an instance of a concept). An attribute can belong to only one record, but the record can have several additional attributes. Therefore, between this concept and the concept "Object attribute" there is a one-to-many link, which is called "Attribute belongs to an object." Attributes may be composite objects (with collections, several properties, etc.). Thus, it is necessary to create one more concept to describe a tree of values – "Object attribute value." Each value belongs to one attribute (i.e., all the tree of values of one attribute belongs only to this attribute). Therefore, between these concepts, there is a one-to-many link, which is called "Object attribute values." Each attribute value may have sub-values (such as property values of the composite object). Therefore, between the attribute values, there is a one-to-many link, which is called "Sub values." In order to see the type difference between values, one requires a link to indicate the type of the value. Each value may have only one type, but there may be several values of the same type, thus, between the concepts "Attribute type" and "Object attribute value" there is a one-to-many link, which is called "Value type of an object attribute." In order to see the type property difference between values one requires another one-to-many link (each value can describe only one type property, but each type property can have several values in different objects) between the concepts "Attribute type property" and "Object attribute value", which is called "Type property value". The Figure 7 shows links between the additional concepts.

There exists a certain set of the fields to store the information about the various WIQA application objects. For example, the information source is described by the following set of the fields: name, link, description. However, it might be required to store an extra field (attribute), which is not provided

Figure 7. The use of additional attribute for linking objects

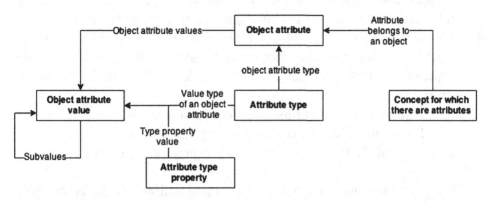

by the application developers. E.g. the relevance field might be required in the case with information sources.

Additional attributes can have a different structure (type). For example, like in the previous case, the relevance field might have a type consisting of two values: "Yes" or "No". In order to provide the functionality to expand the types of additional attributes, the "Additional attributes" component supports the mechanisms for constructing user types, based on the existing base types.

In order to understand how the type system works and how to interact with it, it is necessary to consider the following list of abstract types, called "meta types" in the application.

1. **Primitive Types:** This meta type includes all the types that are required to construct more complex types. The current version has the following primitive types:
   a. **String:** The value of this type might be a string of any length.
   b. **Number:** The value of this type might be an integer.
   c. **Date:** The value of this type is any date.
   d. **List:** The value of this type is a different-type set of the values. It means that an object of the list type can simultaneously contain strings, complex objects, lists and so on.
   e. **Dictionary:** The same type of the list, but each separate value is marked with an additional string key.
2. **Application Object Link Types:** This meta type includes all the types, which identify specific application objects. In the current version of the application, there is only one type that belongs to this meta type.
   a. **QA-Unit Link:** The value of this type is the existing QA-unit.

3. **Enumerated Types:** This meta type includes all the types, which have a limited number of values. For example, months of the year.
4. **Composite Types:** This meta type includes the complex object types. Each type is determined by a set of the properties that can have any value type. For example, "human" type can be described with the following properties:
    a. **Name:** The type of this property can be a string.
    b. **Surname:** The type of this property can be a string.
    c. **Date of Birth:** The type of this property can be a date.

The application user can create enumerated and composite types only. Thus, the component type system provides the functionality to describe the objects of any structure.

In order to merge a set of attribute types WIQA application uses attribute type groups, which are characterized by the following set of the fields:

1. Group name.
2. System group name.
3. Group description. This field can be used to define a set of characteristics, which can define the type group membership.

Every type group can contain the subgroups and the types that belong to this group. For additional attribute type description the following fields are used:

1. Type name.
2. System type name.
3. **Metatype:** This field is automatically assigned and can have the following set of the values, which are described in the previous paragraph:
    a. Primitive
    b. Enumerated set
    c. WIQA object link
    d. Composite type
4. **Type Description:** This field can be used to describe the type of the values, to describe the methods of using this type and so on.

Depending on the value of the meta type, each type of additional attributes might also be characterized by the additional data. To describe the composite types, type properties are required. They are described with the following set of the fields:

1. Property name.
2. System property name.
3. **Value Type:** This field is used to determine the set of the values of this property. For example, if the property has the "string" type, then the set of the values of this property can be a string of any length.
4. **Property Description:** This field can be used for additional notes about the type property (e.g. its purpose).

For the enumerated types description, it is necessary to specify a set of the values of this type. Every enumerated type value is described by a single line, which determines this value.

1.4. Ontology

While working with a domain ontology, it is necessary to separate the ontologies. To do this, there is a concept "Dictionary." In any domain, there are structured sections, subsections and so on, and to store the information about them, one requires another concept "Group of concepts." Each dictionary contains a list of root groups (root sections of a domain), each root group belongs only to one dictionary, therefore, between these entities, there is a one-to-many link, which is called the "Dictionary group." Each group contains a set of subgroups (subsections), but each group has only one parent group. Therefore, between the groups, there is a one-to-many link, which is called "Subgroup of a group."

To store the information about a concept of an ontology one requires a concept "Concept." Each concept is included into one group, but a group can contain many concepts. Therefore, between the concepts "Group of concepts" and "Concept" there is a one-to-many link which is called "Concept from a group." While describing a concept, one requires its definition. One concept may have several definitions depending on its context or method of using the ontology. Therefore, there is a concept "Concept definition." The definition belongs only to one concept, thus, between these concepts, there is a one-to-many link, which is called "Definition belongs to a concept."

Ontology is not only a set of concepts classified but also links between these concepts. The links can also be classified. To do this one requires a concept "Link type." To store information about a link, there is a concept "Link." Between these concepts, there is a one-to-many link (link type may contain several links, but a link can belong to only one type), which is called "Link belongs to a type."

Each concept can have a link to several other concepts; thus, between them, there is a many to-many links, which is called "a concept has a link to a concept." The link has a special type (connection between concepts) and direction. For example, there are two concepts with a partwhole link – a car and an engine. If one "reads" a link in one direction, the concept "car" is a whole for the concept "engine." If one "reads" a link in the opposite direction, the concept "engine" is a part of the concept "car."

Project ontology consists of the same concepts but is different by the physical implementation. An additional concept is required for the ontology. Since every concept of the project must be related to its implementation, it is necessary to classify the cases when a concept belongs to a certain part of the implementation. So, there is a concept "Materialization type." Each concept from the project ontology may have only one materialization type, but to each materialization type, several concepts may belong. Therefore, between the concepts, there is a one-to-many link, which is called "Concept materialization type." Each materialization type may have specifying subtypes, thus, between the types, there is a one-to-many link, which is called "Materialization type subtypes."

It is clear that a materialization type of the concept is only one, but there can be several places where this concept is used. Therefore, a new concept "Concept materialization" is required. Taking this into account, between the concept "Concept" and the concept "Concept materialization" there is a one-to-many link, which is called "concept materializes into." The following Figure 8 shows all the concepts and the links between them.

Figure 8. Framework for Ontology

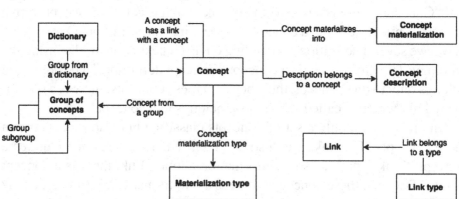

Ontology is closely related to information sources. That is why they are described in this section. To store information about information sources, there is a concept "Information source." To classify and unite sources according to certain features there is a concept "Group of information sources." Each group can contain several information sources, which can belong to only one group. Therefore, between the concepts, there is a one-to-many link, which is called "Information source from a group."

Many existing concepts can be related to a set of information sources (on the base of which they could have been built). Therefore, for them, there is a many-to-many link (each information source can be related to several concepts), which is called "Information sources of an object."

Apart from the ontological concepts, ontology subsystem allows creating keywords for some concepts. To do this, there is a concept "Keyword." Keywords are not classified – they are a set without any repetitions. Each concept can have several keywords, and one keyword can be attached to different concepts. Therefore, between the concepts, there is a many-tomany link, which is called "Keywords of an object." Figure 9 shows all the described concepts and the links between them.

There is no doubt that any project refers to a subject field. In its turn, the subject field includes a certain set of concepts, which are connected via relations (links). Concepts, in their turn, can be classified into groups, which correspond to specific domains of a subject field. In order to support projects with such classification, WIQA application includes Ontology component. The purpose of the component is not only to support the concept system of projects but also to describe various subject fields in general (without reference to a project). It can be useful for topical research and information accumulation. But the ontology of a specific domain can also be introduced into the ontology of a project (project ontology).

Figure 9. Access to units of the ontology

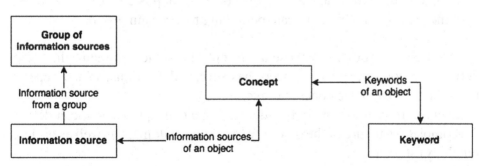

The Ontology component also supports flexible and extendable system of concepts relations (links). For instance, the concept automobile and auto can be connected by the link synonym (in a certain context). The system also has a basic set of relations, classified according to links types, which can be enough for a description of most subject fields.

The component refers to the project ontology not only as a set of classified and connected concepts but also as a materialization (use) of these concepts in project implementation and description. For this purpose, extra functions for ontology concepts were implemented, which enable to define the place and type of the concept usage.

In the Ontology component for the complex concepts, which take part in ontology description, functions for accumulation and simple keywords (tags) assignment are introduced.

Dictionaries are used to divide ontologies into subject domains. Each dictionary is described with the following fields:

1. **Name:** The field can be used as a name of a subject domain or, probably, as a name for a group of concepts.
2. **Description:** The field can be used for a more detailed description of a subject domain, specified by the dictionary.

Concept groups are used to describe subject domains of a larger subject field. Groups can also be used for simple classification of concepts: to divide a large number of concepts into several small groups. A group of concepts has the following fields:

1. **Group Name:** The field may be used as a name of a subject domain, which the current group (domain) refers to.
2. **Group Description:** The field may be used for various purposes. For instance, to describe a subject domain, which the current group refers to; to outline the reasons why the current group is created; to describe the properties which indicate belonging to a certain group.

One field is enough to choose a concept of a subject domain; this field defines the concept. Every concept has several definitions, which depend upon the context of the concept usage.

Every definition is a plain text describing a concept. Thus, it can define the complete structure of the ontology (of a subject domain as well as project ontology) storage.

Every dictionary can contain a set of child groups, which in their turn can contain subgroups and so on. Every group can contain a set of concepts referring to this group. Every concept can include several definitions. For this reason, a tree structure was used for dictionary structure, where dictionaries are tree roots, and concept definitions are tree leaves.

For classification of concepts relations links types are used. They have the following fields:

1. Link type name, e.g. association links.
2. System name.
3. **Description of the Relation of the Concept:** The field can be used to describe properties, uniting concepts into one group.
4. To describe a relation (link), the following fields are used:
5. Name.
6. System name.
7. **Text for Relation With Depending Concept:** While relations are defining one of the concepts as main exist, the text of the relation depends upon the direction of the relation. For instance, between the concepts, automobile, and engine a relation part-whole may be set. Which in one direction is: the automobile is the "whole" for the engine. In the other direction: the engine is a part of the automobile.
8. The text of the relation with the main concept.
9. **Whether the Relation is Symmetrical:** There are also relations which are nondirected, e.g. synonyms. That is why the text for both directions is the same.
10. **Relation Description:** The field may be used to describe concept properties, which enable to set a relation.

As it was mentioned above, the ontology is supplemented with functionality for the definition of concepts materialization. For that purpose, extra objects are implemented. In order to describe the place of concept in the project the object materialization type is introduced, which has the following set of fields:

1. Name.
2. System name.
3. Description of materialization type. The field can be used for the definition of the concepts properties, which can be materialized this way. This field can also describe the means of materialization.

The application has a starting set of materialization types which covers a quite wide range of concept materialization ways. Every materialization type may have a set of subtypes. For instance, a concept describes a method of certain data type check. The concept can have materialization type "method." But this type is very abstract, to define it more precisely a new type can be created, and it will be a subtype of the type "method."

The current version supports concepts materialization only in a file, which means that for every concept beside materialization type may also be marked with the exact location in the certain file. For one materialization record the following fields in the file are used:

1. **File Path:** The field defines the exact file, where concept materialization should be found.
2. **Location in the File:** The field describes the exact location of the concept materialization in the file.
3. Materialization description.

2. PSEUDOCODE PROGRAMMING IN THE SEMANTIC MEMORY

2.1. Structure of Language

QA-reasoning can be used by designers when they create different conceptual models of tasks, for example, in formulating the task statement or in the cognitive analysis of the formulated statement or in (pseudocode) programming the solution plan of the task. The toolkit WIQA supports the creative work of designers with all indicated conceptual modes and conceptual models of the other types.

When any QA-object is uploaded in QA-base, this object is mapped in the definite structure of data that can be visualized on a monitor screen as an interactive question-answer scheme (QA-structure) of this object. Below we will use the designation "QA-model of data" to underline this feature of QA-object.

Its visual structure is one side of any QA-object. This structure opens access to other its characteristics. Any Q-object or A-object of has a basic subset of characteristics such as the type of the object, its textual description, the name of the creator, time attributes, the indicator of changes, the attribute of inheritances and others.

QA-objects of other kinds opens the access to characteristics of all their nodes each of which is Q-object or A-object. For any of such QA-object, its basic characteristic is assigned to the root node.

Our answer the second question had two complementarity versions:

1. The first version concerned QA-objects created in frames of the task view and logically linguistic view. Operations of this version specified the kernel of WIQA.
2. The operations corresponding to the second version applied in plug-ins of WIQA for which (at the first stage) mechanisms of plug-ins were basic means of its evolving. For some plugins., for example for plug-ins provided the work with the model of the model of the designers' team, we applied "QA-model of data" for coding the team model in the view shown in Figure 10.

The use QA-models of data in plug-ins of WIQA for expanding its functionalities prompted the interpretation of QA-base as s semantic memory (or QA-memory) the cells $\{C_i\}$ of which are intended for mapping of QA-objects. This interpretation defined our research to the inclusion of pseudocode programming defined above QA-memory.

In our understanding, QA-memory is a construction intended for providing the work with QAobjects from the viewpoint of data or, by other words, cells

Figure 10. Model of the team

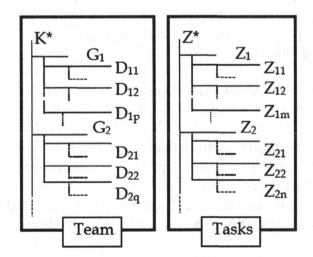

of QA-memory save QA-models of data (or shortly QA-data) corresponded QA-objects.

Originally, QA-data had been suggested and developed for the real-time work with such interactive objects as <Tasks>, <Questions> and <Answer> which were kept in QA-base) and used by designers in the corporate network. It is necessary to notice that <Task> is a type of a question and <Solution of the Task> is an answer to such question.

On the logical level, QA-model of data can be interpreted as the specialized hierarchical model of data emulated using the relational model of data. In the toolkit WIQA, this model is realized with the use of MS SQL SERVER.

The QA-database, which is built on the base of the QA-model of data, has the following useful characteristics:

1. Allocation on the server with the client access to the content of data in the corporate network with an opportunity of the access from the Internet;
2. Visualization on the monitor screen with the possibility of the interactive access to corresponding objects;
3. Personification of Z-, Q- or A-units as the registration of the responsible designer and the group of "support";
4. Textual definition Z-, Q- and A-units with an opportunity of the transformation to the language of the logic of predicates;
5. Transformation of the text for the each unit to the XML-version with positive effects which are being achieved by such form of data.

Enumerated positive characteristics are only a part of value belonging the QAdatabases which can be used not only in the development of SIS. Moreover, it is possible to expand in the interpretation of the connected pair of QA-units by following ways:

1. <Question> → "Cause" and <Answer> → "Effect";
2. <Question> → "Condition" and <Answer> → "Reaction".

The possibility of useful interpretations of QA-data and their materializations in QA-memory have led to the development of a pseudocode language L^{WIQA} embedded to the toolkit WIQA.

This language is oriented towards on its use in experiential interactions of designers with accessible experience when they create programs of their activity and investigate them. Step-by-step, L^{WIQA} has been evolved until an executed state with the following components:

1. Traditional types of data, for example, such as scalars, lists, records, sets, stacks, queues and the other data types.
2. The data model of the relational type, describing the structure of the database.
3. Specialized types of data that provide programming a logic of workflows, agile managing of works, their figuratively semantic maintenance and the use of a project ontology.
4. Basic operators, a set of which includes traditional (pseudocode) operators, for example, Appoint, Input, Output, If-Then-Else, GOTO, Call, Interrupt, Finish and the others operators.
5. SQL-operators in their simplified subset, including Create Database, Create Table, Drop Table, Select, Delete From, Insert Into, and Update.
6. Operators that provide processing of data of specialized types.
7. Behavioral operators that specify switching the execution of (pseudocode) programs on designers' actions as in mental space so in a technological environment.

The inclusion of behavioral operators in resources of pseudocode language L^{WIQA} open the possibility for the controlled intertwining of the human and computer actions that originally were oriented on processing the conceptual objects of question-answer types. Based on this, at an early stage of becoming the language L^{WIQA}, it was named "pseudocode language for QAprogramming." Now, L^{WIQA} is qualified as the language of conceptually algorithmic programming.

Explicit behavioral commands are written as imperative sentences in the natural language in its algorithmic usage. When a designer visually interacts with descriptions of questions or answers and uses them as causes for designer actions, then, such descriptions can be interpreted as implicit commands written in L^{WIQA}. For example, textual forms of questions are a very important class of implicit commands. To underline specific features of the language L^{WIQA}, programs on this language were called QA-programs.

2.2. Emulation of Data and Operators

In the general case, a QA-program can include data and operators from different enumerated subsets. However, the traditional meaning of such data and operators is only one aspect of their content. The other side is bound with attributes of QA-units in which data and operators are uploaded. As described above, QA-data and QA-operators inherit the attributes of corresponding cells of QA-memory. They inherit not only attributes of QA-units but also their understanding of "questions" and "answers."

Originally, QA-data had been suggested and developed for real-time work with such interactive objects as "tasks," "questions" and "answers," which were stored in the QA-database and used by designers in the corporate network. It is necessary to recall that "task" is a type of question and "decision of the task" is an answer to a question.

On the logical level, any QA-data can be interpreted as the specialized hierarchical model of data emulated using the relational model of the data. Two hierarchical trees of data, the units of which are connected to questions and answers, is one of the specificities of QA-data. The general version of QA-data includes the dynamic tasks tree of the units, which are united with a system of QA-models for corresponding tasks.

Let us recall that any unit of such a model is the interactive object with a unique name and symbolic expression, which are visually accessible to designers in the task tree or in the corresponding QA-protocol. Other characteristics (for example, such basic attributes as the name of the creator, time attributes, indicator of changes, and attribute of inheritances) have been discovered and used in different planned actions with the data unit.

One way of broadening the interpretation of QA-data is connected with the abstract type of data with named attributes and features, including the accessible set of commands. Such an interpretation allows for the developers to use the abstract QA-type for the emulation of types of data that are necessary for pseudocode programming.

The emulation is based on the use of Q-objects and corresponding A-objects for the following presentation of any normative types:

1. "Question" – " name of the variable for the simple type of data," and "answer" – "its value";
2. "Definite composition of questions" – " typical data" (for example, array, record, set, an array of records or table, stack, queue and others types of composite data) and "corresponding composition of answers" – "its value."

There are sufficient reasons for the interpretation of variables (names of variables) as questions and their values as corresponding answers. As a result, QA-data can be used for emulating data of many known types. As told above in WIQA, there is a special mechanism for assigning the necessary characteristics to a specific unit of QA-data. It is the mechanism of additional attributes (AA) that provides the possibility of expanding the set of basic attributes for any Z-, Q- or A-object stored in the QA-database.

The mechanism of AA implements the function of the object-relational mapping of QA-data to program objects with planned characteristics. One version of such objects is the classes in C#. The other version is fitted for pseudocode programming. The scheme that is used in WIQA for the object-relational mapping is presented in Figure 11.

The use of the AA is supported by the specialized plug-ins embedded in WIQA. This plug-in helps the designer declare the necessary attribute or a group of attributes for specific QA-units. At any time, the designer can view declared attributes for the chosen unit. Any necessary actions that have assigned additional attributes can be programmed in C# or in the pseudocode language L^{WIQA}.

Broadening of the abstract type of QA-data using additional attributes helps to emulate any traditional data types, such as scalars, arrays, records lists, and others. Moreover, means of additional attributes open the possibilities for assigning to simulated data their semantic features. An example of specifying the array with elements of the integer type is presented in Figure 12, where a set of additional attributes is used for translating the array declarations to computer code.

Figure 11. Creation of additional attributes

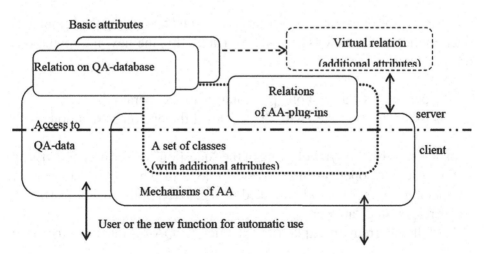

Figure 12. Declaration of array

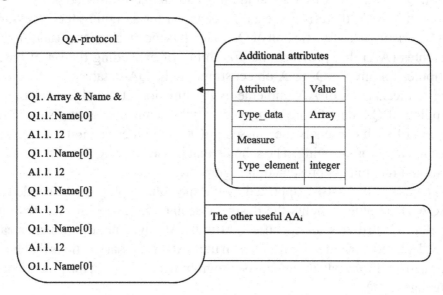

Attributes that are assigned for the array are visually accessible for the designer at any time and can be used for more than for translating. The designer can add useful attributes to the set of array attributes, for example, to describe its semantic features, which will be checked in creating and executing the QA-program. Any designer can create any necessary type of data, for C#-programming as well as for pseudocode programming.

2.3. Emulation of Operators

The second type of pseudocode strings is intended for writing the commands (operators). Similar to for QA-data, we can define the next interpretations for operators:

1.   "Question" is " a symbolic presentation of an operator";
2.   "answer" is connected with the results of the operator execution.

In other words, the symbol string of the "question" can be used for writing (in this place) the operator in the pseudocode form. The fact or the result of the operator execution will be marked or registered in the symbol string of the corresponding "answer."

The following remarks explain the specificity of QA-operators and their use:

1. Any sentence in any natural language includes the interrogative component, which can be indicated explicitly or implicitly. In QA-reasoning, this component is used obviously, while in the pseudocode operator, the question is presented implicitly.
2. Named interpretation opens the possibility of registering pseudocode programs in QAmemory in the form of programmed QA-models of the corresponding tasks.
3. In this case, any pseudocode operator presented by the pair of coordinated interactive objects of Q- and A-types is written on the "surface" of the corresponding QA-unit in QAmemory.
4. Thus, the used QA-unit can be interpreted as the "material for writing" of the corresponding operator of the source pseudocode. This material has useful properties, which are presented figuratively by attributes of the QA-unit in Figure13 Interactive QA-unit.

This "material" comprises visualized forms for writing the string symbols that were originally intended for registering the texts in the field "textual description" of the corresponding QAunit. The initial applicability and features of such a type of strings are inherited by data and operators of pseudocode programs. It is possible to assume that data and operators are written on "punch-cards," the features of which (basic and useful additional attributes of corresponding QA-units) can be accessible for their processing together with textual descriptions if it is necessary.

Thus, the traditional grammar of pseudocode languages can be extended by the use of indicated attributes of QA-units and the operations with them. This reason was one of the principal reasons for qualifying QA-programs as the new type of pseudocode programs.

Figure 13. Writing of the pseudocode operator

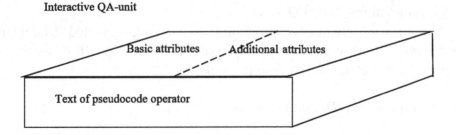

Interactive QA-unit

Basic attributes   Additional attributes

Text of pseudocode operator

2.4. Examples of QA-Programs

QA-programs are implemented for the programming of the condition part and the reaction part of any precedent separately. The condition part should help to solve the task of the precedent choice from the base of precedents. The typical scheme of QA-programs for the conditioned parts has the following view:

QA-PROGRAM_1 (condition for the access to the precedent):

N1 Variable &V_1& / Comment_1: symbolic indicator "N"(Name) is used as a type of "question"

V1 Value of V_1. / "V" indicates value of variable N2 Variable &V_2& / Comment_2?

V2 Value of V_2.

..

NM Variable &V_M& / Comment_M?

VM Value of V_M.

ON F = Logical expression (&V_1&, &V_2&, ..., &V_M&) EN Value of Expression.

OP Finish.

It is necessary to notice that the designer can build or modify or fulfill (step by step) a specific example of similar programs in real-time work with the corresponding precedent, which the designer creates or reuses. In the presented typical scheme, the logical expression of choice is programmed as the program function (QA-function).

The next fragment of a QA-program is used in plug-ins called "System of Interruptions" for the calculation of a priority of the interrupted QA-programs being executed by the designer in parallel:

O 1.11 Procedure &DiscardPriority&

O 1.11.1 &P&:= &Pmax&/

O 1.11.2 Label &DP1&/ "O 1.11.2"-unique index name (Address)

O 1.11.3 &Priority&:= &P&

O 1.11.4 CALL &GetTaskByPr&

O 1.11.5 &base& -> &TaskPriority&:= &base& -> &TaskPriority&+1

O 1.11.6 CALL &ChangeTask&

O 1.11.7 &P&:= &P& - 1

O 1.11.8 IF &P& < &base& -> &Pmin& THEN &base& -> &NewPriority&:= &Pmin& ELSE GOTO &DP1&

O 1.11.9 ENDPROC &DiscardPriority&

This QA-procedure is translated by the compiler (not by the interpreter) because it is processed by the computer processor (not by the I-processor). Therefore, A-lines of operators are excluded from the source code.

It is necessary to mark that creation and execution of any QA-program is implemented in an instrumental environment, which includes two translators (interpreter and compiler), editor, debugger and a number of specialized utilities for working with data declarations (Sosnin, 15).

2.5. Instrumental Environment of QA-Programming

The language L^{WIQA}, as any other applied language, is not separated from the means of its usage. Methods of QA-programming have been developed and embedded into WIQA during its evolution. The creation and use of QA-programs are fulfilled in the instrumental environment presented in Figure 14.

Creation of a specific QA-program involves beginning from the choice of the point in the tasks tree and the declaration of the new task for this program. The index name of this task (1) will be used as the initial address

Figure 14. Environment of QA-programming

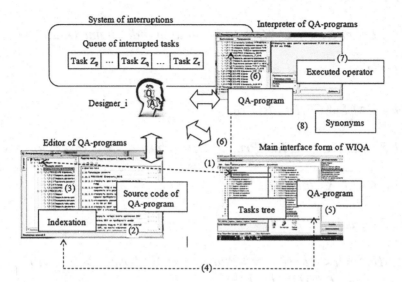

for computing the index names for any line of source code of a QA-program that is written in the area (2) of the text editor. The indexed copy of the source code is registered in the editor memory, and it is visualized in the area (3). After saving the current state of the source code, its indexed copy transfers (4) to the QA-database (5). At any time, any QA-program from the database can be uploaded to the editor.

Any QA-program in any of its states can be uploaded (6) to the interpreter for execution. Any executed operator of a QA-program is visualized in the special area (7) of the interpreter, and at any time, the designer can declare a new synonym for the chosen keyword (8) or variable. There are other useful possibilities that are accessible for the designer in the main interface forms presented above in Figure 14.

The reality of the designer activity is that there is parallel work involving many simultaneous tasks. Therefore, a special system of interruptions is included in WIQA. This system provides the opportunity to interrupt any executed task or QA-program (if it is necessary), to work with other tasks or QA-programs. The interruption subsystem supports the return to any interrupted task or QA-program to the point of the interruption.

3. SOME REMARKS TO THE CHAPTER 4

1. Reifying the question-answer approach has led us to developing the toolkit WIQA in a number of versions as for a team of designers (WIQA. Net) so for the personal use also (OwnWIQA).
2. There are differences among versions, but in any version, the central place occupies its kernel that provides a reflection of a project on the corresponding tree of tasks and a set of QA-models of tasks, both of which are placed in the specialized base of data (QA-base)
3. We interpret QA-base of the toolkit as a semantic memory of question-answer type (QAmemory), cells of which help to designers to create the semantic memory with the necessary content.
4. QA memory is created by transforming the relational data model, which is implemented by using MS SQL Server into a set of hierarchical data structures that intend to store simple and complex information-visualized Q- and A-type objects.
5. QA-memory with its cells is intended for registering the conceptual content of reflected units with taking into account the semantics of their textual descriptions. The necessary semantics is fixed in basic attributes of the cell and in additional attributes that can be added by the designer if it will be useful for a simple object stored in the cell.
6. Any cell helps to register for the stored object its unique identifier (address in QA-memory), type, description, the name of the creator, time of storing or last modification, the name of the parent object, the quantity of "children" and some other characteristics. These attributes with their values and the definite subsystem of operations (commands) support interactions of designers with visualized object stored in the corresponding cell.
7. Additional attributes are attached to the simple definite object for enriching its computerized potential, for example, to enrich semantics of the object representation in QA-memory. It is necessary to note that additional attributes are applied in some system processes implemented with the toolkit WIQA.
8. The WIQA-kernel includes the system of commands providing manual operations with cells of QA-memory and QA-objects uploaded in this memory. The set of commands opens for its use in programming on the specialized language embedded in WIQA.

9. In the general case, QA-object has a graph structure that can contain several types of nodes, so, the database should contain a concept describing all the necessary information about the node type (QA-unit type).

10. Around this concept, we defined a number of frameworks providing as understanding the structure of QA-memory so playing the roles of generative grammars that help to build the necessary constructions in QA-memory.

11. One of such framework specifies creating the ontologies for different goals, for example, ontologies the becoming of which accompany the creation of project theories.

12. In QA-approach, there are two regimes for the use of QA-objects uploaded in QA-memory, the first of which provide manual modeling in the conceptual space of this semantic memory while the second is oriented on the automation of works in this space.

13. In both of these regimes, designers interpret QA-objects in terms of a set of interactive types of data, for example, interactive objects of Z-, Q- and A-types, the use of which allows creating the tree of tasks and a set of corresponding QA-models.

14. The creator of any QA-program, declaring any variable of the traditional type, can significantly expand both declarative and operational components of the type, in particular, by enclosing the required amount of semantics in the specification.

15. The possibility to build QA-data for different goals has led to the development of the pseudocode language L^{WIQA} with instrumental shell that provides executing the corresponding programs (QA-programs) in three modes – an interpretation, compilation and mixed mode.

16. The data and operators of pseudocode programs loaded into the QA-memory of the WIQA processor acquire properties that allow the designer to create programs own activity for their automated reuse. The one kind of useful QA-programs of the behavioral type is those that support thought experimenting.

17. The LWIQA language is specially fitted to the natural language in its algorithmic use that supports human interaction with available experience in the conceptual designing the systems.

18. Language LWIQA can be used to program tasks of different types, but in the means of its use, an important place is occupied by the orientation to tasks behind which stand precedents. That is why this language can be qualified as "precedent-oriented".

19. The complexity of QA-programs that are available to the designer using the WIQA toolkit correlates with the natural programming capabilities (N programming) that the designer possesses.
20. The scheme of the WIQA.Net includes a number of plug-ins, any of which can be qualified as the certain application of the kernel because this application interacts with QA-base. Moreover, plug-ins use data that are also uploaded in QA-base.

REFERENCES

Karray, F., Alemzadeh, M., Saleh, J. A. & Arab, M. N. (2008). *Human-Computer Interaction: Overview on State of the Art Smart sensing and intelligent systems*. Academic Press.

Sosnin, P. (2012a). Question-Answer Approach to Human-Computer Interaction in Collaborative Designing. In Cognitively Informed Intelligent Interfaces: Systems Design and Development. IGI Global. doi:10.4018/978-1-4666-1628-8.ch010

Sosnin, P. (2012b). Experiential Human-Computer Interaction in Collaborative Designing of Software Intensive Systems. *Proc. of 11th International conference on Software Methodology and Techniques*, 180-197.

Sosnin, P. (2012c). Pseudo-code Programming of Designer Activity in Development of Software Intensive Systems. *Proc. of the 25-th International conference on Industrial Engineering and other Applications of Applied Intelligent Systems*, 457-466. doi:10.1007/978-3-642-31087-4_48

Webber, B., & Webb, N. (2010). Question Answering. In Handbook of Computational Linguistics and Natural Language Processing. Blackwells. doi:10.1002/9781444324044.ch22

Yang, F., Shen, R., & Han, P. (2003). Adaptive Question and Answering Engine Base on Case Based and Reasoning Technology. *Journal of Computer Engineering*, 29(1), 27–28.

ADDITIONAL READING

Card, S. K., Thomas, T. P., & Newell, A. (1983). *The Psychology of Human-Computer Interaction*. London: Lawrence Erbaum Associates.

Hewett, T.; Baecker, R., Card, St., Carey, T., Gasen, J., Mantei, M., Perlman, G., Strong, G., & Verplank, W. (2002). *ACM SIGCHI Curricula for Human-Computer Interaction.*ACM Technical Report. P. 162.

Hirschman, L., & Gaizauskas, R. (2001). Natural Language Question Answering: The View from Here. *Natural Language Engineering*, *7*(04), 67–87. doi:10.1017/S1351324901002807

Jacobson, I., Ng, P.-W., McMahon, P., Spence, I., & Lidman, S. (2012). The essence of software engineering: The SEMAT kernel. *Queue*, *10*(10), 1–12.

Software Intensive systems in the future. (2006) Final Report//ITEA 2 Symposiu*m,* from http://symposium.itea2.org/ symposium2006/ main/ publications/ TNO_IDATE_study_ITEA_SIS_ in_the_future_Final_Report. pdf

Xu, S., & Rajlich, V. (2005). Dialog-Based Protocol: An Empirical Research Method for Cognitive Activity in Software Engineering. In *Proc. of the 2005 ACM/IEEE International Symposium on Empirical Software Engineering*, pp. 397-406.

Xu, S., & Rajlich, V. (2005). Dialog-Based Protocol: An Empirical Research Method for Cognitive Activity in Software Engineering. In *Proceedings of the 2005 ACM/IEEE International Symposium on Empirical Software Engineering*, pp. 397-406.

Yang, F., Shen, R., & Han, P. (2003). Adaptive Question and Answering Engine Base on Case Based and Reasoning Technology. *Journal of Computer Engineering*, *29*(1), 7–28.

Chapter 5

Question–Answering in Conceptual Designing of Software–Intensive Systems

ABSTRACT

Potential of Question-Answer approach and means of its realization were evolved during many years of research and its applications, in which we used a number of interpretations of the toolkit WIQA, for example, question-answer processor, Instrumentally, technological environment, and shell for developing the new applications. This Chapter discloses the retrospection of our activity and a number of architectural views on the toolkit that was developed in several versions as for collective so for personal uses. Among results of our works, the especial place occupies a set of reflections of important essences (used in designing the SISs) onto the semantic memory. A set of these essences includes a project, task, workflow, team, a member of a team, and others. Reflections of such artifacts uploaded in the semantic memory helped to program our versions of Kanban and Scrum that take into account an unpredictable appearance of new tasks

DOI: 10.4018/978-1-5225-2987-3.ch005

1. INSTRUMENTAL SUPPORT OF QUESTION-ANSWERING IN CONCEPTUAL DESIGNING

1.1. Retrospective View on Question-Answer Approach

For more than ten years, our research has focused on the use of question-answering in the conceptual design of software intensive systems. This choice was due to the following reasons:

1. Lack of sustained progress in enhancing the success of the development of this class of systems.
2. Availability of long-term statistical reports containing information on the positive and negative factors that influence the success in designing the SISs (reports of the Corporation
    Standish Group in the first place)
3. Our awareness of that very important source negatives is the human factor from the problems of the designer's interaction with available experience and its models.
4. Our research results achieved at that time in the use of QA -reasoning in solving the approach tasks that we could try to evolve in the context of improving the degree of success in the development of SISs.

Beginning this phase of our research, we decided to orient on the best technology used for developing the SISs as sources of typical tasks and workflows as well causes and forms of human-computer interactions and their implementations. As a basic source, we chose Rational Unified Process, developers of which did not use obvious requirements and solutions for interactions of designers with the available experience and models of its items.

After that, stage by stage, the interests of which are reflected in Figure 1, we investigated possibilities and effects of question-answering in the context of positive and negative factors that influence the success in the development of SISs.

At the first stage, we have created and investigated a set of new models, methods, and means that provide the controlled inclusion of QA-reasoning in conceptual designing the SISs. The use of created way of working had allowed us to define the specialized approach (QAapproach) for conceptual work with tasks in designing. This approach (partially described in chapters 3 and 4) has following features:

Figure 1. Retrospective view of stages of our research

Factor of successfulness	1994	....	2012
User Involvement	1	....	2
Executive Management Support	2	....	1
Clear Statement of Requirements	3	....	
Proper Planning	4	....	
Realistic Expectations	5	....	
Smaller Project Milestones	6	....	
Competent Staff	7	....	4
Ownership	8	....	
Clear Vision and Objectives	9	....	7
Hard-Working, Focused Staff	10	....	
Project Management		....	5
Minimized Scope		....	10
Standard Tools and Infrastructure		....	6
Formal Methodology		....	3
Reliable Estimates		....	8
Agile Requirements Process		....	9
Optimizing Scope/Optimization		....	2
Financial Management		....	1
Emotional Maturity		....	
Execution		....	
Other		....	

1. The dynamics of the QA-approach is being represented with the current state of its tree of task $Tr(Z*, t)$ that is built by the team $T*$ of designers {Dvs} with the use of the stepwise refinement applied to the initial statement $St(Z*, t_0)$ of the root task $Z*$.

2. For each node Z, expressed in the tree $Tr(Z*, t)$ by the statement $St(Z, t)$ of the corresponding task Z, the designer (responsible for this task) performs question-answer analysis (QA-analysis) in the form of the stepwise refinement also.

3. The tree $Tr(Z*,t)$ and the result of QA- analysis for each task of the tree are recorded in a special database (question-answer base, QA-base) in hierarchical forms any of which is visually accessible as a whole and at the level of its nodes (any node or a group of nodes).

4. Tasks of the tree $Tr(Z*,t)$ are distributed among designers of the team, the organizational structure of which is also registered in the QA-base.

5. Designers interpret and apply any indicated artifact, and any component of this artifact as a visual model that helps them to interact with used the natural experience in the real-time.

For the estimation of the possible diversity of chosen artifacts and their components, we have used the RUP. Estimation helped us:

1. From the viewpoint of questions and answers, to specify the system of types for nodes of hierarchical structures shown in Figure 2. The used viewpoint opened the possibility for the description of any type with sim2ilar models of data in QA-base.

Figure 2. Relations of Artifacts in QA-approach

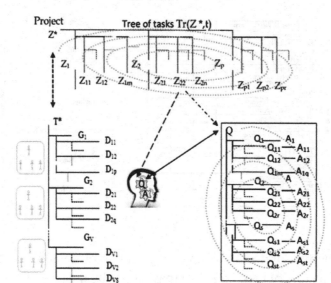

2. Chose for the task its normative question-answer model (QA-model) that can be adjusted by the designer as the example of the QA-model of the task for the definite case.

3. Develop the appropriate net version of the toolkit WIQA.

The QA-model of the task is a model of collaborative reasoning in the real time process of solving the task. Any QA-model is a set of interactive objects such as <question>, <answer> and <Task> with the certain attributes and operations.

Therefore, specifications of the QA-models will be presented from the interactive system viewpoint or another word as specifications of a specialized software intensive system SIS^{QA}. Such position gives the possibility to use the experience of the SIS to the SIS^{QA}, first of all, the experience of the architectural description. We defined and investigated the QA-model of the task that is architecturally presented in Figure 3.

In the scheme, any view indicates the definite set of functions that can be activated when the designer or designers will use this view of QA-model. In this work, the designer will use definite instrumental means, and technics provided a necessary act of modeling that will be useful for the corresponding task. That is why combining all views in a wholeness can be interpreted as the specialized SIS^{QA} with the toolkit that was named WIQA.

Figure 3. Architectural description of QA-model

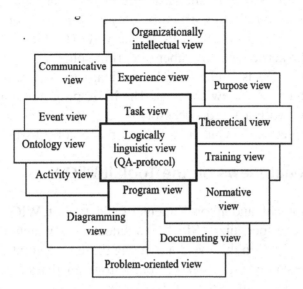

In such whole, the central occupies following vies:

1.   The task view that leads to the model QA(Z(t)) as an interactive task tree including the interactive model of Z(t) with models of all subordinated tasks. This view visually corresponds to the tree Tr(Z*,t) where any node is understood as a question of the <Task> type for which an answer has the type "solution of the task."

2.   The logical-linguistic view that presents QA(Z(t)) within frames of logic and linguistics of questions and answers. The visual representation of the view includes a system of registered QA-reasoning as a set of QA-protocols corresponding to the task tree of Z(t). Each QA-protocol is a tree of questions and answers (QA-tree) which present the reasoning used in the decision process of the corresponding task.

The set of means providing the work of designers with both these views is the kernel of WIQA to extend the functionality of which we have used the mechanism of plug-ins. Let us notice that other views of QA-model of the task explicitly or implicitly concern the central views because they help to solve additional technological tasks. For example, the documenting view is responsible for the development of normative documents each of which defined by the corresponding question-answer pattern. The work with such patterns supports the kernel of WIQA and plug-ins "Documentation."

The component structure shown in Figure 4 corresponds to one of the versions of the toolkit. In this structure, only a number of components have names indicating on views because the typical way of the view implementation is the use of the kernel and a number of definite plugins.

The toolkit WIQA is implemented as a client-server system that has been evolved architecturally view by view. The basic programming language is C#. By analogy with a Wordprocessor (for example, Microsoft Word), the toolkit is interpreted as a Question-Answer processor (QA-processor).

1.2. Functional Views on the Toolkit WIQA

In the development and improvement of the toolkit WIQA, we use its interpretation as a specialized SIS, the architecture of which integrates a set of viewpoints reified in this system. Among these viewpoints, for example, there was understanding the toolkit as an environment that supports modeling any task at the conceptual stage of designing.

Based on this, we created a complex of workflows for the conceptual solution of project tasks and registering the solutions in forms for future reuse. These workflows evolved in parallel with the evolution of the toolkit till its current state. The main feature of such technological process is interactions of designers with the accessible experience in the real-time. That is why the complex of workflows has name "Interactions with experience," and its kernel provides the work of designers with logically linguistic and tasks views shown in Figure 3.

Figure 4. Components structure of WIQA

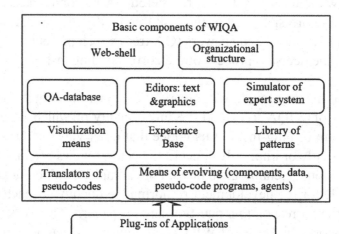

Our experience of applying the toolkit WIQA in the development of systems for documenting, automated training, technological preparing the production, as well as in solving a number of navigation tasks has shown that this toolkit can be used as a shell for developing the applications, in which human-computer interactions fulfill the fundamental role.

The shell that is inherited by the application should be adapted to its subject tasks, and this adaptation should take into account an adequate interpretation of the toolkit. One can use following versions of interpretation:

1. Instrumentally technological interpretation: Collaborative development environment providing the conceptual solution of project tasks.
2. Processor interpretation: Specialized processor for pseudocode programming.
3. Communicative interpretation: Environment supporting experience-based HCI.
4. Shell interpretation: Shell for developing the specialized applications based on the use of the semantic memory of QA-type.

In any its interpretation, a set of technics combined in workflows supports applying the toolkit. When the kernel of WIQA united with its (technological) applications, workflows are also combined as it is schematically shown in Figure 5.

The scheme demonstrates that, in the process of conceptual designing, a team of designers has to solve a number of additional classes of technological tasks in conditions when specialized workflows provide the work in corresponding classes of tasks. In practice, designers have to interrupt their work for the transition between specialized workflows. For this, in WIQA, we use agile management that will be described below.

Called interpretations reflect the becoming of the toolkit WIQA including the development of its versions. Nowadays, this toolkit exists in two last versions correspondingly for collaborative development of systems (WIQA.Net) and a personal work of a designer (OwnWIQA). For each of this versions, we use own way of evolving. For the version WIQA.Net, we use plug-ins way while for OwnWIQA we use pseudocode programming in language L^{WIQA}. Below, when it is important, we will use names of versions. For other cases, we will save the name WIQA.

Finalizing this subsection, we mark that combining the different interpretations, an embodiment of which is logical to consider as models of the WIQA usage, leads to the use of uniform tools (resources) in the processes

Figure 5. Workflows' structure of WIQA

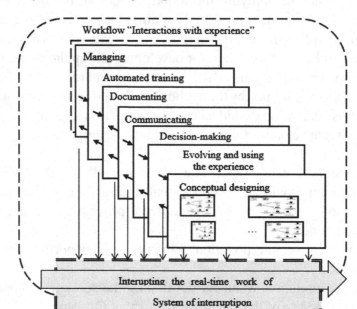

of interaction of designers with the process of conceptual design. The use of modes simplifies the complexity of the interaction.

1.3. The Use of QA-Processor in Human-Computer Interactions

The process of "Conceptual designing" is open for three interpretations, the sense of which can be clarified by the scheme shown in Figure 6.

The scheme presents the use of QA-processor by the designer who plays the role of a Humanprocessor (H-processor). The phrase "Human processor" and partially its understanding we take from results of investigations published in a number of papers, for example in (Card et al. 1986) where authors have described Model of Human Processor (MHP). The main idea of MHP is existence (in the human brain) of a number of specialized <processors> that processes input information in coordination.

In the scheme, the question is understood by the author as the natural phenomenon which appears (in human brains) at the definite situation when the human interacts with the own experience. As told above, in this situation, the <question> is a symbolic (sign) model of the appropriate question. Used

Figure 6. Collaboration of Human processor with QA-processor

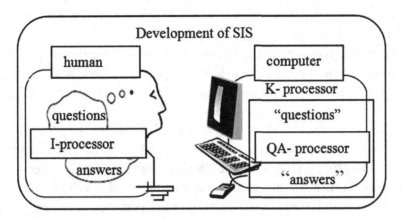

understanding helps to explain the necessity of fitting the <question> in QA-processes. Implicit questions and answers exist in reality while <questions> and <answer> present them as sign models. Once again, we note, the task is a type of questions.

Thus, question-answer reasoning reflects processes in the consciousness of designers when they interact with their experience. Explicit question-answer reasoning helps in controlling interactions with experience. This type of reasoning is expedient for the creation and use of experience models that present the designer's behavior.

In our case, H-processor provides processing <question>, <answer> and their compositions embodied in QA-base as a part of QA-processor. The basic aim of such processing is access to the necessary or useful items of the human experience. In turn, in back reactions based on activated items, the human activates necessary commands or functions of QA-processor, for example, for following aims:

1. Correcting the sign models of registered questions and answers;
2. Evolving QA-items in corresponding QA-models.
3. Choosing the necessary item for its use for the restore of the necessary state of mind.
4. The use of the necessary items for modeling.

All named actions to indicate that, in solving the task Z, the designer plays two roles:

1. In the first role, the designer using H-processor "interacts" with natural experience, and this interaction is provoked by definite observable components of the corresponding QAmodel.
2. The second role is based on the use of QA-processor that help to visually choose the necessary components of QA- model and activate them for organizing the necessary influence on H-processor of the designer.

Collaborative execution of described roles can be interpreted as the interaction between two active roles each of which is fulfilled by the same designer. This process is aimed at the realtime use of the designer's experience. That is why workflows provided the use of the toolkit WIQA were named "Interactions with Experience"(with natural experience of the designer). At the first stage of our research, the potential of these workflows was sufficient only for QAmodelling in the conceptual design of SISs.

1.4. Human-Computer Interaction in Forms of QA-Modeling

Question-answer models, as well as any other models, are created "for extraction of answers to the questions enclosed in the model." Moreover, any model is a very important form of the representation of questions, answers on which are generated during interaction with the model. In WIQA, we understand questions as a natural-artificial phenomenon which initiate, orientate and control the definite speech activity of developers and users of the created SIS. The attribute "natural" indicates that the cause of the speech activity is the development of the SIS. The attribute "artificial" reflects that any <question> is being expressed in the language of the SIS project.

The essence of QA-modeling is interactions of designers with artifacts included to the QAmodel in their current state. For such interaction, the developer can use the special set of QAcommands, their sequences and a set of WIQA plug-ins.

The main subset of positive effects of QA-modeling includes:

*   Controlling and testing the reasoning of the developer with the help of "integrated reasoning" and "integrated understanding" included into the QA-models;
*   Correcting the understanding of designer with the help of comparing it with "integrated understanding";

- Combining the models of collective experience with individual experience for increasing the intellectual potential of the designer on the definite working place;
- Including the individual experience of the developer by request on the other working places in the corporate network.

Any developer can get any programmed positive effect with the help of QA-modeling as <answer> on question actually or potentially include in the QA-model (Figure 7).

As it is shown in this scheme, any component of the QA-model is the source of answers accessible for the developer as results of interactions with QA-model. At the same time, the potential of the QA-model is not limited by the questions planned at defining and creating the QA-model. Another source of useful effects of QA-modeling is an additional combinatorial "visual pressure" of questions and answers, which are caused by influence on brain processes in their contacts with components of QAmodel. There is no difference, who has created QA-model.

There are different forms for building answers with the help of QA-modeling, not only linguistic forms. In any case, the specificity of QA-modeling is defined by the inclusion of additional interacting with "question-answer objects (QA-objects)" into dynamics of the integrated consciousness and understanding (into the natural intellectual activity of designers).

The description of any behavioral unit composed of designer interactions with the QA-model in accordance with a specific scenario can fulfill the role of a model of such a designer activity. To distinguish this type of model from other types of models that were used in our approach, they can be

Figure 7. QA-model as a source of answers

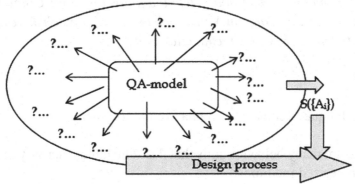

named "QA-models of the designer activity." Any such scenario as a specific program reflects designer interactions (actions) aimed at understanding the corresponding task and its solution. In the discussed case, the scenario is a text that comprises instructions that indicate the designer's actions, which should be executed in the reuse of the behavioral unit in the WIQA-medium.

Similar scenarios can be created for human actions that are not limited to the WIQA-medium. Their content, form, and appointment are demonstrated by the following technique:

//Reset of Outlook Express O1. Quit all programs.

O2. Start On the menu Run, click.

O3. Open In the box regedit, type, and then OK the click.

O4. Move to and select the following key:

HKEY_CURRENT_USER/Software/Microsoft/Office/9.0/Outlook O5. In the Name list, FirstRunDialog select.

O6. If you want to enable only the Welcome to Microsoft Outlook greeting, on the Edit menu, Modify, click the type True in the Value Data box, and then the OK click.

O7. If you also want to re-create all of the sample welcome items, then move to and select the following key:

HKEY_CURRENT_USER/Software/Microsoft/Office/9.0/Outlook/Setup

O8. In the Name list, select and delete the following keys: CreateWelcome First-Run O9. In the Confirm Value Delete dialog box, click Yes for each entry. O.10. On the Registry menu, click Exit.

O11. End.

This technique is chosen to emphasize the following:

1. There are many behavior units that describe human activity in different computerized mediums.

2. Descriptions of similar typical activities help in the reuse of these precedents.
3. Descriptions of techniques have forms of programs (N-programs) that are written in the natural language LN in its algorithmic usage.
4. Such N-programs are made of operators that are fulfilled by humans interacting with the specific computerized system. In the example of the N-program, its operators are marked by the symbol "O" with the corresponding digital index.

Thus, there are no obstacles for uploading the N-programs into QA-memory. This method is used for uploading the techniques that support the designer activity in the WIQA-medium.

Thus, the other way of coding the designer activity is connected with its programming in the context of the scientific research on the task. All of the tasks indicated above are uploaded to QA-memory with the rich system of operations with interactive objects of the Z-, Q- and Atypes. Designers have the opportunity to program the interactions with necessary objects. Such programs are similar to the plans of the experimental activity during the conceptual design of the SIS. Operators of programs are placed in Q-objects. Corresponding A-objects are used for registering the facts or features of the executed operations.

2. REFLECTION OF OPERATIONAL SPACE ON QUESTION-ANSWER MEMORY

2.1 Features of Reflections

As told above, the proposed QA-approach is aimed at the creation and use of the Experience Base in collective designing of the SIS family. In this case, the designer should operate in an operational space the general scheme of which is presented in Figure 8.

Specificity of named actions is expressed by a reflection R^{QA} of the operational space to QAmemory of the WIQA toolkits. On the scheme, this reflection shows that all what involving in designing of the family of SIS is found their expression as models in the QA-memory. It can be written by the following expression:

Figure 8. Operational space

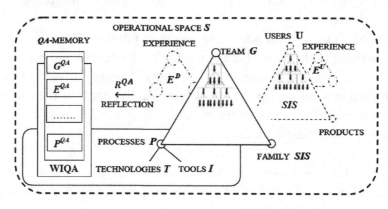

$$WW(P, G, E^D, E^{QA}, E^{Pr}, \{SIS_j\}, t) \rightarrow G^{QA}(t+\Delta t) \cup E^{QA}(t+\Delta t) \cup P^{QA}(t+\Delta t) \cup SIS^{QA}(t+\Delta t), \tag{1}$$

where *WW* is a Way-of-Working used by designers and all other symbolic designations corresponds to the names of essences in Figure 8. Let us additionally note that results of the reflection R^{QA} are dynamic objects, $S^{QA}(t_j)$ models all relations among essences, $E^{QA}(t_j)$ presents models corresponding to the used professional experience E^D which is mastered by members $\{D_k\}$ of the team $G(\{D_k\}$.

At the conceptual stage of designing, means of WIQA are used by designers for the following aims:

1. Registering of the set of created projects each of which is presented by the tree of its tasks in the real time;
2. Parallel implementing of the set of workflows $\{W_m\}$ each of which includes subordinated workflows and project tasks $\{Z_n\}$;
3. Pseudo-parallel solving of the project tasks on each workplace in the corporate network;
4. Simulating the typical units of designers' behavior with using the precedent framework.

These details of operational space are opened on the scheme presented in Figure 9 where the space structure is reflected in QA-memory.

For the process P_l of designing the project $PROJ_l$, all indicated aims are achieved by the following reflections:

$$WW(P_l)=WW(PROJ_l, \{W_m\}, \{Z_n\}, t) \to ZP_l^{QA}(t+\Delta t) \cup \{ZW_m^{QA}(t+\Delta t)\} \cup \{Z_n^{QA}(t+\Delta t)\}, \tag{2}$$

$$\{Z_n^{QA}(t) \to Pr_n^{QA}(t+\Delta t)\},$$

where symbol Z underlines that model has a task type, $Pr^{QA}(t)$ designates a model of precedent for the corresponding task, $R^{QA}(X)$ indicates that the reflection RQA is applied to the essence or artifact X. For example, $R^{QA}(Z^{QA})$ designates applying this reflection to the model Z^{QA} of the task Z. In WIQA-environment, the model of such kind is called as "QA-model of the task."

The second scheme includes a designer's model with feedback, which shows that, in the proposed approach, a set of precedents mastered by the designer can be used for the creation of the designer model.

2.2. Reflection of Processes

If designers of SIS use the toolkit WIQA, they have the opportunity for conceptual modeling the tasks of different indicated types. In this case, the current state of tasks being solved collaboratively is being registered in QA-base of the toolkit and this state is visually accessible in forms of the tree

Figure 9. Reflections of operational space on QA-memory

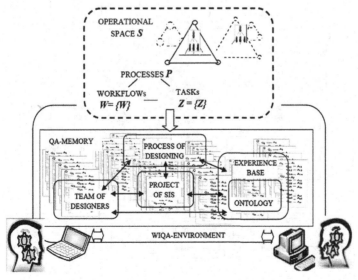

of tasks and QA-models for corresponding tasks. The named opportunity is presented figuratively in Figure 10.

The scheme demonstrates relations of designers with tasks and forms of their coding in the question-answer memory (QA-memory). In the toolkit WIQA, this type of memory is materialized as a system of cells (units) which are destined for keeping the attributive descriptions of tasks, questions, and answers.

The following classes of tasks are shown in the scheme:

1. Class of domain tasks $Z^D=\{Z^D_i\}$ contents of which connect with the application domain of the SIS to be created;
2. Class of normative tasks $Z^N=\{Z^N_j\}$ embedded to the technology applied by designers;
3. Class of adaptation tasks $Z^A=\{Z_j\}$ which support the adaptation of appropriate normative tasks to the solving processes of domain tasks;
4. Classes of tasks $\{Z^W_m\}$ and $\{Z^W_n\}$ any of which corresponds to the definite workflow in SIS or in the used technology;

Figure 10. Reflections of Process

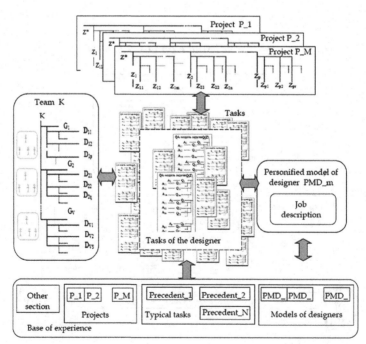

5. Classes of tasks $\{Z^G_p\}$ and $\{Z^G_p\}$ any of which corresponds to the definite group of workflows in SIS or technology.

Let us notice that normative tasks $\{Z^N_j\}$ are invariant to the application domain of the future SIS. Such invariance is a cause of the necessity to adopt any used Z^N-task to its application for solving the definite Z^D-task. Moreover, the adoption should be put into practice in coordination with other normative tasks used for solving of the corresponding Z^D-task. From this point of view, the use of normative tasks in solving of the definite Z^D-task can be interpreted as decomposing this task into a series of normative tasks $Z^D_i(t) = \cup\ a_j\ Z^N_j$, where a_j is a factor reflecting the specificity of the task Z^N in the decomposition.

Thus conceptual designing as the activity includes a very important kind of the designer subactivity aimed at adequate decompositions of Z^D-tasks on the basis of Z^N-tasks. With the automation of such sub-activity, we bind the class of Z^A-tasks. To define and solve the definite Z^A-task the designer should use personal and collective experience and their models in the real time.

Details of the operational space that are presented in Figure 10 not only indicate on reflections of projects on the QA-memory, but it also demonstrates structures that should find their representations in such memory. For example, models of the project and its components in QAmemory correspond to the following rules of GR^{QA}:

PROJ = ZP;

ZP = (Z, "↓", {Workflows };

Workflows = ZW $|$ (Workflows, "↓",{ZW}); ZW = {Task};

Task = Z $|$ (Task, "↓", {Z});   (3)

Z = QA-model $|$ (Z, "↓", {QA-model});

QA-model = {QA} $|$ (QA-model, "↓",{QA}); QA = (Question, Answer),

Question= Q $|$ (Question, "↓",{Q});

Answer = A $|$ (Answer, "↓",{A}),

where "Z," "Q" and "A" are typically visualized objects stored in cells of QA-memory, symbol

"↓" designates an operation of "subordinating." Let us note, these objects have the richest attribute descriptions. For example, a set of attributes includes the textual description, index label, type of object in the QA-memory, the name of a responsible person and the time of last modifying. Any designer can add necessary attributes to the chosen object by the use of the special plug-ins "Additional attributes" (object-relational mapping to C#-classes).

Thus, in reflections of the process of conceptual designing the system, the central place occupies by the tree of tasks and QA-models of corresponding tasks. The tree combines domain tasks, normative (technological) tasks, tasks of adaptation and tasks corresponded to workflows. To distinguish types any of which requires assigning the certain additional attribute to tasks of this type. Such assignment helps to separate components of the theory $Th^P(t)$ from models of this theory.

2.3. Reflections of Workforces

As told above, the success of designing the family of SISs depends on from the occupational maturity of used human resources in the essential measure. Therefore, modeling the team of designers as a whole and members of the team should play an important role in the project activity. In the toolkit WIQA, modeling of the team is supported by the specialized plug-ins Organizational structure.

First of all this plug-in is intended for real-time appointing of tasks to members of the team T*. This function is demonstrated in general in Figure 11 where one can estimate the scale of the used database.

The scheme in Figure 11 also shows the reflection $R^{QA}(T^*)$ of the team on its question-answer model which opens the possibility for the use of this model in corresponding practices of the standard P-CMM 2.0. The second reflection $R^{T^*}(Z)$ presents the distribution of project tasks among designers. In the offered approach, such distribution is implemented with using the personified models of designers (PMD).

As told above, the set of attributes of any Z-object of any tasks' tree includes the personified name of the designer who has been appointed as the solver of the corresponding task. For any designer, it gives the opportunity for extracting from indicated structures the following information:

1.   Lists of the solved task as for tasks of ZPr-type so for tasks of ZO-type;

Figure 11. Organizational structure

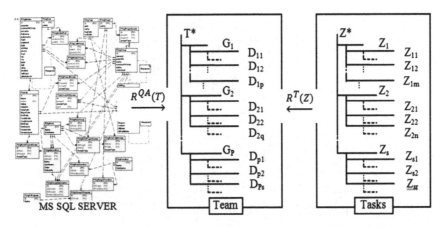

2. The list of the used precedents models;
3. The list of precedents models created by the designer;
4. The other professional information.
5. The list of groups $G = \{G_p\}$ in which the designer has been worked or is working.

The denoted opportunity is used for creating the PMD framework on the base of precedents' models, which have been successfully applied by the designer in the solved tasks.

The first step of such work is bound with grouping the precedents mastered by the designer. The grouping is oriented on the use of mastered competencies and roles being executed. In the suggested approach, a competency is understood as "a measurable pattern of knowledge, skills, abilities, behaviors, and other characteristics that designer needs to perform work roles or occupational functions successfully"(http://apps.opm.gov/ADT/Content.aspx?page=103 &AspxAutoDetectCookieSupport=1&JScript=1). The basis of measurability is a set of successfully solved tasks that have been appointed to the designer who used precedents' models.

This understanding has led to the solution of using the precedents' models as units for "measurement" of competencies. Therefore, competencies and roles have been specified in grammar GR^{QA}. Competency K of the designer is expressed structurally by the following grammar rules:

K = (Name, Definition, FPr);

Figure 12. Details of organizational structure

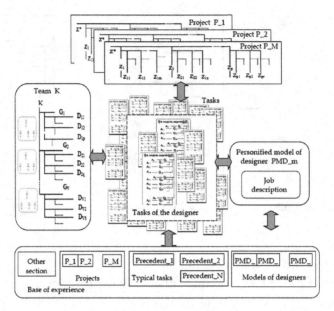

$$K = (Name, Definition, ``\gamma1", \{FPr\}); \quad (5\text{-}4)$$

$$K = (Name, Definition, ``\gamma2", \{K\}); \quad Competencies = \{K\};$$

$$Role = (Name, Definition, ``\gamma2", \{K\}); \quad Roles = \{Role\},$$

where **Definition** is a verbal description for the corresponding **Name**, $\gamma1$ and $\gamma2$ are operations of grouping.

Rules underline that some competencies can be expressed through a number of subordinated competencies. It helps the use of generalization, in brief, describing the occupational experience mastered by the designer. The rule for the role fulfills the similar function, but roles are, usually, used for qualifying the occupational area of designer responsibility, for example, an architect, programmer or tester.

The opportunity of the precedent-oriented description of designer competencies opens the question about their systematization. In the management practice of workforces, the job descriptions are widely used. "Job descriptions are written statements that describe the duties, responsibilities, most important contributions and outcomes needed from a position, required qualifications of candidates, and reporting relationship and coworkers of a particular job" (http://humanresources.about.com/od/ job descriptions/ a/ develop_job_des.htm).

Documents of this kind can be written as a result of job analysis in different forms. In our case, these documents should be oriented on the personified modeling of any member of the team designing the family of SISs. Furthermore, the personified job description should systematize the measurable competencies of the designer.

Traditionally, a normative text of the job description (JD) includes the following sections: Job title; General Summary of job; Key relationships; Education and Experience (Minimum qualifications); Knowledge, skills and abilities; Principal duties and essential functions; Major challenges; Physical, mental, sensory requirements; and Working conditions.

In the section structure, the Italic indicates elements the main content of which can be presented by names of competencies and references to models of precedents. For this reason, JDdocument has been chosen as a kernel of the PMD. This choice requires the use of reflecting the documents on the QA-memory.

In the WIQA-environment, the work with documents is supported with using their QApatterns, which should be previously developed and stored in the specialized library. Two its patterns present the typical model of each document. The first pattern reflects the document structure and the second defines it printed version. The specialized plug-ins "Documenting" provides adjusting of both patterns on conditions of their use.

As told above, the JD-documents are created in the process of the job analysis. In the described case, one stage of this analysis should be aimed at forming the list of competencies. Such work should be implemented with using the generalization for the net of competencies. The net of competencies should be reflected in JD-documents without details.

In the proposed approach, JD is used as a kernel of the personified model of the designer because JD-components have the constructive references on models of precedents stored in the Experience Base. The framework of the PMD with such a kernel is presented in Figure 13.

The scheme demonstrates the PMD in the context of its forming and creating. In grammar G^{QA}, the PMD is described by the following rules:

PMD = (DName, JD, {List of Features});

JD = {Section};

Figure 13. Framework of the PMD

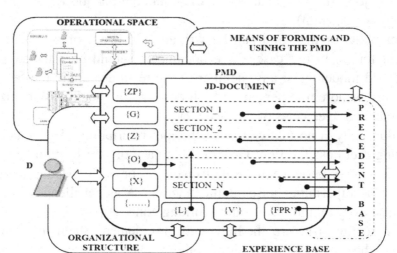

Section = Text -{[Role]} -{[K]}- {[O]} - {[L]}; (5-5)

List of Features = (Type, {F}, {[AF]});

F = ZP │ G │Z │ O │ L │ V' │FPR';

AF = Additional Feature,

where units of **O**-type present the results of estimating the designer actions, units of **L**-type register the results of experiential learning, lists of **FPR'** indicates the precedents' models built by the designer and units of **V'**-type are the references to the other values that are created by the designer. Lists **{X}** and **{....}** indicate that PMD is opened for the extension.

The PMD is not separated from its use for solving a set of tasks connected with the management of human resources including the management of workforces. The representative system of such tasks is described and specified in the standard P-CMM 2.0. Furthermore, this standard defines the steps of continuous improving the work with human resources. The called standard is aimed at solving the following main classes of tasks:

1. Rational forming the project team and groups of designers;
2. Managing the efficient use of workforces;
3. Continuous improving the project team.

3. WAY OF AGILE MANAGEMENT

3.1. Preliminary Bases

The question "How will project success be affected by changing the way of working?" occupies the central place in the search for innovations in SEMAT aimed at reshaping the software engineering. Let us remind, in normative documents of SEMAT, a way of working used by a team of designers is defined as "the tailored set of practices and tools used by the team to guide and support their work."

This definition indicates some directions of possible changing among which we can mark the search of innovations in managing of personal and collective human-computer activity. One of these directions is an innovative development of agile approaches in the project management.

Below we present combining of Agile managerial mechanisms with the managing of human-computer interruptions. The choice of such combining is caused by inevitable multitasking in a personal behavior of designers with multitasking in their collective activity. Moreover, the main feature of the offered approach is the use of intellectual processing the creative situations that often arise as the reasons for human-computer interruptions or unplanned events during their processing. The suggested solutions facilitate increasing the adequateness in specifying the work of the designer and open the possibility for the use of experimenting in processing the reasons of interruptions.

Interruptions inevitably accompany any human activity. They can be caused by different reasons and can lead to negative or positive effects. For example, they can be caused by made errors and can lead to other mistakes or they can be bound with a discovery of a more effective idea for the task being solved.

Taking into account the inevitability and importance of interruptions, reactions on them should be managed by the definite type of the human activity, reasons for interruptions and aims of their processing. The offered approach is developed for human-computer interruptions in the human-computer activity in the setting of multitasking.

The typical understanding of multitasking is the "ability to handle the demands of multiple tasks simultaneously" while a useful definition of the interruption is "the process of coordinating abrupt changes in people's activities". It should be noted; that multiple tasks can be simultaneously implemented by a group of designers each of which can operate with a set of multiple tasks switching among them in planned or situational conditions. This

Figure 14. Operational environment of project management

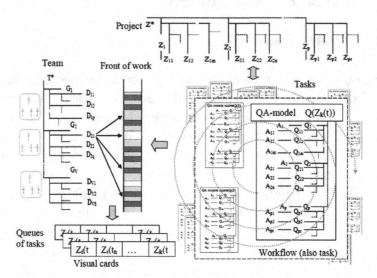

indicates that the multitasking behavior of the designer is very complicated kind of the interrupted activity which additionally has a creative character. It is this kind of the human activity occupies the central place in the approach described below. We shall describe the offered approach from the viewpoint of its use by a single designer.

Nowadays, agile methods are widely used for managing the collaborative work of designers with multiple tasks. These methods suggest a reflection of the activity process and its state on their descriptions, estimations of which are applied to managerial aims. For example, Kanban method orients the designer on the use of a set of visualized cards registering the information about the tasks being solved.

These cards are prepared for interactions with them any of which fulfills the role of the corresponding interruption. Thus, any access to the chosen card or a queue of cards can be interpreted as interrupting the previous item (task) of the designer's behavior for the planned or situational processing in accordance with the definite Kanban-rule. It should be noted that Kanban-rules are specified and being implemented under following basic restrictions:

1. On any card presenting the corresponding task, intermediate states of its solution are not reflected.
2. Arising the new tasks (creatively generated by the designer in the real time) is out the responsibility of Kanban mechanisms.

However, in the reality of designing, an interruption can happen at an intermediate step (and state) of the task solution, and creative generating the new tasks is the very important reason for self-interruptions initiated by the designer in a real-time solving of project tasks.

Except the above, there are other reasons for interruptions of human-computer activity that are taking place but not managed with using of Kanban rules. All of these reasons notes prompt combining of the managerial potential of interruptions with Kanban mechanisms.

The creation of the offered version of combining had two stages the first of which has dealt with developing a kernel of version. This kernel includes a set of agile means that was extended by the use of programmable queues of tasks. Features of our solutions embedded in the kernel were described in the paper (Sosnin, 2014) where Figure 15 presented the workspace of the offered version of combining.

The scheme of the workspace consists of following components:

1. The organizational structure that reflects relations among team K^*, its groups $\{G_p(\{D_{ps}\})\}$, their members $\{D_{ps}\}$ and project tasks $\{Z_i\}$ in real-time.
2. A number of means that can be fitted on agile project management in Kanban or Scrum or Scrum-ban version.
3. A number of means, including Editor, Interpreter, Compiler and Library, which support conceptually algorithmic programming the work with queues of tasks.

Figure 15. The workspace of the flexible management

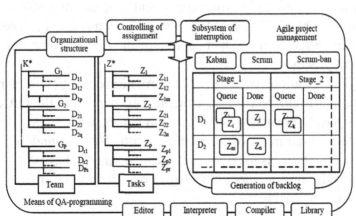

4.   Subsystem "Controlling of assignment" that allows appointing the estimated characteristics of time for planned work with each task Z_i included to the front of tasks (backlog of Kanban or Scrum or Scrum-ban).
5.   The subsystem of interruption that supports the work with tasks in parallel and in pseudo-parallel mode.

Four positions of this list were presented in our publications (Sosnin, 2016) and where the interruption subsystem was only mentioned. At that moment, the necessity of this component was envisaged, but it was specified in general without deep delving and without the possibility of using in practice. Developing the second stage of our approach was aimed at an extension of the kernel by instruments supporting of the personal multitasking that is implemented in coordination with the agile management by taking into account the human-computer interruptions. Moreover, the main attention was paid on self-interruptions that can be inevitable without interactions with natural experience and its models.

3.3. Features of Intellectual Processing the Self-Interruptions

The offered approach helps to manage the human-computer interruptions in any of their cases, but the more interesting class of these cases is self-interruptions when the designer discovers the necessity to include a new task in in the implementation of the multitasking work. The typical scheme of processing for this type of self-interruptions is presented in Figure 16.

This scheme indicates that the designer D_{ps} (as a member of a definite group G_p of the designers' team) implements the delegated task Z_i that has been chosen, for example, from the corresponding queue of the Kanban board. (label 1 on the scheme). In accordance with Kanban rules, it can be any task that has been extracted from the task tree of the corresponding project in a management process.

In analyzed situation, the necessary information describes the task Z_i in the corresponding visualized card (Z_i-card) that is mapped in the QA-memory. Such cards have a normative structure and can be used as units of data in pseudocode programming of interactions with any card and/or queues of cards. Such possibility is useful for an automation of behavioral actions not only in the agile management but also in the interruption management in conditions of multitasking.

Figure 16. Steps of processing the self-interruption

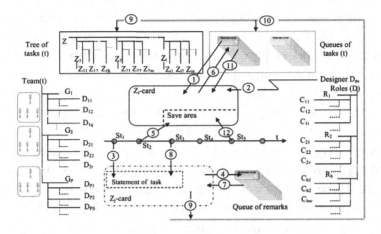

Let us assume, when the designer implements a current task Z_i, it is unpredictably appeared a reason of a self-interruption (label 2) that must get its expression in the consciousness of the designer for explicit initiating the process of the corresponding interruption. Let us additionally suppose that such reason potentially leads to the new task Z_j. In this case, the first step St_1 of such initiating should aim at registering the arisen reason outside of brains with using the appropriate description (for example in the form of a number of words and phrase as keys for remembering the reason). Similar description must be sufficient for formulating an initial statement of the task Z_j. Without such registering, there is a danger to "lose" the reason or incorrectly recover it. In the described research, the special utility activated by the designer creates the card (for the potential task Z_j) where the designer registers the keys in the field "statement of task" (label 3). After registering, the Z_j-card relocates to the queue of temporal remarks (or basket of pending tasks, label 4).

Only after that, it is better to start the second step St_2 of preparing the task Z_i for the future resumption. Actions of this step are similar to actions of the computer interruptions when the system of interruption registers the necessary information in the save area (label 5) that extends the informational structure of the card used in the Kanban management. It should be noted, the point between the first and the second steps can be the point of the next self-interruption if it is necessary or useful for the designer. Therefore, for ordering, the Z_i-card relocates to the corresponding queue of tasks (label 6) after the second step.

In the offered approach, at the third step St_3, extracting the Z_j-card from the queue of temporal remarks (label 7), the designer defines the task Z_j in a form that adequately reflects the interruption reason for its successful processing. Such work is creative, and it requires interactions with accessible experience or, by other words it requires intellectual actions of the designer. More definitely, the designer creates the statement of the task (label 8) by interacting with the Experience Base and Ontology as the part of this Base.

In this step, the task Z_j is included in the tree of project tasks (label 9) and in the set of queues of tasks (label 10) that are solved by the designer. The choice of the appropriate queue is caused by the priority of the new task Z_j and its type. If the priority is low then the task Z_i embeds in a backlog of the used agile managing. In another case, the task Z_j is located in the definite queue of tasks for its solving in multitasking mode.

The fourth step St_4 suggests processing of the reason when the designer creatively solves the task Z_j. This step will begin and fulfill by normative rules of the described management that are applied to an ongoing set of tasks. Solving the tasks corresponding the interruption reasons, the designer can use conceptual experiments any of which helps to understand the reason, outline the way of its processing and check the preliminary solution of the task Z_j. All of these actions include using the interactions with the experience. After conceptual experimenting, the task Z_j will be a member of a multitasking set, and it will be managed similarly as other members of this set.

At the fifth step St_5, after activating Z_i-card (label 11), actions of the designer provide the recovery of the task Z_i from the point of its interruption. Actions of this step use data from the corresponding save area (label 12). In the described approach, these tasks are reflected in a set of queues oriented on types of tasks and roles played by the designer in solving the tasks.

In concluding this section we note, the offered approach of agile management is realized in the instrumental environment WIQA, which supports conceptually algorithmic programming of designer's actions. In this case, solutions of tasks are described by behavioral programs that are executed by the designer who fulfills the role of the (intellectual) processor. Thus, the activity of the designer divided on parts corresponding operators that facilitate their interruptions. Moreover, the designer has the opportunity of using the interpreter of behavioral programs, and this interpreter provides step-by-step executing the operators of such programs.

Therefore, ways of computer interruptions can be used as a source of inheritance for the interruption management of behavioral programs.

3.4. Some Features of Agile Management

Focusing on SEMAT documents, underlining the important role of way-of-working in software engineering, we have studied the new version of the work management based on the controlled use of human-computer interruptions.

Called documents pay special attention to applying the Agile management means in the real-time work of designers. Solutions described in these documents are based on visualized cards registering the current states of tasks being solved in predefined points of their life cycles. It was assumed that designers use appropriate possibilities and means for (human-computer) interacting with these cards. The lack of SEMAT recommendations for useful forms of human-computer interactions with the cards has led us to the intention of developing our approach to the Agile management.

Expectations of novelty and effects from the development of this approach were caused by features of the toolkit WIQA that provides the experiential kind of human-computer interaction with the process of designing. Moreover, these expectations were confirmed.

The implementation of the approach included two steps. The first step has led to the management version that combines Agile means with programmable queues of tasks. Basic components of this version are presented above.

In this version, the designer can work with cards and queues of cards only in their predefined states that correspond to the normative division of the life-cycle of the task on stages. Sets of these states and stages were depended on the model of the life cycle used by designers. Technologically, in the WIQA-environment, any normative stage is defined by the corresponding practice previously programmed in the pseudocode language for its implementation by the designer. This feature leads to following useful possibilities:

1. Tasks solved by the team at the definite stage are reflected on their queue that uses a priority for each task. The programmable access to all queues of tasks helps to build the personal queue in interacting with which the designer uses priorities.
2. Additionally, the designer can interrupt the own work with the active practice at any point of its (pseudocode) program. The basic aim of interruptions is to conduct the useful conceptual experiments (Sosnin, 2015).

In the first version, interruptions were used, but the interruption management was absent. This managerial function is included in the second version supporting the multitasking mode that simulates mechanisms of computer interruptions. The scenario simulation is described in the previous section. This scenario provides controlled intertwining offered managerial functions. First of all, such intertwining is achieved by the use of the special area on the visualized card for saving information that provides the resumption of the interrupted task. So, in the definite moment of time, life-cycles of tasks can be crossed in any their points (not only in predefined points). The additional feature of the second version is bound with the offered way of processing the reason of the self-interruption caused by the appearance of the new project task. The above, we described this reason and its processing without details.

It should be noted that both versions of offered means are realized and successively applied (the first for two years, the second with last October) in the project organization (about 2,000 employees). This fact indicates that offered approach was tested in the real designing.

The following conclusions can be drawn from the present study of human-computer interruptions in the multitasking mode. The use of programmable queues of tasks for combining the agile management with interruption management facilitates increasing the level of automation in the behavioral activity of designers' team. In conditions of pseudocode programming the designer' behavior, such way-of-working helps to organize and control the multitasking work of any designer by analogies with computer interruptions and the use of visualized cards for registering the recovery information. The offered mechanisms open the important possibilities for self-interruptions, and especially for their class that is bound with appearing the new tasks.

In this case, the designer can creatively build the owned behavior that can include formulating the statement of the new task and experimenting with its conceptually algorithmic solution. Useful intellectual and practical effects are achieved, first of all, by using the interactions of the designer with the Experience Base and Ontology located in the environment of the toolkit WIQA. Offered combining is possible for any version of agile management that uses the board of visualized cards.

3.5. Preparation to Managing

Let us assume that a technology workflow task Z^W_n is included to the tree of tasks and a group of designers $G_p(\{D_{ps}\})$ should implement the task Z^W_n with a subordinated set of tasks $\{Z^N_j\}$. After that, the following programmed procedures will be executed:

The leader of the group distributes tasks $\{Z^N_j\}$ among members $\{D_{ps}\}$ of the group in accordance with them competences.

A specialized (pseudocode) programmed agent registers all appointments in tables of "Controlling of Assignments". A fragment of the agent source code has the following view:

```
&OrgProject&:= QA_GetProjectId ("Organizational structue")
&ProjectsTask&:= QA_GetQaId(&OrgProject&, "Проекты")
&cnt&:= 0
&max&:= QA_GetDirectChildsCount (&OrgProject&, &ProjectsTask&)
LABEL &L1&
IF &cnt& >= &max& THEN GOTO &L2&
&Pid&:= QA_GetDirectChildId (&OrgProject&, &ProjectsTask&, &cnt&)
&Pname&:= QA_GetQAText(&Pid&) &npid&:= QA_
    GetProjectId(&Pname&)
if &npid& == &current_project& THEN GOTO &L3&
&cnt&:= &cnt& + 1
GOTO &L1&
LABEL &L2&
```

This code is only presented for a demonstration of syntax L^{WIQA}. The code of this agent is processing by the WIQA-compiler.

1. The leader of the group uploads the necessary typical QA-program for the task Z^W_n from a library of QA-programs. The uploaded pattern is adjusted to the specificity of the executed work and, after that, QA-program of the task Z^W_n is executed. Results of the execution register in "Controlling of Assignments" for each task Z^N_j in the form of "pseudocode of condition opening the opportunity to start work with this task."

2. If the pattern for the task Z^W_n is absent, then the necessary QA-program is created and processed in accordance with points (p.1 - p.3).

3. Additionally, the leader of the group sets the estimated characteristics of time for planned work with each task Z^N_j.

4. The responsible member of the group specified a next sprint (list of tasks being solved, values of story-points for tasks, real estimates, the initial velocity of the team and other characteristics).

This part of the work is implemented in the operational conditions presented in Figure 17, where some labels are used because of all interface forms in Russian.

The other program agent that is responsible for the current state of the Kanban board visualizes a number of characteristics for each task Z^N_j in two-side cards in corresponding cells of the board. An interface of the visualization is presented in Figure 18.

Figure 17. Tasks' queues on the board

Figure 18. Tasks' queues on the board

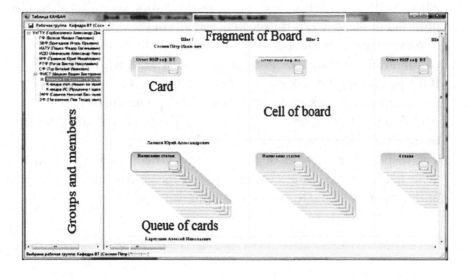

3.6. Real Time Work

The real-time work of designers with tasks of any workflow is based on the following actions:

1. Informational interactions with queues of tasks that are located on the board of cards include possibilities of visual and touchable navigation (on groups, members of groups, previous sprints), sorting and selecting of cards, their dynamic visualizing and choosing of the necessary card.
2. Informational interactions with the choosing card include choosing of the necessary side of the card, analyzing of information on the visual side and activating of the necessary actions from the card.
3. Programmable interactions of the designer with the personal queue of the appointed tasks the scheme of which is figuratively presented in Figure 19.

In the discussed case, the queues with which the designer works is expediently interpreted as a special type of program (M-programs), which manages the activity of the designer. Any queue in M-program includes the names of the tasks and attributes that indicate conditions in which the work with the corresponding task can be begun or interrupted. Any unit of such a queue is interpreted as an operator of an M-program.

Figure 19. Operational conditions of programmable managing

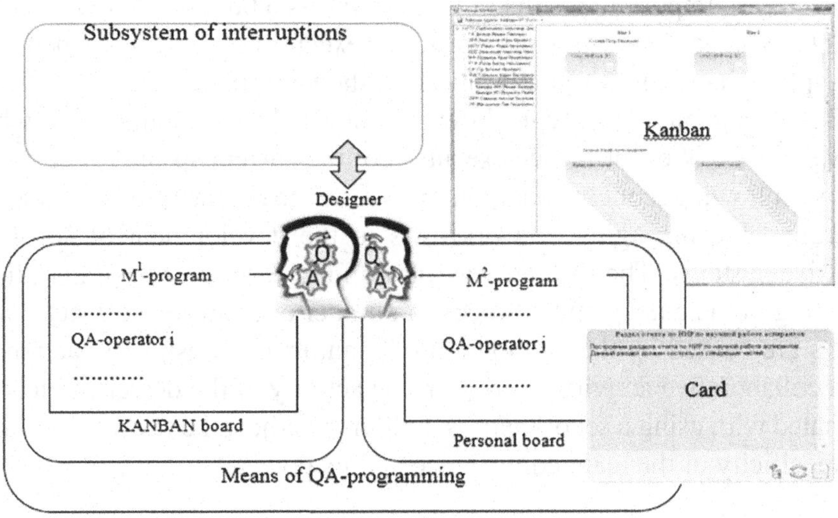

A program character of such an interpretation is clarified by an abstract example with a workflow contains a sequence of three tasks:

Z0: &IsEnabled&:= 1
Z1:IF &idZ0&.STATE == &running& THEN &IsEnabled&:= 1 ELSE &IsEnabled&:= 0 Z2:IF &idZ1&.STATE == &done& THEN &IsEnabled&:= 1 ELSE &IsEnabled&:= 0Z.

There is a possibility of using two types of M-programs in the WIQA-environment. The first type M1 provides the pseudo-parallel solving of tasks (QA-programs) by the designer playing a role of I-processor (Sosnin, 2013) Such an opportunity is supported by the plug-in "System of interruption."

Any M2-program manages the execution of tasks by the group of designers in the workflows, which are processed collectively with the use of other means presented in Figure 2. In this case, it is necessary to take into account an inheritance among conditions that are opening the possibilities for the work with tasks in the group. In both cases, the access to the queues includes priorities of their units.

3.7. Analysis of Sprint Execution

The analysis (inspection) of the sprint execution is the principal part of a Scrum process. This part of the work helps to define the characteristics of the definite team activity that will allow more adequately planning of the next sprint. The most of the data for analysis is gathered from daily Scrums.

One of the important results of the analysis is a burn-down diagram that helps to manage the sprint work during its execution. In the described case, this type of diagrams is visualized as it is shown in Figure 20.

There are a number of typical trends of a watched diagram curve, which show evolving of events in the execution of the current sprint.

The following conclusions can be drawn from the present study of programmable managing of workflows in the development of software-intensive systems. The offered way-of-working for such managing allows including in the management process a number of additional effects. These effects are caused by the automation of a number of designers' actions in them collaborative activity. Moreover, the activity of the designers' team is estimated with using a set of metrics, helping to adjust the executed work on the specificity of the team competence and its power.

Figure 20. Burn-down diagram

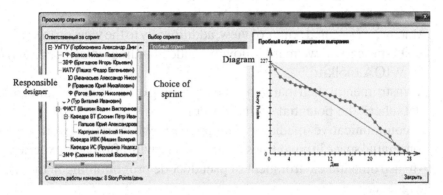

The offered approach correlates with innovations declared in SEMAT for program engineering. The positive effects of managing are achieved by using: the means of pseudocode programming oriented on the memory that is specified for the registration of QA-reasoning of designers; the programmable activity of designers; the visualized cards in the frames of Kanban and Scrum means. In conceptual designing, all workflows, including of programmable managing, can be implemented in WIQA environment.

4. SOME REMARKS TO THE CHAPTER 5

1. By the initial intent, the WIQA environment has been created for the instrumental support of the team of developers in the conceptual designing the systems with the software. This intention found its expression in a view on the toolkit as QA-processor in a sense similar to the Word-processor of Microsoft Office.
2. This understanding helped us to build some applications of the WIQA in the form of "kernel+plug-ins." A set of applications included plug-ins "Organizational structure of the team," "Project Documenting," "Communicating among member of a team" and "Automated professional learning." In all these applications, we used QA-models of tasks corresponding to domains of applications.
3. In the indicated creation and improvement of the WIQA complex, we also used its interpretation as a specialized SIS, whose architecture integrates into a single whole the set of viewpoints on the complex.

That has led to the toolkit state, in which the set of useful viewpoints has been evolved before material embodiment.

4. Among investigated points of view, additionally to the view on the WIQA as QA-processor, we mark following understanding (interpretations) of the WIQA toolkit:

5. An instrumental shell that supports developing on its basis of applications that inherit the potential of this system;

6. A communicative mediator that provide collaborative work in the conceptual space in conditions of interactions with affordable experience;

7. An instrumental environment of pseudocode programming in the L^{WIQA} language.

8. Step-by-step, a set of viewpoint was evolved before architectures of the current versions of the WIQA toolkit. These architectures reflect features of collaborative and personal works of designers with project tasks in their conceptual solution.

9. During the becoming of the WIQA toolkit, including its workflows, we built and tested reflections onto semantic memory for a number of important essences of designing the systems. Some of these reflections are disclosed above in the context of their applications. The main goal of disclosing is only to demonstrate the potential of QA-approach tested in our research and development.

10. Reflections on the semantic memory (on the conceptual space, C-space) were investigated in the context of the operational space for the process, a team of designers and designed systems taking into account the applied experience.

11. In reflections of the process of conceptual designing the system, the central place occupies by the tree of tasks and QA-models of corresponding tasks. The tree combines domain tasks, normative (technological) tasks, tasks of adaptation and tasks corresponded to workflows.

12. To distinguish types any of which requires assigning the certain additional attribute to tasks of this type. Such assignment helps to separate components of the theory $Th^P(t)$ from models of this theory.

13. For reflections of the team and its members (in reflections of workforces), the special plugins "Organizational structure" was embedded to the WIQA-toolkit. In this plug-ins, the model of the team is similar to the tree of tasks. Such hierarchical structure expresses only subordinations among members of the team. Additional attributes help to mark other relations among designers.

14. One of the important functions of the organizational model is a distribution of tasks among designers. Results of distribution help are used in project management for implementing of which the WIQA contains sub-system of agile means.

15. Reflections of workforces include personal models of designers. A base of any of such

16. model is a job description, the text of which includes references to normatively assigned roles, mastered competencies, assigned tasks and other characteristics that help to use this model not only in organizational aims (for example, managing the workforces). Models of designers can be used into pseudocode programs automating the tasks corresponded to the standard P-CMM

17. The tree of tasks and models of the team and its members are also the base for reflections of agile means of the real-time managing the project process onto the semantic memory. This kind of reflections is oriented on Kanban and Scrum means that are reified with the use of a complex of pseudocode programs. The choice of the L^{WIQA} language was intentional in order to estimate its power.

18. The principle features of developed agile means are their extending by the multitasking mode and taking into account an unpredictable appearance of new tasks during the solutions of tasks already included in the tree of tasks.

19. Let us notice again, the main goal of this chapter is to demonstrate on which base of our research and development we present our version of experience-based human-computer interactions. That is why the content of the chapter discloses the toolkit and its workflows only schematically without important details that can be found in our previous publications indicated in the reference section of the book.

REFERENCES

Adler, R. F., & Benbunan-Fich, R. (2013). Self-interruptions in discretionary multitasking. *Computers in Human Behavior*, *29*(4), 1441–1449. doi:10.1016/j. chb.2013.01.040

Held, M., & Blochinger, M. (2009). Structured collaborative workflow design. *Future Generation Computer Systems*, *25*(6), 638–653. doi:10.1016/j. future.2008.12.005

Sosnin, P. (2012). Question-Answer Approach to Human-Computer Interaction in Collaborative Designing. In Cognitively Informed Intelligent Interfaces: Systems Design and Development. IGI Global. doi:10.4018/978-1-4666-1628-8.ch010

Sosnin, P. (2013). Role Intellectual Processor in Conceptual Designing Of Software Intensive Systems. In *Proc. of the 11-th International Conference on Computational Science and Applications, Part III.* Springer. doi:10.1007/978-3-642-39646-5_1

Sosnin, P. (2015). Combining of Kanban and Scrum Means with Programmable queues in Designing of Software Intensive Systems. *Communications in Computer and Information Science, 532,* 367–377. doi:10.1007/978-3-319-22689-7_28

Sosnin, P., Lapshov, Y., & Svyatov, K. (2014). Chapter. In A. Moonis (Eds.), Programmable Managing of Workflows in Development of Software-Intensive Systems (Vol. 8481, pp. 138–141). LNAI. doi:10.1007/978-3-319-07455-9_15

Sosnin, P., & Maklaev, V. (2014). Question-Answer Reflections in a Creation of an Experience Base for Conceptual Designing the Family of Software Intensive Systems. Springer International Publishing.

Sosnin, P., & Pertsev, A. (2014). An Approach to Creating a Personified Job Description of a Designer in Designing a Family of Software Intensive Systems. LNCS, 8583, 51–62.

ADDITIONAL READING

Basili, V. R., & Lindvall, V. R., V. R. & Costa, P. (2001) Implementing the experience factory concepts as a set of experience bases. In Proc. of SEKE, pp. 102-109.

Bass, L., L. Clements, P., R. Kazman, R. & Klein, M. (2008) Models for Evaluating and Improving Architecture Competence, Technical Report, CMU/SEI-2008-TR-006.

Borges, P., Machado, R. J., & Ribeiro, P. (2012). Mapping RUP Roles to Small Software Development Teams, In *Proc. of International Conference on Software and System Process,* pp. 190-199. doi:10.1007/978-3-642-27213-4_5

Jin, J., & Dabbish, L. A. (2009). Self-interruption on the computer: a typology of discretionary task interleaving. In *Proc. of the SIGCHI Conference on Human Factors in Computing Systems* (CHI '09). ACM, New York, NY, USA, pp. 1799-1808. doi:10.1145/1518701.1518979

McFarlane, D. C., & Latorella, K. A. (2002). The scope and importance of human interruption in human-computer interaction design. *Human-Computer Interaction*, *17*(1), 1–61. doi:10.1207/S15327051HCI1701_1

Rational Unified Process (RUP). (2017). Available at http://www-01.ibm.com/software/rational/rup/

Roglinger, M., Poppelbuth, J., & Becker, J. (2012). Maturity models in business process management. *Business Process Management*, *18*(2), 328–346. doi:10.1108/14637151211225225

Sosnin, P. (2013) Scientifically experimental way-of-working in conceptual designing of software intensive systems. In Proc. of the IEEE 12th International Conference on Intelligent Software Methodologies, Tools and Techniques, pp. 43-51.

Sosnin, P. (2013) Role Intellectual Processor in Conceptual Designing Of Software Intensive Systems. In Proc. of the 11-th International conference on Computational Science and Applications, Part III, LNCS 7973 Springer, Heidelberg, 2013, pp. 1-15.

Sosnin, P. (2016). Precedent-Oriented Approach to Conceptually Experimental Activity in Designing the Software Intensive Systems. *International Journal of Ambient Computing and Intelligence*, *7*(1), 69–93. doi:10.4018/IJACI.2016010104

Systems Engineering Competency Framework. (2010), Available at http://www.incoseonline.org.uk/Documents/zGuides/Z6_Competency_WEB.pdf

Von Rosing, M., Moshiri, S., Gräslund, K., & Rosenberg, A. Competency Maturity Model Wheel, Available at http://www.valueteam.biz/downloads/model_cmm_wheel.pdf

Chapter 6
Precedent–Oriented Approach to Human–Computer Activity

ABSTRACT

In our research that was aimed at study of reflecting the various essences involved in designing the SISs onto the semantic memory, we have been conscious of the principle role of tasks (and especially new tasks) in the design process. New tasks are a useful source of experience units, models of which can be better prepared for reusing in personal or collective activity. This chapter represents our version of such models (as models of precedents for corresponding tasks). The basic feature of our version is the use of analogies between intellectual processing a solution of a new task and intellectual processing the conditioned reflexes that lead to generating the natural forms of human experience. The kernel of our version is a framework of the precedent model that includes components for expressing verbal, logical, analytical, graphical and programmatic views on reusable models of task that fulfill the role of experience models.

1. MODEL OF PRECEDENT AS UNIT OF HUMAN EXPERIENCE USED IN SOLVING THE PROJECT TASKS

1.1. Behavioral View on Problem-Solving

At this section, we focus our research on a behavioral side of the designer's activity in solutions of project tasks. Above some features of this side, we

DOI: 10.4018/978-1-5225-2987-3.ch006

told at the end of section 3. For this side of a human-computer activity, in our research, we use the following position.

The life of any person exists and evolves via interactions with the naturally artificial world. The human side of interactions consists of behavioral units the most of which are repeatable. Such repeatable units of the human behavior are often referred to as precedents. Human life is based on precedents.

The precedent form of human activity was (created) by Nature in an evolution of a phenomenon called "conditioned reflex." This step of the natural evolution as any prior steps can be interpreted as evolutionary experiments conducted by Nature. Therefore, it is possible to consider, that any precedent appears as a result of the corresponding experiment conducted by persons who solved the definite task and prepared its solution for the reuse.

An analysis of the richest set of practices of the experimentation as a type of the human activity suggests following their natural features (discovered by Nature and embodied to the human life):

1. Using the natural language for interactions with surrounding (environment of experimenting) on the base of the natural experience
2. Using other intellectual abilities (additional to the use of the natural language) inherent to man.

These features can be generalized in the following assertion "The precedent form of the human life is based on the intellectual processing of conditioned reflexes." This understanding of the human behavior occupies the central place in our research described in this manuscript where we agree with the following definition "précédents are actions or decisions that have already happened in the past and which can be referred to and justified as an example that can be followed when the similar situation arises" (Precedent, 2011).

Thus, when creating SIS, designers solve the tasks of the project and develop models of tasks in forms of precedents for their future reuse. In this activity, they intellectually process the solution of tasks similarly "intellectual processing of conditioned reflexes." The similarity suggests explicitly or implicitly conducting "experiments" results of which evolve the occupational experience of designers.

There are three ways for the appearance of the precedent and its model providing the reuse. The first way is connected with the intellectual processing of the definite behavior which happened in the past but was estimated by the human as a potential precedent for its reuse in the future. The second way is the creation of the precedent in parallel with its first performance, and the third way is an extraction of the precedent model from another's experience and its models.

The toolkit WIQA supports all of these ways in the implementation of which designers use the specialized framework for the model of the precedent. We defined the structure and semantic of this framework with the orientation on the following positions:

1. As told above in section 2, an important feature of designing the SIS is the work of designers in conditions of a high complexity that can be expressed by the use of the Kolmogorov measure oriented on the length of the program P providing the creation of the system. To reduce the complexity, the program P should divide on the complex of parts each of which is a certain program object (P-object).

2. Any P-object as a program of actions defines the way-of-working the use of which helps to the designer or designers to build the corresponding artifact in definite conditions. Let us notice that a very important kind of such artifacts is a prototype version of future program units. In this case, P-objects describe algorithmically the prototypes in actions being executed by designers. The prototypes are being created not only for program units, but such objects are always used in experimental aims. Therefore, investigating algorithmic prototypes, the designers investigate usually the units of the own behavior. Such understanding prompts that P-objects can be used for planned experimenting with behavioral units of designers embedded into ways-of-working.

3. Experimenting, the designers focus own attention on "how to do" but not on "what to build" and this correlates with cardinal principles of SEMAT. Experimenting the designers acquire units of an experience which they should register in forms of models providing the future reuses of experiments. It is necessary to notice that typical (reused) units of human behavior are named "precedents."

4. Natural precedents are based on conditioned reflexes which are intellectually processed and included to the human experience as its units. Interpretation of behavior units as precedents prompts the necessity of their intellectual processing aimed at the planned reuse.

1.2. Experimenting With Behavioral Units of Designers

In a general case, a system of the SIS-type involves software that is combined with Peopleware and other different components. Any such system can be interpreted as a naturally artificial world, the processes of which are implemented by specific cause-and-effect laws (regularities). Some of these regularities are laws of nature, while others have a normative character.

In designing a SIS and its cause-and-effect regularities (or shortly regularities), the designer must find a reflection of the design in the software components. In software engineering, the reflected regularities are bound with requirements and restrictions that are embodied in the created software. Such embodiments are implemented when designers formulate and solve the corresponding project tasks. Embodiments of requirements and their subsets are distributed between project tasks. It is necessary to note that this part of way-of-working is based on the experiences of requirements engineering.

Thus, in a general case, the project task concerns a set of specific regularities, the coexistence of which should be confirmed for SIS, which otherwise is not be constructed. Under such conditions, the necessary confirmation can be implemented by the designer who performs the appropriate actions, with a scheme for the corresponding part of the SIS.

Thus, acting by the created scheme, the designer should be convinced that the scheme of actions leads to the necessary use of cause-and-effect regularities in the task. Moreover, for mutual understanding and collaborative work, the designer should specify the scheme for reuse by other members of the team. A similar responsibility is expected of a scientist who has solved an experimental task.

Therefore, simulating the scientists' activity in experimenting with activity units of designers is a promising way of improving the ways-of-working when designing the SISs. This position focuses on the system of cause-and-effect regularities, which manages the processes in the naturally artificial world of SIS; it correlates with the empirical nature of software engineering.

There were several reasons for the choice of conceptual design as an activity domain for the constructive use of the analogy between designing and experimental scientific research. The first reason is connected with the high cost of errors that mainly arise from an incorrect understanding of the cases that the designers are working on.

Any conceptual project is aimed at a description of the system that is being created, allowing for its structure and behavior to be coordinated with natural laws and normative rules the system should satisfy. Hence, designers should prove that the used models of "cause-and-effect regularities" provide the required coordination. This approach should be put into practice in the conceptual design of a specific SIS as early as possible. The aim of any scientific experiment is an existence of the confirmation of a corresponding cause-and-effect regularity. The similarity of the obligations of designers and scientists was the second reason for this choice.

The third reason is the lack of methods that are included, especially modern technologies for supporting the experimental activity of designers at the conceptual stage of design. It is necessary to note that, at the conceptual stage of design, the investigated scheme of the designer's actions can be a simplified version of the task solution, demonstrating only how regularities of the task can be materialized and will be used.

1.3. Normative Model of Precedents

In the offered approach, the work with regularities is considered from the viewpoint of the designers' behavior in the solution processes of the project tasks. Moreover, the approach is oriented toward the analogy between projects completed by designers and scientists. In specific circumstances, any designer plays the role of a scientist who prepares and conducts experiments with P-type behavior units. In such experiments, the designer works in the naturally artificial world of SIS, which is developed in the technological medium used. Any experiment is connected with solving the corresponding task appointed to the designer on the team.

As told above, natural precedents are based on conditioned reflexes, which are intellectually processed and are included as models to the human experience, as its units. No one knows how these models are embodied in human brains' structure. In the same time, there is a possibility for controlled influencing on such "models" by their models that are built outside brains. Below models of "models" will be called as models of precedents.

In the design processes, models of precedents should be created with using of intelligent processing for the solutions of project tasks. Such way of their creating will facilitate the conformity and compatibility among models of precedents and corresponding "models" localized in designer brains. Therefore, interactions with any model of the definite precedent will be transferred to the corresponding model.

Thus, controlled interactions of designers with units of the natural experience can be implemented through interaction with models of corresponding precedents. Such understanding of "interactions with experience" is used in the QA-approach in any its versions. Moreover, in the approach, modeling of precedents is controlled by a typical model P^M that integrates a number of subordinate models reflecting precedents with a number of important points of view.

Basic features of the QA-approach are bound with the logical model Pr^L_i of the precedent Pr_i that has the structure shown in Figure 1.

This model has a human-oriented view, the human interaction with which activates the internal logical process on the level of the second signal system in human brains. Such logical processes have a dialog nature, and therefore, for keeping the naturalness, interaction processes of interaction of human beyond brains with computerized means should be implemented the dialog form also. That is why, in our research, this model has been chosen for creating the models of precedents.

Logical descriptions of models $\{Pr^L_i\}$ are very important constructs of the project theory $Th^P(t)$. A semantics net for a logical description of a precedent Pr_i consists of a connected set of nodes corresponding such types of answers as a motive, aim, condition and references (on guide describing the reaction and alternative models of precedents). Thus, this model has a generative potential as for creating its samples so for a full specification of precedent' description.

The model Pr^L fulfills the role of a kernel for the model Pr^M of the precedent Pr and applies for specifying other its components that we use for modeling the precedents.

Figure 1. Logical model of the precedent

Name of precedent P_i:

c
h
o
i
c
e

    while [logical formulae (F) for motives $M = \{M_k\}$]
        as [F for aims $C = \{C_l\}$]
            if [F for precondition $U' = \{U'_n\}$],
                then [plan of reaction (program) r_q],
            end so [F for post conditions $U'' = \{U''_m\}$]
    ----
    there are alternatives $\{P_j(r_p)\}$.

Figure 2. Framework for models of the precedents

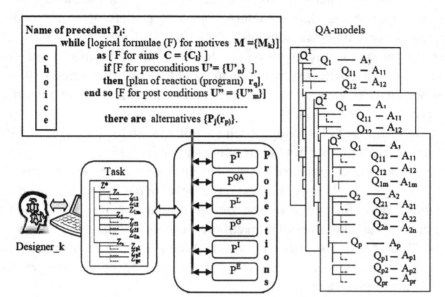

Our version of a framework of an integrated normative model Pr ^{M} is shown in Figure 2.

First of all the subordinated model Pr^L helps to formulate and structure the textual model Pr^T as a statement of a task for the corresponding precedent. Such help is additional for the work with the statement Pr^T which, in the general case, begins with its initial state Pr^T(t$_0$) describing the new task. In this case, the normative logical model prompts the steps of QA-analysis, results of which evolve as Pr^T(t) so Pr^L(t) till their adequate descriptions.

The model Pr^T generalizes results of the QA-analysis conducted on the base of QA-reasoning that can be effective used as a question-answer model (QA-model) of the task, or, that the same, the question-answer model Pr^{QA} of the corresponding precedent. the theory Th^P(t), the model Pr^{QA}) describes a fragment that presents a corresponding task.

An effectiveness of understanding in work with the model P^M(t) can be increased if this model will include subordinated model Pr^G that presents block-and-line descriptions of the Pr^M. In the QA-approach, the model Pr^G is specified so that it supports the diagrammatic reasoning of designers in their interactions with the model Pr^M. Additionally, built schemes reflected diagrammatic reasoning could be aimed at on a simulation of a necessary perception coordinated with QA-reasoning.

The model Pr^T includes the reaction r$_q$ that should implement if the corresponding precedent Pr will be chosen. In the QA-approach, any reaction

176

r_q can be defined as a conceptually algorithmic model Pr^I in the form of the executable pseudocode program that presents a conceptual solution of the corresponding task. If the model Pr^I fulfills the role of the precedent prototype for its programming in another executed version Pr^E, then the version Pr^E is also included the integrated model Pr^M the typical scheme of which is presented in Figure 2.

The model Pr^M is shown in the activity context when the designer solves the task Z as the reuse of the precedent Pr. Any of its subordinated models or a definite their group can be interpreted as a projection of the precedent model. One of the important projections is the QA-model of the task.

It should be noted, the model Pr^M and its subordinated models Pr^T, Pr^L, Pr^{QA}, Pr^G, Pr^I have a common feature. They are created in a semantic memory that is oriented on the implementation of question-answer processes.

Thus, the applied logical scheme allows integrating the natural and normative regularities in the precedent model. Natural regularities are reflected in pre- and post-conditions, while normative regularities are specified in such constructs as motives and aims.

In the grammar GR^{QA}, the precedent framework is described by the following set of rules:

$$\left.\begin{aligned}
Fpr &= (\text{``}r\text{''},\ ZPr); \\
FPr &= \left(Keys,\ TPr,\ LPr,\ QAPr,\ GPr,\ IPr,\ EPr\right); \\
VFPr &= FPr - \left[QAPr\right] - \left[GPr\right] - \left[IPr\right] - \left[EPr\right]); \\
VFPr &= (\text{``}p\text{''},\ FPr); \\
Keys &= \left\{Key\right\},
\end{aligned}\right\} \qquad (1)$$

where "ρ" presents the reflection $R^{QA}(Z^{QA})$ in the operation form, ***VFP*** designates a variant or projection of the precedent use, and π is an operation of projection. The possibility of projecting is included in the potential of reflections for adjusting the precedent models on conditions of their reuse.

At the level of tasks, the rules of the set (6.1) can be detailed with the help of the following grammar rules:

$$
\left.
\begin{aligned}
FPr &= ((ZPr,\ \text{"-"},\big(TZ,\ LZ,\ QAZ,\ GZ,\ IZ,\ EZ\big));\\
TPr &= TZ;\ /\ specialized\ Z\\
QAPr &= QAZ;/\ specialized\ Z\\
LPr &= LZ;\ /\ specialized\ Z\\
GPr &= GZ\ /\ specialized\ Z\\
IPr &= IZ\ /\ specialized\ Z\\
EPr &= EZ\ /\ specialized\ Z
\end{aligned}
\right\}
\qquad (2)
$$

In this version, the task structure (**ZPr, TZ, QAZ, LZ, GZ, IZ, EZ**) is represented the precedent model by means of QA-objects. The use of described model of precedents in designing the systems corresponds to our approach to solving the project tasks. In our research, this approach was named as "Precedent-oriented approach" (Sosnin, 2013).

1.4. Pseudocode Programming of Precedents

The work of the designer as a type of activity is initially oriented to the use of experiential practices. Any new SIS project is evolved through the real-time solution of the technological and subject tasks that are distributed among members of the team. This distribution accounts for the personal experience of any member with real-time access to the collective experience and its models.

It is easy to agree that the contribution of any designer to the general work depends on an essential measure both from the accessible experience and from the used means of the access. With any newly solved task, any designer evolves their experience, further enhancing the current state of the commonly accessible experience. Such a process is similar to experiential learning under the conditions of designing a specific SIS. The most important aspect of experiential learning is the fact that the learner (in our case, the designer) should actively participate in purposeful actions and reflect them when using the accessible experience.

Thus, one can interpret the designing of SISs from the viewpoint of experiential learning in the team of designers. This viewpoint indicates an important area for rationalizing (improving) the real-time actions of designers aimed at interactions with the accessible experience. Rational workflows of such interactions can increase the degree of success in the development of SISs. The continuous improvement of the used practices is recognized as a reliable way of achieving the sustainable success of the team of designers and their project organization.

In active practice, the person usually represents their behavior using a plan that is written in a natural language based on its algorithmic usage. Repeatable work that is fulfilled by people is represented by techniques that are also written in a natural language based on its algorithmic usage. This approach prompts the designer to use this technique in planning experiments, which was the reason behind choosing a pseudocode language for programming the units of the designer's ideas. Interacting with such programmed models of behavior, the designers will apply their experience in the use of natural language.

The logical scheme of the precedent specifies two parts of its model because of their separate pseudocode programming. The first part must define the access to the precedent model, while the second part must describe the corresponding reaction that must be implemented by the designer.

It is necessary to remind about the M- and P-types of programs that were chosen to describe the designers' activity in the offered approach. Creating of instrumental means for an explicit work with M- and P-type artifacts essentially depend on their understanding. In an approach described in this book, these artifacts are understood as models of designers' behavior that are created for scientific experimentation on the corresponding behavior units included in the wayof-working. Therefore, the indicated instruments should have the potential for the creation and use of the artifacts of M- and P-types in experiments with behavioral units of designers' activity. Moreover, the means of supporting the experimental work should help the designers create solutions for investigating tasks and opening the possibility for their confirmatory reuse in the designers' team.

Let us clarify the difference between these types of programs. P-programs are destined for simulating the units of the designer's behavior in the solutions of the appointed tasks, while Mprograms describe the collaborative work of the designers. Thus, M-programs are destined for controlling the activity of the designers, while they work in parallel and coordination. This type of program is also suitable for controlling the pseudo-parallel work of the designer, with a number of appointed tasks. In general, the M-programs automate the implementation of the workflows.

Workflows in conceptual designing are formed according to the planned schemes. Thus, they conform with the current situation. Workflows of the planned type can be programmed in advance, but workflows of the second type are to be programmed by working designers (not professional programmers) in real time. Hence, the language of pseudocode programming, which will be used by designers for the creation of P-programs, can be used for the creation of M-programs also.

Creating of instrumental means for an explicit work with M- and P-type artifacts essentially depend on their understanding. In an approach described in this book, these artifacts are understood as models of designers' behavior that are created for scientific experimentation on the corresponding behavior units included in the way-of-working. Therefore, the indicated instruments should have the potential for the creation and use of the artifacts of M- and P-types in experiments with behavioral units of designers' activity. Moreover, the means of supporting the experimental work should help the designers create solutions for investigating tasks and opening the possibility for their confirmatory reuse in the designers' team.

The specificity of the precedent-oriented approach is defined by the following features:

1. The investigated units of behavior are interpreted as precedents, with which the designers use interactions to obtain helpful experience, and models are used.
2. Experimenting with the chosen unit of behavior, the designer creates the corresponding precedent model that fulfills the function of "experimental setup."
3. Any such "experimental setup" is built to confirm the existence of a specific "cause-andeffect regularity (or regularities)" in the "naturally artificial world" of the SIS that is being created.
4. The existence of any investigated "cause-and-effect regularity" should be confirmed not only by an author of the experiment but also by other members of the designers' team.
5. Interactions of designers with the experience and its models (i.e., the accessible experience) are based on question-answer reasoning.
6. The approach is aimed at the conceptual stage of designing because a system of SIS regularities should be formed, checked and confirmed during the design as early as possible.
7. Artifacts of M- and P-types (which are included in models of precedents) are programmed in a specialized pseudocode language that is used by designers in coordination with question-answer reasoning.

2. STEP-WISE REFINEMENT IN CREATING THE MODEL OF PRECEDENT

2.1. Step-Wise Refinement in Conceptual Solving the Project Task

As told above, in the general case, a project task that will be solved by a designer can occur in the form of a new task Z, statement $St(Z, t_0)$ of which has a view of an intention of achieving the certain useful aim. From this point of time, the task starts its life cycle, during which the task will be to move from state to state, enriching its content to a state in which it will receive the necessary decision and its material realization. At the conceptual stage of the life cycle, the task Z achieves its conceptual solution.

Before the statement $St(Z, t_0)$ acquired the observable shape of a text written in the language of the project, this statement has been created in the mind of a designer as a reaction to the corresponding task situation. This process includes mental imaginations, the activity of consciousness and other requested intellectual activities.

Let us suppose, that statement $St(Z, t_0)$ has the observable shape as a text written in the language of the project, and this text is observable on the monitor screen. In order to move forward, the designer should check the lexical items used in the text and its understandability. These checks can be fulfilled with the use of the following actions:

1.   Comparison of the used words with the current state of the ontology that is created in the process of project designing from its beginning.
2.   Reflection of $St(Z, t_0)$ on an appropriate visual image or images that will activate the mental imagery and other intellectual activities in the mind of a designer who will register the result of the reflection beyond brains (in our case on the screen of the monitor).

Both kinds of checks lead to service tasks the first of which is disclosed below. Our version of the second service task was described in publications (Sosnin, 2013). Here we also mark, the reflection on graphics support the achievement and expression of understanding, without which either personal or collective work of designers are impossible.

Processes of checking and finding errors will lead to the expansion of the information content of $St(Z, t_0)$, which the designer should analyze to

Figure 3. Conceptual solution of the task

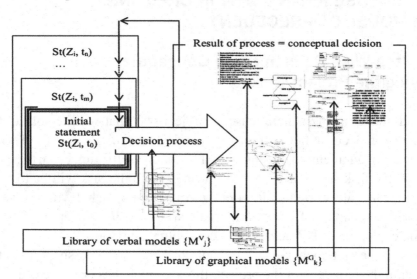

create and to register the next state $St(Z, t_0)$ of the task Z. Thus, step by step, the designer will build the conceptual solution of the task. This process is presented in Figure 3 in a general way.

The scheme also includes two sources of conceptual models (verbal models $\{M^V_j\}$ and graphical models $\{M^G_k\}$) applied to the solution process. They are conditionally called libraries, but this only emphasizes that such models are useful to gather in a whole for the possible reuse.

In the described research, the way of coordination was materialized in the instrumental environment WIQA where a designer creates and evolves the statement $St(Z_i, t)$ by the use of its stepwise refinement based on question-answering analysis and modeling, results of which are registered in the form of a question-answer tree (QA-tree). Dynamic of this process has an iterative process and includes precedent-oriented simulation.

The system of tasks of conceptual designing the SIS is being formed and solved according to a method of the stepwise refinement. The initial state of the stepwise refinement is defined by the system of normative tasks of the life cycle of SIS which includes the main project task $Z^*(t_0)$. The base version of normative tasks corresponds to standard ISO/IEC 12207.

The realization of the method begins with the formulation of the statement for the main task in the form which allows starting the creation of the prime conceptual models. The initial statement of the main task formulates as the text $Z^*(t_0)$ which reflects the essence of the created SIS without details. Details of SIS are being formed with the help of QA-analysis of $Z^*(t_0)$ which evolves the informational content of the designing and includes subordinated project tasks $(Z1(t_1), \ldots, ZI,k(t_n), \ldots, ZJ,r(t_m))$ in the decision of the main task.

The detailed elaboration of SIS forms the system of tasks, which includes not only the project tasks connected with the specificity of SIS but also service tasks, each of which is aimed at the creation of the corresponding conceptual diagram or document. The solutions of project and service tasks are chosen from libraries of normative conceptual models $\{M^k\}$ and service QAtechniques $\{QA(M^k_i)\}$.

During conceptual decision of any task (included in a tasks tree of the SIS project) additional tasks can be discovered and included in the system of tasks as it shown in Figure 4. The tasks tree is a dynamic system which is evolved iteratively by the group of designers. The step-wise refinement is used by any designer who fulfills QA-analysis and QA-modeling of the each solved task. General conceptual decision integrates all conceptual decision of all tasks included in a tasks tree of the project.

Figure 4. Task tree of development process

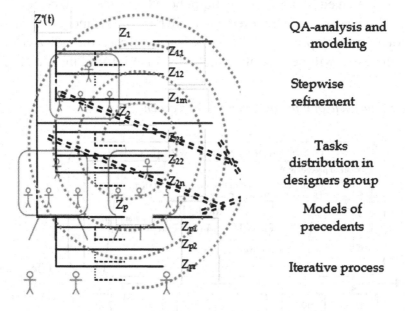

<table>
<tr><td>QA-analysis and modeling</td></tr>
<tr><td>Stepwise refinement</td></tr>
<tr><td>Tasks distribution in designers group</td></tr>
<tr><td>Models of precedents</td></tr>
<tr><td>Iterative process</td></tr>
</table>

The conceptual solution is estimated as the completed decision if its state is sufficient for the successful work at the subsequent development stages of SIS. The degree of the sufficiency is obviously and implicitly checked. Useful changes are being added for achieving an adequate conceptual representation of SIS.

Thus, the conceptual solution of the main project task is defined as a system of textual units and conceptual diagrams with their accompanied descriptions at the concept language the content of which are sufficient for successful coding of the task solution. Which conceptual diagrams are included to the solution depends on the technology used for developing the SIS.

2.2. Life Cycle of Precedent Model

The basic way is the creation of the precedent in parallel with its first performance. Any task (and the task of precedent creation) can be presented by a number of its state in its life cycle. Moreover, with any useful state of the task solution, the designer includes additional items in components of the corresponding precedent model as it is shown in Figure 5.

In the development of the definite SIS, the life cycle of any created precedent is being embedded into the life cycle of the created SIS. If it is being implemented in the RUP-medium, both life cycles will correlate with standard ISO/MEK-12207. Moreover, it will be so in any modern technology supported the development of SISs. Thus, in general case, the indicated models of the precedent will be evolving iteratively. In WIQA all indicated models

Figure 5. Life cycle of integrated model of precedent

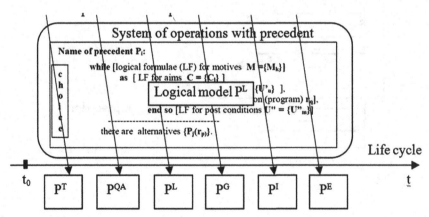

are being registered in the QA-database (or, by other words, with using the means of QA-reasoning). The life cycle $P_i(t)$ of any new precedent P_i begins from the initial statement $T(Z(P_i,t_0))$ of the corresponding task $Z(P_i,t_0)$. This statement fulfills the role of model $P^T_i(t_0)$ at the moment of time t_0.

During designing statement $T(Z(P_i,t))$ usually changes from a current state $T(Z(P_i,t_j))$ to a state $T(Z(P_i,t_{j+1}))$ which describes precedent $P_i(t)$ more adequately. The basic reason of changing is a question-answer analysis (in the form of QA-reasoning) fulfilled by the designer who is responsible for solving the task $Z(P_i,t_0)$. For the simplification of such analysis, the designer can use the means of the task analysis engineering included to the libraries of WIQA. Methods of cognitive task analysis are the kernel of these means.

The representation of QA-analysis results has a value for the future reuse of precedent $P_i(t)$. Therefore these results are combined in the model P^{QA}_i of precedent $P_i(t)$ as the QA-model of the task $Z(P_i,t_0)$.

A very important source of questions for evolving the statement $T(Z(P_i,t))$ and its understanding is the logical framework. Filling this framework by the content from the current informational description of the precedent $P_i(t)$ leads to its model P^L_i.

The model P^G_i reflects the content of the precedent $P_i(t)$ by graphical means, and it supports as creating the richer state of the precedent $P_i(t)$ and its reuse.

Figure 6. The model of the precedent

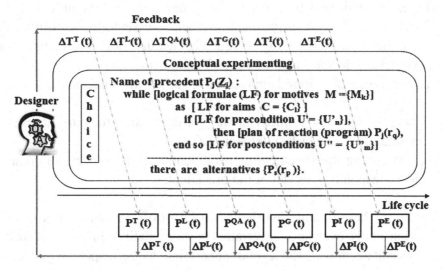

2.3. Iterative Creating the Example of Precedent Model

One important specificity of the used multitasking environment is the use of models of precedents that are generated in designing and accumulated in the Experience Base. The designer creates any of such unit with applying the normative scheme (framework, FP) that is shown in Figure 6.

The scheme reflects the structure of the created model MP(Z) and its step by step development regarding the life cycle. Let us remind, the structure includes following subordinated models: textual model P^T of the solved task; its model P^{QA} in the form of registered QA-reasoning; logical formulae P^L of modeled regularity; graphical (diagram) representation P^G of precedent; pseudocode model P^I in QA-program form; and executable code P^E.

Note, in step by step development of MP(Z), the reason for any step is caused by increments of textual units that are created in forming the statement of the corresponding project task.

Let us clarify this feature of the model MP(Z) in detail. As told above, the task Z and its model MP(Z) begins their life with zero-states when even the initial statement of the task is absent.

As it was in section 3.3.1, on our profound believ, the initial statement must be formulated with the short text that most abstractly (but in the sufficient measure) expresses the essence of the task.

After creating the initial statement of the task, the designer turns to an analysis of its text and implementing the other normative actions of the used technology. During these actions, step by step, the statement S(Z, t) will be enriched while its uncertainty will decrease.

The enrichment will be caused with generating increments $\Delta S(Z_j, t_1)$, $\Delta S(Z_j, t_2)$, ..., $\Delta S(Z_j, t_K 1)$ prioritization of which essentially determines the characteristics of the task being solved. This feature indicates the necessity of managing the development of the task statement.

For managing, the offered approach uses following solutions:

- Using the stepwise refinement way for decreasing the current level of uncertainty of the task statement $S(Z_j, t)$;
- Coordinating the statement development with the process of creating the corresponding model of the precedent.

The first of these solutions is oriented on the use of question-answering in its application for discovering of uncertainty portions, their coding by appropriate questions and decreasing the level of uncertainty by corresponding answers.

The feature of the second solution is the use of iterative creating the precedent model in the real-time work of the designer with the new task. The designer creates any component of this model on the base of the task statement in its current state $S(Zj, t)$. It may happen that steps of such creation will be sources of information for enriching the state $S(Zj, t)$ or its corrections. This new informational unit can have not only the textual form. They can also be diagrams, pictures, tables, formula and algorithmic units.

So, in its turn, any changing the state $S(Zj, t)$ can be a reason for corrections any of the components P^L, P^{QA}, P^G, P^I, P^E. In other words any increment $\Delta S^x(Z_j, t)$ can lead to the increment $\Delta P^Y(Z_j, t)$ where $Y \in (T, L, QA, G, I, E)$. In its turn, any increment $\Delta P^Y(Z_j, t)$ can be the source of a textual increment $\Delta T^Y(Z_j, t_1)$, that can be a reason for corrections $\Delta S^x(Z_j, t)$ and so on. Thus, components P^T, P^L, P^{QA}, P^G, P^I, P^E are results of the iterative development in coordination with the feedback that is shown in Figure 3.

2.4. Precedent-Oriented Base of Experience

For the use of QA-approach, the main aim of creating the models of precedents is their reuse in situations of the <Task> type during conceptual designing. Therefore, such artifacts are better to unite in the system that has been called "Experience Base." In the version of the toolkit WIQA provided designing the family of SISs by the design company, this system is intended for assembling the useful assets of a design company that creates the family of SISs. Any asset is presented in the Experience Base as the model of the precedent that presents the inclusion of the corresponding asset in designing. The definite model can be realized by the framework of the precedent model or as the appropriate form of its projection.

In the current state, the Experience Base is divided into section each of which includes assets of the definite type some of which are shown in Figure 7. The greater part of assets is stored in the corresponding section in forms of their models. For example, the section of "Human resources" saves personified models of designers (PMD). Section "Projects" is intended for registered the information about developed projects of SISs.

There are two versions of the access to models of experience the first of which is provided by the catalog of the experience base. The second version uses the search by keys that are included in the set of the controlled vocabulary.

Only one part of assets is placed in Precedent Base. The greater part of assets is stored in corresponding libraries where they are presented in forms

Figure 7. Structure of the Base of Experience

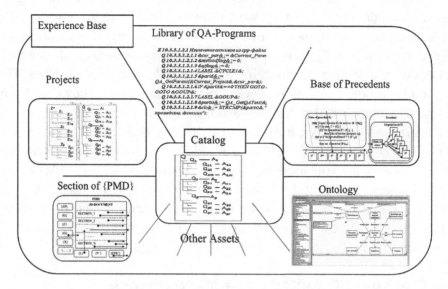

of precedent projections. As told above, components stored in QA-memory can be bound with the attached files that are placed in corresponding libraries too. One of such libraries includes programs written in C# that can be used in pseudocode programming.

Potential of L^{WIQA} is sufficient for QA-modeling and QA-programming the assets of following kinds: previous projects, valuable project solutions, prototypes, documents, interface samples, schemes of reports, standards, frameworks, guides, patterns, samples of different types, schemes of modeling, structure of the software, packages of the source code, tools, platforms, infrastructure and other valuable units.

Models of assets are registered in the catalog of Experience Base and allocated in the specialized area of QA-memory.The use of a large set of different assets (with orientation on precedents) leads to questioning about means of their systematization. In the described case, this function is fulfilled by the project ontology, concepts of which are also stored in QAmemory.

3. EXPERIMENTS IN PRECEDENT-ORIENTED APPROACH

3.1. Space of Conceptual Experimenting

In the described case, conceptual experimenting is defined as a version of conceptual thinking a part of which is automated and transformed to a specialized doing that also includes in the intertwining of designer's actions bound by appropriate models and flows of information. Features of conceptual experimenting are defined by the use of a set of models that are mapped in the semantic memory.

The central place in this set occupies models of concepts combined in the main section of project ontology. Each of other sections presents a subset of axioms that correspond to the definite application of the ontology. One of such application is a systematization of the Experience Base that supports the occupational activity of designers. By other words, the ontology includes the part of the Experience Base, and this part provides a regulation of accessible experience units. The place of the ontology and Experience Base in the operational space of designing is shown in the scheme presented in Figure 8.

The scheme indicates that the operational space includes a conceptual space (C-space) as an activity area where designers fulfill the automated part of own conceptual thinking when they conduct conceptual experiments. It should be noted, the C-space is a kind of the actuality, that inherits definite regularity from the operational space, and it has own regularities expressed the behavioral nature of the human activity.

Figure 8. Operational space

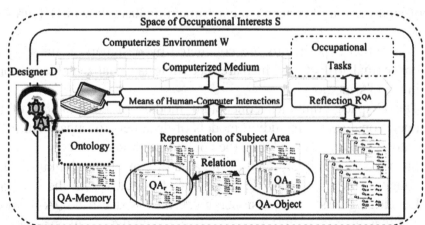

The C-space is a system of declarative and procedural artifacts that are results of reflecting the actuality of the operational space of designing on the semantic memory of the toolkit WIQA the memory of which is intended for question-answer specifications of chosen components of the operational space.To underline this intention, the semantic memory has been called "QAmemory."

In solutions of project tasks $\{Z_j\}$, any result of the reflection (or shortly R^{QA}) is accessible for any designer as an interactive object (QA-object). Conceptually thinking, designers work in the C-space. In such actions, they interact with necessary concepts, units of the Experience Base and other components (QA-objects) of the C-space. In conceptual experimenting, these actions are instrumentally supported by a computerized environment that is realized as a subsystem of the toolkit WIQA.

Thus, the C-space is the system of conceptual artifacts that are created and used by designers in processes of conceptual thinking when they conceptually solve the project tasks. In this kind of the activity, the C-space models essences and processes of designing, and such modeling is oriented on their reflections in the consciousness of designers. It is provided by the reflection of the operational space on the specialized semantic memory. It can be said, that the C-space is additional for the space of consciousness. Doing in this additional area is automated actions of conceptual thinking. Processes of such doing are supported by instrumental means of the computerized environment that additionally facilitates the intertwining of doing and thinking in the conceptual activity of designers.

3.2. Features of Conceptual Experimenting

The offered version of conceptual experimenting has following features:

1. Conceptual experiments are conducted by designers in the C-space conceptual artifacts of which are accessible as visualized objects stored in the QA-memory.
2. The C-space combines conceptual models of components of the operational space, including models of designers, occupational tasks, ontology and units modeling the applied experience.
3. Such C-space is interpreted as the area of conceptual thinking that is aimed at the conceptual development of systems with the software. Developing the systems, designers create the C-space in the QA-memory, and they interact with this space for achieving the useful purposes.

4. In the C-space, its processes are managed by interactions with the experience the typical units of which are models of precedents that are defined below.

5. Models of precedents obviously or implicitly reflect the regularities of the C-space or, by other words, "laws" of this space. These regularities reflect regularities of the operational space (regularities of the subject area of SISs, norms of the used technology, requirements and restrictions managed by developing of SISs).

A set of useful purposes that can be achieved by conceptual experimenting includes:

1. Discovering the regularities of the C-space that exists in QA-memory;
2. Evolving the C-space by an inclusion of the additional regularities into a system of the space regularities;
3. Reusing the definite regularity or their composition in designing;
4. Adjusting the definite regularity or their composition in designing;
5. Understanding the definite regularity or their composition in designing;
6. Learning the definite regularity or their composition in designing.

It is necessary to remind that processes in the C-space activate processes in the consciousness of designers who participate in these processes. All these processes are being implemented on the base of interactions with the accessible experience.

Thus, conceptual experiments are automated thought experiments that are conducted in the Cspace and implicitly supported by processes in the consciousness of designers who participate in experimenting.

3.3. Instrumental Support of Conceptual Experimenting

Any conceptual experiment has a behavioral nature. Any precedent model helps in simulating the definite unit of the designer behavior. In the described case, any such model is understood as an "experimental setup" with instructions for this use that confirms the "existence" of the definite regularity or a group of cause-and-effect regularities in the operational space of designing (or in the C-space).

As it is known, any experiment should be prepared, conducted and documented in the understandable form, so that is suitable for the reuse.

Figure 9. Environment of conceptual experimenting

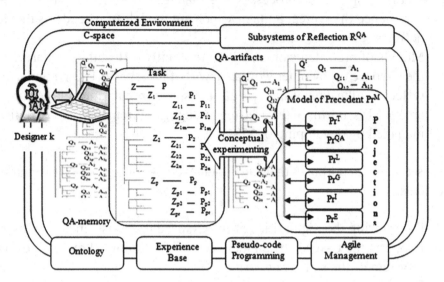

In conceptual experimenting, such work is fulfilled in the instrumental environment presented in Figure 9.

To conduct the definite experiment, its idea, for example, in the form of an initial statement of task, should be formulated. The question-answer analysis of this statement helps to discover and reflect necessary components that will be involved in experimenting. The designer fulfills this work with the help of "Subsystem of Reflection" that is a kernel of the toolkit WIQA.

In parallel, the designer creates the experimental setup in the form of a conceptually algorithmic description of behavior that leads to the conceptual solution of the investigated task. In this stage of experimenting, the designer uses functionalities of subsystems "Ontology," "Experience Base" and "Pseudocode programming," artifacts of which are located in the QAmemory. In conducting the experiment, the central place occupies the use of subsystem "Pseudocode programming" that supports all kind of works been typical for programming. Additionally, there are features that includ the programmed access to the semantic of objects and process (till an execution of any chosen operator), possibility for step by step interpreting the code of QA-programs, including the work with (pseudocode) programmed scheme in the process of experimenting and the use controlled human-computer interruptions in behavioral activity (Sosnin, 2014).

The designer applies the normative scheme of precedent model and means of the subsystem "Experience Base" for registering the results of experimenting.

All actions of experimenting are fulfilled under the control of the subsystem "Agile Management" where the designer can adjust the work on Kanban or Scram or Scramban management.

3.4. Conceptual Experimenting With Behavioral Actions

The principal feature of the proposed approach is an experimental investigation conducted by the designer with the programmed behavior, which has led to the conceptual solution of the appointed task. Any solution of such a type should demonstrate that its reuse meets the necessary requirements when any designer of the team will act in accordance with QA-program of the investigated behavior.

As described above, to achieve the goals, the designer should work in a way similar to a scientist who prepares and conducts experiments with the behavior units of the M- or P-types. In the discussed case, the designer will experiment in the environment of the toolkit WIQA. In this environment, to prove that the aim of an experiment has been achieved, the designer has the possibility of experimenting with any QA-operator of an investigated QA-program and/or with any group of such QA-operators or with the QA-program as a whole. Describing the experiment for reuse, the designer should register it in an understandable form for the other members of the team.

To begin a specific experiment, the initial text of the QA-program should be built. In the general case, such a project would include the following steps:

1. Formulation of the initial statement of the task.
2. Cognitive analysis of the initial statement with the use of QA-reasoning and registering it in QA-memory.
3. The logical description of the "cause-effect relation" reflected in the task.
4. Diagrammatic presentation of the analysis results (if it is necessary or useful).
5. Creation of the initial version of the QA-program.

The indicated steps are fulfilled by the designer with the use of the accessible experience, including the personal experience and useful units from the Experience Base of WIQA.

Only afterward can the designer conduct the experiment, interacting with the QA-program in the context of the accessible experience. The specificity of interactions can be clarified on examples of QA-operators of any QA-program or its fragment, for example, the following fragment of QA-program coding the well-known method of SWOT-analysis (Strengths, Weaknesses, Opportunities, and Threats):

Q 2.5 PROCEDURE &SWOT main&

Q 2.5.1 &t_str&:= QA_GetQAText(&history_branch_qaid&)

Q 2.5.2 SETHISTORYENTRIES(&t_str&)

Q 2.5.3 CALL &ShowHistory&

Q 2.5.4 IF &LastHistoryFormResult& == -1 THEN RETURN

Q 2.5.5 IF &LastHistoryFormResult& == 0 THEN &current_action_qaid&:=

QA_CreateNode(&current_project&, &history_branch_qaid&, 3, "") ELSE

&current_action_qaid&:= &LastHistoryFormResult&

Q 2.5.6 &t_str&:= QA_GetQAText(&current_action_qaid&)

Figure 10. Experimenting of designer with QA-program

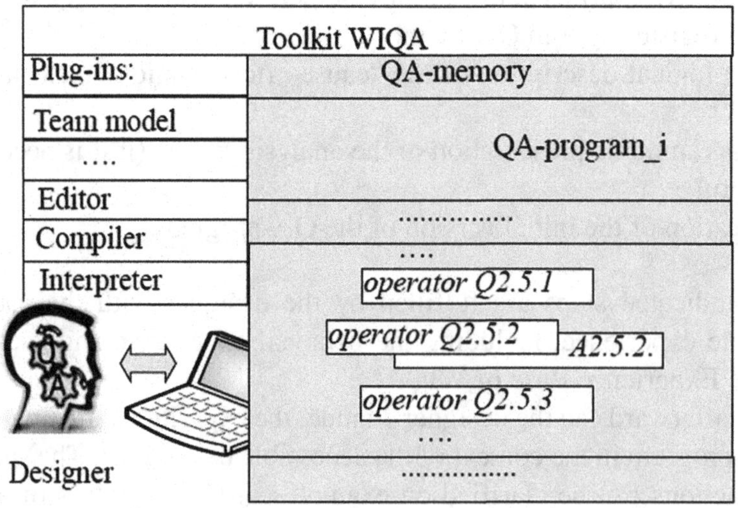

Q 2.5.7 SWOT_DESERIALIZE(&t_str&) Q 2.5.8 &t_int&:= SWOT_SHOWMAINFORM()

....

Q 2.5.14 FINISH

This source code demonstrates a typically used syntax, but features of the code are opened in interactions of the human with it. Conditions and methods of experimenting are shown in Figure 10, where one of the operators (with address name Q2.5.2) is shown in the context of previous and subsequent operators. Any QA-program is executed by the human step-by-step, in which each step is aimed at the corresponding QA-operator. In this study, the human uses the plug-in "Interpreter" embedded into the toolkit.

Interpreting the current operator (for example, Q2.5.2), the human can fulfill any actions until its activation (for example, to test existing circumstances) and after its execution (for example, to estimate the results of the investigation), using any means in the toolkit WIQA. When the human decides to start the work with the QA-operator, this work can include different interactive actions with it as with corresponding QA-units or with their elements. The human can analyze values of their attributes and make useful decisions.

Moreover, the human can appoint the necessary attributes for any QA-operator and any unit of QA-data at any time. By appointments, the human can include changes in the source code of the QA-program being executed (investigated). Such work can be fulfilled in QA-memory with the help of the plug-ins "Editor."

The current QA-program or its fragments can be executed or used step-by-step by the human or automatically as a whole with the help of the plug-in "Compiler." Therefore, all of the work described above with the QA-operator can be used for any of the groups and any QA-program as a whole. For this reason, the execution of QA-operator by the human is similarly experimentation. Thus, the human has a flexible possibility to perform experimental research on any task that is solved conceptually. This feature is the principal feature that distinguishes pseudocode QA-programs from programs written in pseudocode languages of different types, including the class of Domain-Specific Languages.

The specificity of the described type of human activity is the work controlled by the QAprogram and executed by the human interacting with the accessible experience. To underline this specificity, the specialized role of "intellectual processor" was constructively defined and is effectively supported in the use of WIQA (Sosnin, 2013). This role is added to the other types of roles that applied in the conceptual design.

3.5. Intellectual Processor

Indicated interactions with the accessible experience are a kind of the specialized designer activity which can be implemented as the role "Intellectual processor" (or, shortly, I-processor) that plays by any designer in parallel with other appointed roles.

Any modern technology used for designing the SIS includes modeling the work of designers with the help of roles. For example, the current version of Rational Unified Process (RUP) supports activities of designers playing approximately 40 roles. RUP is a "heavy" technology therefore for small teams the quantity and specifications of used roles are decreased and simplified.

In existing technologies, the role provided interactions with experience is being fulfilled by designers without its explicit specifying and special instrumental support. In the QA-approach, the content of the role is defined for its use by designers in WIQA-medium, but the role can be materialized by the other ways.

The essence of I-processor is being defined by features enumerated below.

1. So first of all I-processor is a role being played by any designer solving the appointed tasks in conceptual designing the SIS. In the life cycle of any SIS, its conceptual stage is an area of intensive modeling the tasks being solved. The invention of UML and its obligatory use in conceptual designing is a confirmation of it. Means used by I-processors open new useful possibilities in conceptual modeling of SIS but they support the work with UML diagrams also.

2. In any case, the role is a special version of a designer behavior which satisfies to the definite set of rules. Role specifications depend on appointed tasks and tools supporting their preliminary solving and reuses of solutions.

3. I-processors are intended for experimenting with tasks the solving of which are problematical without explicit real-time access to the personal experience and/or collective experience and/or models of useful experience.

4. In its activity, any I-processor interprets tasks as precedents and interacts with experience units as with models of precedents.

5.   The real-time work of any I-processor is being accompanied by QA-reasoning and its models being registered in QA-memory of the toolkit WIQA.

6.   The choice of QA-reasoning as the basic form for I-processor is determined by the intention to model the dialog nature of consciousness. For that, the implicit QA-reasoning accompanying the cognitive processes inside I-processor should "be translated" and transferred to QA-memory as the model QA-reasoning.

7.   And contrary any used model of QA-reasoning activates the corresponding internal QAreasoning in the brain structures of the designer playing the role of I-processor.

8.   QA-reasoning is used by I-processor for creating QA-models of tasks in different forms including their versions as QA-programs.

9.   The use of QA-reasoning in interactions of I-processor with QA-programs is being implemented in the pseudocode language LWIQA. Knowing and effective using of this language by I-processor is a very important its feature.

10.   In general case, the activity of I-processor is similar to the experimental activity of the designer who creates QA-model of the task for experimenting with the prototype of its solution. In such experimenting with tasks I-processor can use as means of QA-modeling so and means of QA-programming.

11.   In our case, the competence providing the effective use of the toolkit WIQA can be included to the number of I-processor features also.

As told above the use of QA-programs by I-processor for experimenting with tasks is the very essential its feature. That was a cause to create the library of the specialized QA-programs providing some versions of such experimenting. This library includes a number of QAtechniques for cognitive tasks analysis, decision-making and typical procedures of estimations. For example, the library section of QA-techniques for cognitive task analysis includes widely known methods and the other methods.

4. SOME REMARKS TO THE CHAPTER 6

1.   The life of any person exists and evolves via interactions with the naturally artificial world. The human side of interactions consists of behavioral units the most of which are repeatable. Such repeatable units

of the human behavior are often referred to as precedents. Human life is based on precedents.

2. The precedent form of human activity was (created) by Nature in an evolution of a phenomenon called "conditioned reflex." This step of the natural evolution as any prior steps can be interpreted as evolutionary experiments conducted by Nature.

3. There are three ways for the appearance of the precedent and its model providing the reuse. The first way is connected with the intellectual processing of the definite behavior which happened in the past but was estimated by the human as a potential precedent for its reuse in the future. The second way is the creation of the precedent in parallel with its first performance, and the third way is an extraction of the precedent model from another's sources of natural experience and its models.

4. It is possible to consider, that any precedent appears as a result of the corresponding experiment conducted by persons who solved the definite task and prepared its solution for the reuse. Such way is similar to scientifically experimental task, in which the central place occupies by the corresponding experiment that conducting must be prepared for the reuse.

5. Simulating the scientists' activity in experimenting with activity units of designers is a promising way of improving the ways-of-working used for conceptual designing the systems.

6. The conceptual project of any system is, first of all, a system of tasks solved conceptually. The conceptual solution of a task is a state of its solution registered in a natural-professional language in its algorithmic use and containing diagrammatic models and tabular constructs, if necessary.

7. Any conceptual solution of the task is a model of its solution, the degree of adequacy of which is able to confirm by its experimental verification for compliance with requirements, or the material implementation of the solution for this model.

8. If the conceptual solution of the task is intellectually processed with an orientation on the future reuse, then this version of the conceptual solution can play the role of a precedent model for this task.

9. We sure, for intellectual processing the solution of the project task, the designer should build corresponding precedent model with the use of framework regulated the structure and content of the model in the process based on thought experimenting.

10. This belief has led us to the development of the precedent-oriented approach that is additional to QA-approach and focuses on creating the units of experience while QAapproach is responsible for interactions with such units.

11. Both of these approaches are applied at the conceptual stage of designing when designers conceptually solve the project tasks and build models of corresponding precedents.

12. In our research and developments we invent and verified in numerous applications the framework for models of precedents. This framework is coordinated with reflecting the task on the theory of the project, and this reflection for the certain task is its precedent model that integrate a set of theoretical constructs and models.

13. At the level of components the framework consist of following normative sub-models – textual, logical, question-answer, graphical, conceptually algorithmic and program submodels, which except the program sub-model have their semantic representation.

14. In creating a new precedent model with the use The WIQA toolkit, it is need to take into account and apply our way of solving the tasks of the project. This way is based on QAanalysis and modeling, stepwise refinement, distribution of tasks in groups of designers, the use of models of precedent and iterative processes.

15. Almost all mechanisms of this way, the designer uses in the work with the certain task, applying the stepwise refinement to the statement of the task in creating its model of the precedent.

16. In this work, the task fulfills a role of mediator between the process of designing and the theory of the project construct. We understand any task of the project as the certain application of the theory for verifying the new construct and models of which the designer must use conceptual experimenting (sub-section).

17. Implementing this role, the designer is active in the conceptual space embodied in the semantic memory of the WIQA toolkit.

18. Conducting the conceptual experiments is one of the important responsibilities of the role "Intellectual processor" fulfilled by the designer in the WIQA environment. Interactions of the designer with accessible experience define basic features of this role.

REFERENCES

Jeffery, D. R., & Scott, L. (2002). Has Twenty-five Years of Empirical Software Engineering Made a Difference. *Proc. 2nd Asia-Pacific Software Engineering Conference*, 539-549. doi:10.1109/APSEC.2002.1183076

Sjoberg, D. I. K., Dyba, T., & Jorgensen, M. (2007). The Future of Empirical Methods in Software Engineering Research. *Proc. of Workshop Future of Software Engineering*, 358-378. doi:10.1109/FOSE.2007.30

Sosnin, P. (2012). Question-Answer Approach to Human-Computer Interaction in Collaborative Designing. In Cognitively Informed Intelligent Interfaces: Systems Design and Development. IGI Global. doi:10.4018/978-1-4666-1628-8.ch010

Sosnin, P. (2013). Role Intellectual Processor in Conceptual Designing Of Software Intensive Systems. *Proc. of the 11-th International Conference on Computational Science and Applications, Part III*. Springer. doi:10.1007/978-3-642-39646-5_1

Sosnin, P. (2016a). Precedent-Oriented Approach to Conceptually Experimental Activity in Designing the Software Intensive Systems. *International Journal of Ambient Computing and Intelligence*, 7(1), 69–93. doi:10.4018/IJACI.2016010104

Sosnin, P. (2016b). *Conceptual Experiments in Automated Designing*. In R. Zuanon (Ed.), *Projective Processes and Neuroscience in Art and Design* (pp. 155–181). IG-Global.

Sosnin, P. (2008). Conceptual Solution of the Tasks in Designing the Software Intensive Systems. *Proc. of the 14th IEEE Mediterranean Electrotechnical Conference (MELECON 2008)*, 293 – 298. doi:10.1109/MELCON.2008.4618450

Southekal, H., & Levin, G. (2011). Formulation and Empirical Validation of a GQM Based Measurement Framework. *Proc. 11th International Symposium on Empirical Software Engineering and Measurement*, 404-413. doi:10.1109/ESEM.2011.59

Wiel, W. M., Hasberg, M. P., Weima, I., & Huiskamp, W. (2010). Concept Maturity Levels Bringing structure to the CD&E process. *Proc. of Interservice industry training, simulation and education conference*, 2547-2555.

ADDITIONAL READING

Alberts, D. S., & Hayes, R. E. (2005). *Campaigns of Experimentation, Washington, DC: CCRP Alberts, D.S.,& Hayes, R.E., (2006).Understanding Command and Control.* Washington, DC: CCRP.

Bass, L., Ivers, J., Klein, M., & Merson, P. (2005). *Reasoning Frameworks, Software Engineering Institute, Tech. Rep. Carnegie Mellon University* (pp. 2005–TR-007). Pittsburgh, PA: CMU/SEI.

Booch, G., & Brown, A. W. (2003). Collaborative development environments. In M. Zelkowitz (Ed.), *Advances in computers, 59*. San Diego, CA: Academic Press. doi:10.1016/S0065-2458(03)59001-5

Burger, J. et al.. (2001). *Issues, Tasks and Program Structures to Roadmap Research in Question & Answering (Q&A).* Tech. Rep. NIST.

Cares, C., Franch, X., & Mayol, E. (2006). Perspectives about paradigms in software engineering, in *Proc. 2nd International workshop on Philisophiocal Foundations on Information Systems Engineering*, pp. 737-744.

Crystal, A., & Ellington, B. (2004). Task analysis and human-computer interaction: approaches, techniques, and levels of analysis. In *proceedings of the Tenth Americas Conference on Information Systems*, New York, New York, pp 1-9.

Henninger, S. (2003). Tool Support for Experience-based Software Development Methodologies. *Advances in Computers, 59*, 29–82. doi:10.1016/S0065-2458(03)59002-7

MCM-0056-2010, (2010). NATO Concept Development and Experimentation (CD&E) Process. Brussels: NATO HQ.

Nguyen, P., & Chun, R. (2011) Model Driven Development with Interactive Use Cases and UML Models. Available at pnguyen.tigris.org/SER4505.pdf

Pew, R. W. (2007). Some history of human performance models. In W. Gray (Ed.), *Integrated models of cognitive systems* (pp. 29–47). New York: Cambridge University Press. doi:10.1093/acprof:oso/9780195189193.003.0003

Precedent, (2011), from http://dictionary. reference.com/ *browse/precedent.*

Sosnin, P. (2009). Means of question-answer interaction for collaborative development activity", Hindawi Publishing Corporation. *Advances in Human-Computer Interaction*, *2009*, 1–18. doi:10.1155/2009/619405

Sosnin, P. (2010). Question-Answer Programming in Collaborative Development Environment. In *Proc. of CIS-RAM 2010*, Singapore, pp. 273-278.

Sosnin, P. (2011). *Question-Answer Shell for personal Expert Systems/ Chapter in the book Expert Systems for Human* (pp. 51–74). Materials and Automation, InTech.

Chapter 7
Ontological Support of Human–Computer Interactions

ABSTRACT

In the real-time design, conceptual solving any new task is impossible without analytical reasoning of designers who interact with natural experience and its models among which important place occupies models of precedents. Moreover, the work with new tasks is a source of such useful models. The quality of applied reasoning essentially depends on the constructive use of appropriate language and its effective models. In the version of conceptual activity described in this book, the use of language means is realized as an ontological support of design thinking that is aimed at solving a new task and creating a model of corresponding precedent. The ontological support provides controlled using the lexis, extracting the questions for managing the analysis, revealing the cause-and effects regularities and achieving the sufficient understanding. Designers fulfill all these actions in interactions with the project ontology that can be developed by manual or programmed way in work with the task.

1. FEATURES OF PROJECT ONTOLOGY

The success of conceptual designing the systems is based on a personal and mutual understanding of designers and other stakeholders when they operatively use accessible experience in collaborative work. In order to understand something, for example, the designer needs to fulfill the certain work

DOI: 10.4018/978-1-5225-2987-3.ch007

focusing own attention on the object of understanding in appropriate conditions. For this book, the central place occupies the objects of understanding that concern project tasks and processes of their conceptual solutions.

We have developed a complex of means that provide a constructive achievement of understanding in work with tasks at the conceptual level. These means have embedded in the reifying of the precedent-oriented approach and QA-approach. The intertwining use of these approaches includes an ontological support of works aimed at the achievement of sufficient understanding in interactions with tasks. It should be noted, additionally to the support of understanding, the ontology usually helps to achieve the following positive effects: using the controlled vocabulary; systematizing the methods and means used in an occupational activity; specifying the conceptualization; checking the semantics of the built text and applied reasoning; operating with machine-readable and machine-understandable content.

In the fourth chapter, we have described the component "Ontology" that provides creation and use the project ontology at the level of manual operations with cells of the QA-memory. This level is not so suitable for the ontological maintenance in work with understanding. Below, we present an automation of this work. The automation is realized in two following versions:

1. Plug-ins "Ontology" in the complex WIQA.Net;
2. Program complex in the language L^{WIQA} as an extension of the OwnWIQA.

In both of component versions, their reflections on the semantic memory use the specialized structure of the memory cell that is disclosed in Figure 1.

The content embedded to the concept framework corresponds to the following rules of grammar GR^{QA}:

$$concept = QA \ (*in \ QA- \ memory*)$$
$$concept = \left(concept \ name, \ definition, \ \{list\}\right);$$
$$definition = text; \ list = \left\{ \left(relation, \ \{name\}\right)\right\}; \qquad (1)$$
$$relation = is-a \mid part-of \mid association \mid synonymity \mid$$
$$picture \mid key \mid materialization \mid reference.$$

Let us clarify components that are attached to the QA-object presenting the concept. Ontological relations specify a net of ontology units that are bound with the chosen concept. It is necessary to note that the designer has

Figure 1. Typical structure of the concept in the semantic memory

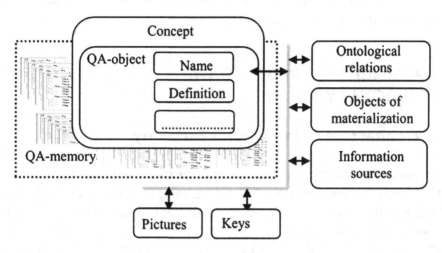

the opportunity for appointing relations such as "isa," "part-of," "attributive," "causative," "associative" (temporal, spatial, synonymous, opposite, following) and relations of pragmatic types. The designer has the opportunity for extending the list of relations.

For the use of the controlled dictionary in implemented projects, the designer should indicate the type of materialization for any used concept.

References to materializations fix relations of concepts with the space of occupational interest of the designer. It allows preventing the use of words from uncontrolled vocabulary in solutions of project tasks. Furthermore, it helps to check the compatibility of used concepts in reasoning and texts.

Concepts can be combined in groups as in frames of project ontologies so as sections in the kernel ontology the content of which is invariant to the specificity of any project fulfilled by designers. Combining is described by the following set of rules:

$$GN = (N, \text{"}C\text{"}, \{N\}); \ (*group \ of \ concepts *)$$
$$PO = \{GN\}; (*project \ ontology*) \tag{2}$$
$$ontology = (kernel \ ontology, \{PO\});$$

It is necessary to note that concepts of the project ontology are, usually, used in definite conditions and that demands to specify variants $\{\Delta N_s\}$ of the concept N into the ontology. Such presentation of the concept opens the opportunity for using the means of the pseudocode programming in the creation and use of ontology units.

2. SPECIFICITY OF REIFYING THE ONTOLOGY IN WIQA.NET

2.1. Architecture of the Project Ontology

Attempts to view the project ontology from the side of creating the specialized SIS^{ONT} leads to questions about its architecture, life cycle and used models which must be coordinated with the evolution of the project ontology. Below we answer these questions.

The architecture of any SIS^{ONT} has a problem-oriented type the materialization of which begins its life cycle from the ontology shell with architectural solutions inherited and kept by the SIS^{ONT} without changing. The main architectural view of the shell (and any SIS^{ONT}) is presented in Figure 2, where the working dictionary plays the role of the "soft" ontology.

For any dictionary entry of the ontology, there is a corresponding analog in the working dictionary. Such analog is used firstly as a representative set of samples registering the variants of the concept usages extracted from statements of project tasks and definitions of project solutions (or shortly from text units). Samples are being gathered naturally in actions of designers

Figure 2. Main architectural view of the project ontology

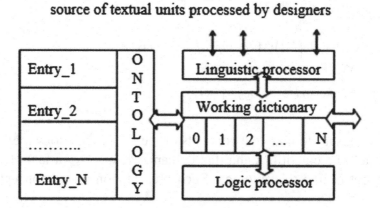

206

who are testing (implicitly or explicitly on different working places) the used concepts on their conformity to the ontology.

Filling the ontology by the content is connected with a specialized project task appointed to an administrator of the ontology. The work of the administrator is managed:

1. By events each of which is generated when the result of comparison of the used concept with the ontology isn't correct;
2. In accordance with a sequence of actions supporting the normative state of the project ontology (current levels of adequacy and systematization).

The necessary informational material for the administrator of the ontology is supplied by designers with the help of the predicative analyzer. Designers must test and confirm the authenticity of concepts which are used in statements of tasks and definitions of project solutions. For achieving such aim, they have to extract firstly the usage of concepts (from the text units) and then to compare them with the ontology. The differences of comparisons (new concepts or additional parts of existing concepts, additional questions which require answers) are used as the informational material for evolving the ontology. Let us notice that any extracted concept usage includes its expression as a simple predicate but not only this (the full expression will be presented below).

Used concepts are the main part of the project ontology which should be expanded by systematizations and axiomatic relations. Means of systematizations are embedded into the ontology component while axiomatic relations are being created with the help of the logic processor.

The logic processor is intended to build the axiomatic relations as formulas of the predicates logic. Such work is being implemented in the frame of the appropriate article (entry) of the working dictionary where the necessary simple predicates are being accumulated. Ontology axioms express materialized units of the SIS and first of all those which corresponds to UMLdiagrams. Any built axiom is registered in the definite entry (article) of the ontology.

The main architectural view presents the project ontology from the side of its components and informational content which defines the dynamics of the life cycle for the SIS^{ONT}. In a typical case, such life cycle is being implemented in the form of the real-time work of several tens of designers who have solved and are solving several thousand tasks. Models which are used in the ontology lifecycle will be presented below.

2.2. Linguistic Processor

The life cycle of the SIS^{ONT} is embedded into the life cycle of the designing SIS from which all (named above) text units are being entered to the linguistic processor.

For testing any text unit, it is transformed into a set of simple sentences, and in such transformation, the pseudo-physics model of the compound sentence or complex sentence of the other type is applied. In the pseudo-physics model of the sentence, all used words are interpreted as objects which take part in the "force interaction" which is visualized on the monitor screen. Formal expressions of pseudo-physics laws are similar to laws of the classic physics.

In accordance with acting forces (forces of "gravitation," "electricity," "elasticity" and "friction") and attributes appointed to the "word-objects," such objects are being grouped in definite places of the interaction area. In the stable state (Figure 3) each group will present the appropriate simple sentence. Let us notice that in the appointment of attributes two mechanisms are applied – the automatic morphological analysis and the automated tuning of object parameters.

After extraction of simple sentences, the designer begins their semantic analysis aimed at test the correctness of each simple sentence (SS_i). In such

Figure 3. Extraction of the simple sentences

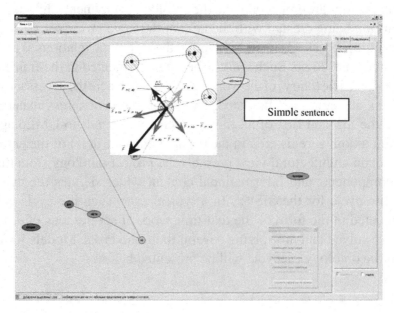

work, the designer uses the model of SS_i and its relations with surrounding which are presented in Figure 4.

The scheme of relations was used for defining and implementing the techniques for their semantic testing. First of all the expression of semantics for SS was chosen. The structure of the semantics value as a set of semantic components $(S_0 \cup (\cup \Delta S_n))$ is schematically presented in Figure 4 where the component S_0 indicates for the sentence SS its conformity to the reality.

Definition and testing of any other semantic component ΔSi help to precise the semantic value of the SS if that can be useful for the design of the SIS. Additionally, the work with any semantic component increases the belief in the correctness of the testable simple sentence (and embedded to it the simple predicate) and can lead to useful questions. In work with additional semantic components, the conditional access to appropriate precedents is used.

Elements of the typical set of semantic components are estimated, applied and tested in the definite sequence. Such work begins from the component S0 which is compared with elements of the ontology. The result of comparing can be positive or can lead to questions which should be registered. The positive result does not exclude the subsequent work with additional semantic components.

Figure 4. Model of the simple sentence

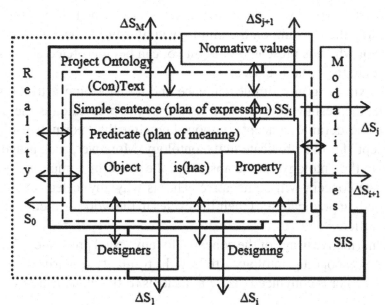

For designers, the semantics of subjectivity and understanding are estimated and tested. The fact of the non-understanding leads to questions or even to the interruption of the work with the testable sentence.

Actual or future material existence of the sentence semantics is a cause for testing the semantic relation of the SS with designing. Such type of relations is used in the ontology for its systematization.

The greater part of semantic relations of the modality type is aimed at defining and testing of the uncertainties of measurable and/or probable and/or fuzzy types.

The semantic relations with normative values suppose the potential inclusion of the SS or its parts into the useful informational sources, for example, into the ontology.

2.3. Working Dictionary

The role of the working dictionary is a very important in creating the project ontology. This component as the soft version of the ontology accumulates all necessary information and distributes informational units between dictionary articles. Carrying out functions of transportation of the information, the working dictionary registers references of text units with their sources.

After extracting the simple sentence with the help of the linguistic processor, the predicate model of this sentence is being included to the virtual article of the working dictionary (the article with the zero index). The zero article is a temporal memory in the working dictionary which keeps predicates till finishing their testing on the ontology conformity. The zero article, the interface of which is presented in Figure 5, can be interpreted as a queue of predicates in their mass service.

After extracting any simple sentence and transforming it to the simple predicate, the designer has to start the test of the predicate (as the definite usage of the definite concept) without knowing the "normative usage of the concept" for this predicate in the ontology. Moreover, such usage of the concept in the ontology can be absent, or the result of comparing with the appropriate concept will be negative. That is why any tested sentence and corresponding predicate start their life cycles in the working dictionary from the zero article.

The "normative usage of the concept" for any tested predicate is localized into the corresponding ontology article. If the result of comparing is negative, but the designer is convinced that "predicate is truth" then the new ontology

Figure 5. Virtual article of the working dictionary

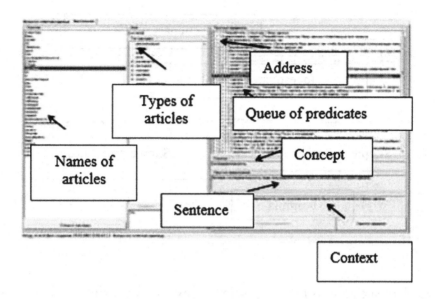

article is to be created, or the new variant of the concept usage is to be built into the existed ontology article. The first of such results requires to create the new article in the working dictionary also and to transport the tested predicate from the virtual article into this new article. The type of the new article in the working dictionary is chosen by designers in accordance with the type of the ontological unit of the designing SIS for the materialization of which the transported predicate will be used.

Processing the second result includes the transportation of the tested predicate but into the existed article (Figure 6) of the working dictionary. In general case, such predicate is transported into several articles of the working dictionary each of which materializes the tested predicate in the definite form.

If the test of the predicate on the conformity to the ontology is positive then this predicate should be transported in the article of the working dictionary, but only in the article of the definite concept for achieving its representativity. So (step-by-step) predicates (and their parent sentences) are being accumulated into corresponding articles of the working dictionary.

There is a set of types of materialized SIS units which are reflected in the project ontology. The set included concepts about "parts" of the reality embedded in the SIS and materialized in its software (in the form of variables, classes, functions, procedures, modules, components and program constructions of the other types) and axioms which combine concepts.

Figure 6. Typical article of the working dictionary

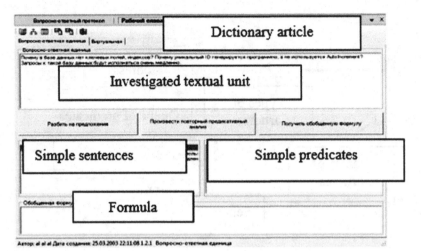

Each of such unit is found as its initial textual expression in statements of project tasks or definitions of project solutions. But when this unit is included in the ontology article it is usually rewritten, redefined and reformulated. All informational material for the execution of the similar work is accumulated in the corresponding article of the working dictionary. After creating the adequate textual expressions and formulas, they are rewritten from the working dictionary to the corresponding articles of the ontology.

2.5. Logic Processor

The logic processor is intended to build the formal description of the text unit from simple predicates accumulated in the definite article of the working dictionary. Such work is being fulfilled by the designer in the operational space presented in Figure 7 where designer assembles simple predicates in the formula watching them in the graphical window. Necessary predicates are being chosen by a designer from the processable article of the working dictionary.

To assemble the predicates the designer has possibilities to use the patterns of two bound predicates, setting the typical relations between predicates, editing the "picture" (using the drag and drop and lexical means), registering the final result as the formula of the first predicate logic.

Figure 7. Assembling the formula of text unit

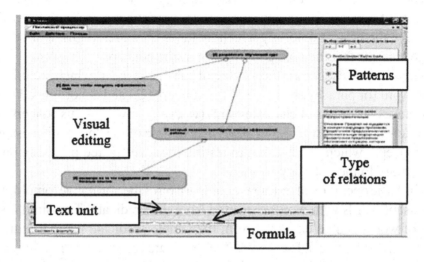

Patterns for two bound predicates has been extracted by the author from the grammars of Russian (46 patterns) and English (32 patterns). Such patterns are formalized as typical formulas of the predicates logic.

Mechanisms of assembling the formulas were evolved with experimental aims till the complex of instrumental means which provide (for statements of tasks) the creation of Prolog-like descriptions. The transformation of the formalized statement of task to the Prolog-like description is being implemented as an automated translating of the formula registered in the appropriate article of the working dictionary. Now the method of translating exists in the preliminary version which will be rationalized by the author.

2.6. Systematization of Ontology

The most important feature of any ontology and the project ontology also is its systematization. In suggested case, the project ontology is defined initially as the Software Intensive System the integrity of which is provided by the system of architectural views. Some of these views are reflected implicitly by screenshots used in this article. But such systematization is only one of possible.

Let us present other means of systematizing. First of all, it is the classification of concepts in accordance with the structures of the SIS and process of its designing. Such system properties of the ontology are formed implicitly through definitions of concepts and corresponding axioms.

The next classification level of the ontology is bound with classifying the variants of concept usages. In this case for any concept is being formed its article in the project ontology which includes the ordered group of concept usage variants and the textual definition of the concept.

The group of usage variants is a list of sub-lists each of which includes the main word (or phrase) as a name of the concept (C_i) and subordinated words (or phrases) as names of characteristics ($w_{i1}, w_{i2}, ..., w_{iN}$) of this concept. The definite sub-list $w_{i1}, w_{i2}, ..., w_{iN}, C_i$ is an example of the "normative usage of the concept" which can be used in testing the investigated predicate on the conformity to the ontology.

The basic operation of testing is a comparison of the normative (ontological) sub-list of words with words extracted from the predicate. Two similar sub-lists of words can be extracted from the simple predicate when it indicates the feature and three subsets when the predicate registers the relation.

After testing the chosen sub-list of words, which expresses the definite variant of the concept usage, the following results of the comparison are possible:

1. Positive result when the chosen sub-list ($w'_{i1}, w'_{i2}, ..., w'_{iN}, C_i$) is included into the normative sub-list;
2. The interrogative result when chosen sub-list crosses the normative sub-list or the tested sub-list is outside all norms (the role of questions was explained above).

The next line of the systematization binds concepts. For uniting the ontology concepts into the system, the following relations are used – basic relations (part and a whole, hereditary, type of materialization), associative relations (similarity, in sequence, time, "space") and causality relations.

To use the concept relation, the designer chooses the necessary concept by its names in the area "keys of entry," and then the designer can switch between groups (nodes of the relations system) up to the necessary relation. In any state of the navigation, the description of any visualized unit can be opened. Let us notice, that all forms of the ontology systematization are inherited by the working dictionary where it opens the possibility for useful switching between its articles.

3. SPECIFICITY OF REIFYING THE ONTOLOGY IN OWNWIQA

3.1. Grounds of Toolset for Automated Creating the Concepts

The ontology in the OwnWIQA system can be accessed via the specific pseudocode functions that request the ontological database in the controlled pseudocode interpretation mode. Here are some examples of such functions (they can be divided into two types – the ones that get data from the ontology and the ones that add data to the ontology):

1. *int Onto_CreateDictionary(string DictionaryName)*: creates a new ontological dictionary with a custom name;
2. *int Onto_CreateWord(int DictionaryName, int GroupID, string WordName)*: creates a new concept in a preset dictionary and a preset dictionary group;
3. *int OntoAddDefinition(int WordID, string Definition)*: adds a new definition in the form of a text string to the existing concept;
4. *int Onto_AddWordRelationship(int WordId1, int WordId2, int RelTypeId)*: adds a new relation of a preset type between two existing concepts;
5. *int Onto_GetDictId(string DictName)*: returns the identification number of the dictionary by its name;
6. *int Onto_GetGrouptId(int DictId, string DictName)*: returns the identification number of the group by its name and the dictionary identification number in which it is stored;
7. *int Onto_GetWordId(int DictId, int GroupId, string WordText)*: returns the identification number of the word by its text and the dictionary and the group identification number in which it is stored;
8. *string Onto_GetWordById(int WordID)*: returns the text of an existing concept by its identification number;
9. *string Onto_GetWordDefinitionText(int WordID)*: returns the text of the existing concept's definition by the identification number of the concept, etc.

We form a set of concepts by stages. We select word forms from the project document, and then the word forms are normalized with the help of a morphological analyzer (parser), this is followed by automatic filtration of the given wordlist, selection of items to include into a vocabulary list and forming collocations based on this list.

Here are the basic steps to forming a set of concepts (the algorithm of automated actions):

1. Select all the word forms from the project document ({WF}) saving their order and punctuation;
2. Normalize a (bring to its original form) set of word forms with the help of a morphological analyzer (parser) and form a list of normalized language units of the project document ($\{WF_n\}$);
3. Filter the list with the help of a stopword dictionary (stopwords are words that do not carry the semantic load), a dictionary of acronyms and unknown symbols (for example, for the Russian language such symbols are Latino ones); form a filtered list of words ($\{WF_f\}$);
4. Remove duplicate words from the resulting list – get the first part of the variant concept list ({VarC});
5. Select the words (this work is done by an expert or a user) and include them into a singleword concept list $\{C_1\}$ (the user may resolve the cases of morphological ambiguity and correct errors made by the morphological analyzer if necessary);
6. Select word collocation variants from the project document which are 2 or 3-words long phrases ({VarCC}) taking into account the punctuation (the phrase cannot be divided by a comma or any other mark);
7. Filter the resulting list of collocation variant with the help of morphological models (described below) to get a list of collocations ({CC});
8. Filter the collocations $\{CC_f\}$ (remove duplicates and those which the ontology already includes) to get the second part of the concept variant list ({VarC});
9. Select the collocations (this work is done by an expert or a user) and include them into a multi-word concept list $\{C_2\}$;
10. Form a set of concepts to be included in the ontology by creating concept groups based on the list $\{C_1\}$. The results obtained at this step provide good potential for detecting relations between the concepts.

This sequence of actions correspond the following implication chain:

$$\begin{cases} T \rightarrow WF \rightarrow WFn \rightarrow WFf \rightarrow VarC \rightarrow C1 \\ (T,C) \rightarrow VarCC \rightarrow CC \rightarrow CCf \rightarrow VarC \rightarrow C2 \end{cases} \quad (3)$$

The Figure 8 opens the structure of these cycles presented them at the level of basic components. As this structure shows, presented task is easily divided into several subtasks that have clear inputs and outputs and can be processed independently. In addition to that, there are two cycles of processing data within our task. Thus, some subtasks can be processed in parallel.

So, the best way to organize a given toolset is to use program agents interacted inside of common environment. The designed set of tools used following program agents:

1. **Agent A:** splitter. Splits text in word forms;
2. **Agent B:** normalizer. Brings words to the original form with the help of a morphological analyzer (for example, the word "*компьютеров*" to the word "*компьютер*");
3. **Agent C:** filter. Filters the list of words, removing stop-words, words with unknown symbols (for example, the words are written in the Latin alphabet), as well as abbreviations (works with a dictionary of abbreviations);
4. **Agent D:** excludes repeating units from the list;
5. **Agent E:** works with a set of words derived from the ontology, if necessary filters the list taking into account the words which the ontology already contains;

Figure 8. Steps of forming a set of concepts

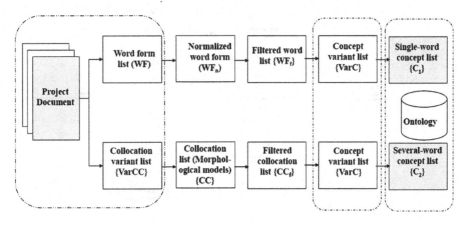

217

6. **Agent F:** selects a word collocation (2-3 words in length) taking into account the list of concepts, the punctuation marks (collocation cannot be separated comma or another mark);
7. **Agent G:** filters the collocations by morphological models.

A number of these agents use the morphological analyzer inside (it can also be called a program agent) – an external program that allows one to determine the part of speech of a word, its grammatical characteristics (gender, number, case, etc.) as well as to bring it to its original (normal) form. The collaborative work of agents is opened in Figure 9 where the used dictionaries are also shown.

We carried out a comparative analysis of four morphological analyzers: LanguageTool, Yandex Mystem, Link Grammar and one designed for WIQA (it uses the AOT morphology inside).

The analysis revealed that the most accurate is the MyStem analyzer, but its main drawback is its close code, so, we cannot be implemented into our work. Link Grammar Analyzer has the highest number of additional opportunities that may be useful for building relations between the concepts, but it works

Figure 9. Interaction between the program agents

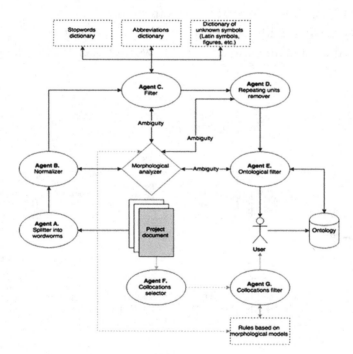

smoothly only in the Linux operating system. Language Tool Analyzer has its advantages but it is written in Java, and thus, it is not possible to integrate it with the WIQA system. Taking into account all this we have decided to use the AOT morphology in the developed complex of utilities.

3.2. Some Basic Tasks and Workflows

The following set of functions helps to solve tasks indicated in subsection 7.3.1:

1. **T1:** To create a new ontological dictionary based on a list of contender words derived from project documentation texts after filtering out stopwords from their wordforms.
2. **T2:** To complement a working vocabulary of concepts in the WIQA ontology using the mechanism of controlled lexis.
3. **T3:** To fetch out the ambiance of concepts in project documentation texts and to add them into the ontology as concepts definitions.

Each of these tasks has several workflows (WF) inside. Some of them are carried out by a software agent only (WF^A), and some of them involve a designer (WF^D).

Let us go into detail on each workflow of the task T1.

1. **T1.WF^D1:** Select a text to process.
2. **T1.WF^A1:** To split the text into wordforms.
3. **T1.WF^A2:** To filter out stopwords from the wordforms and get a list of contender words that can be added to the ontology.
4. **T1.WF^D2:** To select items from the list of contender words, which are consistent with the selected domain and the project task being solved, and add them to the ontology as concepts.

The workflows of the task T2 are partly equal to the ones of the task T1. However, there is one more workflow, which is carried out when adding concepts to the ontology simultaneously with the T2.WF^D1 one. Note that the task T2 can be repeated an unlimited number of times but only after finishing the task T1.

1. $T2.WF^D1 = T1.WF^D1$
2. $T2.WF^A1 = T1.WF^A1$
3. $T2.WF^A2 = T1.WF^A2$

4. $T2.WF^D2 = T1.WF^D2 \parallel T2.WF^A3$. To exercise control over dictionary (check if the concept has already been added to the ontology).

Two agents are involved in solving the tasks T1 and T2. Agent A splits the source text into the wordforms and Agent B filters out the stopwords. The workflows of the tasks T1 and T2 are presented in the figure 10.

Let us go into detail on each workflow of the task T3. This task relates to the working dictionary of a project ontology (or a task ontology) in its current state:

1. **T3.WF^{D}1:** Select a working dictionary to analyze.
2. **T3.WF^{D}2:** Select a text to process.
3. **T3.WF^{A}1:** To fetch out the ambiance of concepts in the ontological dictionary from the selected text and get a list of ambients.
4. **T3.WF^{A}2:** To filter the list of ambients using word collocation syntactic models and some other methods stated below and get a list of concepts "use cases."
5. **T3.WF^{D}3:** To pick up the concept use cases consistent with the natural language rules and the project task being solved. $\parallel$ T3.WF^{A}3. To add the selected use cases into the ontology as concept definitions.

Two agents are involved in solving the task T3. Agent C fetches out the ambiance of each concept (2-3 words before and after each of the concepts) presented in the ontology at its current state and Agent D filters the ambiance using some syntactic models and semantic tokens described below. The workflows of the tasks T3 are presented in the Figure 11.

Figure 10. Workflows of the tasks T1 and T2

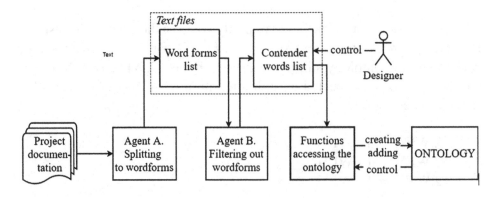

Figure 11. Workflows of the tasks T3

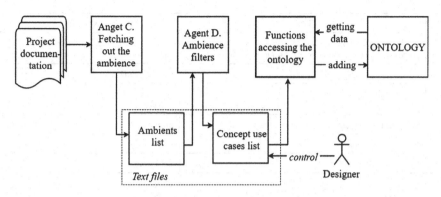

See all the workflows at the generalized scheme below (Figure 12).

In the following we consider the working mechanisms of the Agents B and D because they use some sophisticated linguistic mechanisms inside.

3.3. Functions of Some Agents

- **Agent B. Filtering out Stopwords:** Stopwords are the words that do not have any important semantic meaning in the text and can be ignored in the process of creating a domain ontology which is a semantic model of a text.

We developed the following classification of English stopwords (see Table 1)

We developed the classification after having analyzed a number of open stopword lists used by MySQL, Google and various NLP software systems.

Figure 12. Generalized scheme of project documentation texts processing to form an ontology in the WIQA system

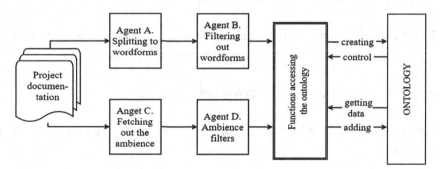

Table 1. Stopwords classification

N°	Type	Examples
1.	Auxiliary parts of speech (articles, conjunctions, particles, prepositions, interjections, pronouns, etc.)	*a the, to, since, that, in, under, oh, whose, mine*
2.	Abbreviations, acronyms	*i.e., etc., PhD*
3.	Words with general meaning	*have, think, become, the universe*
4.	Words expressing assessment and modality	*probably, exactly, can, should, could, perhaps*
5.	Introductory words	*nevertheless, anyway*
6.	Foreign words	*Deutsche, vive*

- **Agent D. Fetching out the Ambiance:** This agent works together with a specific software system – English POS-tagger. It tags a text – the tags define the part of speech (noun, verb, adjective, particle, etc.) of each wordform in a text. See Table 2 to discover the tags and their values of the POS-tagger that we use.

We discovered several syntactic models of English collocations (see Table 3) with the help of which the agent fetches out the ambiance of concepts and forms a list of concept use cases.

Apart from the collocation models we use the following semantic tokens which help to fetch out the ambiance of a concept in a text in order to specify or expand its meaning:

That-token: **<concept> that … .**

If "that" goes after a concept, the rest part (up to the full stop) of a sentence may relate to its definition.

Participle-token: **<concept> V-ing … ./,**

If a Participle I goes after a concept, the rest of the sentence or its part (up to the full stop or a comma) may relate to the concept definition.

Enumeration-token: **…, …, … <concept> …, …, …**

Any enumerations which go before or after a concept may relate to its definition.

Table 2. English POS-tagger tags

Tag	Explanation	Examples
NNP	Proper noun, singular	*Pierre, England*
CD	Cardinal number	*61,three*
NNS	Noun, plural	*researcher, men*
JJ	adjective	*British, new*
MD	modal	*can, ought*
VB	Verb, base form	*be, introduce*
DT	determiner	*the, neither*
NN	Noun, singular or mass	*The spokeswoman, year*
IN	Preposition or subordinating conjunction	*in, because*
VBZ	Verb, 3rd person, singular, present	*has, says*
VBG	Verb, gerund or present participle	*according, rising*
CC	Coordinating conjunction	*so, versus*
VBD	Verb, past tense	*learnt, studied*
VBN	Verb, past participle	*improved, retired*
RB	adverb	*mostly, far*
TO	to	*to*
PRP	Personal pronoun	*they, we*
RBR	Adverb, comparative	*higher, easier*
WDT	Wh-determiner	*why, when*
VBP	Verb, non 3rd person, singular, present	*include, calculate*
RP	particle	*on, away*
PRP$	Possessive pronoun	*their, my*
JJS	Adjective, superlative	*highest, longest*
POS	Possessive ending	*'s*
EX	Existential there	*there*
WP	Wh-pronoun	*whom, whoever*
JJR	Adjective, comparative	*less, closer*
WRB	Wh-adverb	*where, whenever*
NNPS	Proper noun, plural	*angels, motors*
WP$	Possessive pronouns, plural	*whose*
PDT	predeterminer	*quite, such*
RBS	Adverb, superlative	*best, hardest*
FW	Foreign word	*Deutsche, vive*
UH	Interjection	*alas, wow*
SYM	symbol	*@, &*
LS	List item marker	*a, b, first, second*

Table 3. Collocation models classification

Model	Explanation	Examples
Co-Ordinating collocations		
N&N	Noun + conjunction + noun	*sun and moon*
A&A	Adjective + conjunction + adjective	*red and blue*
V&V	Verb + conjunction + verb	*read and write*
D&D	Adverb + conjunction + adverb	*here and there*
Subordinate Collocations		
AN	Adjective + noun	*semantic meaning*
VN	Noun + verb	*filter word forms*
VD	Verb + adverb	*analyze thoroughly*
DA	Adverb + adjective	*very useful*
NN	Noun + noun	*domain ontology*
PN	Participle + noun	*working dictionary*

To sum it all up, both the models and the tokens allow us to get a list of concept ambiance which a designer can add to the ontology.

4. ONTOLOGY APPLICATIONS

4.1. Tool 1. Lexical Control

The ontological tools were developed with the help of the pseudocode functions mentioned above and some extra functions – additional *program agents* integrated with the OwnWIQA environment in the form of dynamic-link libraries (*.dll) written in C# to process data.

The first tool was designed to provide control over the lexical items in project documentation texts and, as a result, to fill the project ontology with new knowledge items (concepts, their relations, definitions, etc.), on the one hand, as well as to make documentation text more accurate in a terminological sense, on the other hand.

Figure 13 shows the overall algorithm of the tool. Firstly the text is analyzed and filtered with the help of a *stopwords list*,] (stopwords are the words that do not have any important semantic meaning in the text and can be ignored in the process of creating a domain ontology which is a semantic model of a text). Then *collocations* are extracted with the help of linguistic models of

Figure 13. Algorithm of lexical control

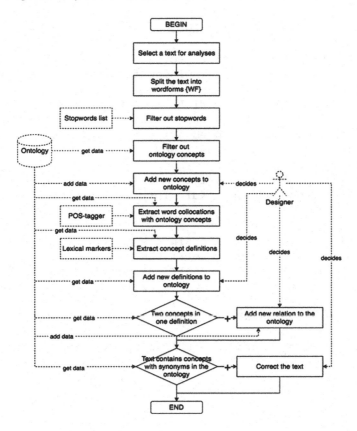

syntaxis. After that *definition* are extracted from the text based on a number of *lexical markers*, such as "that," "which," participles of various forms, etc. After each step, the designer decides if anything (concepts, definitions, relations) should be added to the project ontology. Finally, a text can be corrected if there are any concepts connected with relations of a synonym type in the ontology which means that the document uses some inaccurate terms.

To demonstrate the work of the pseudocode functions, let us represent the part of the program which filters out the items, already presented in the ontology, from a list of words and collocations (for convenience, we wrote the list to a separate text file) and suggests a designer to add some of them to the ontology:

```
PROCEDURE &AddToDictionary&
&dictName&:= INPUTSTRING("Select dictionary", "Enter the target
dictionary name", "Existing dictionary name")
```

```
// select a dictionary in the window form that appears (Figure
14)
&groupName&:= INPUTSTRING("Select group", "Enter the target
group name",
"Existing group name in the selected dictionary")
// select a dictionary in the window form that appears (Figure
15)
&form&:= AddToDictForm("C:\\WIQA\\pretendents.txt")
// call a form where all the words that can be added to the
project ontology are presented (Figure 5) and where a designer
can decide which words to add (they are save in the file
dictconcepts.txt)
&dictID&:= Onto_GetDictId(&dictName&)
&groupID&:= Onto_GetGroupId(&dictID&, &groupName&)
&i&:= 0
LABEL &LCycle& // loop index
&conceptsNumber&:= CountStringsInFile("C:\\WIQA\\dictconcepts.
txt") IF &i& >= &conceptsNumber& THEN goto &LOut&
&word&:= ReadFromFile(&i&, "C:\\WIQA\\dictconcepts.txt")
// read the string with the index i from the file with the
selected concepts
&wordID&:= Onto_GetWordId(&dictID&, &groupID&, &word&) IF
&wordID& == 0 THEN BEGIN
// if the ID of the word is equal to 0, that means that such
word does not exist in the ontology
&conceptID&:= Onto_CreateWord(&groupID&, &word&)
END
&i&:= &i& +1
GOTO &LCycle&
LABEL &LOut&
ENDPROC &AddToDictionary&
```

The user interface, which helps to add data to the ontology (Figure 14-16), was integrated with the pseudocode program with the help of dynamic-link library developed in C#.

4.2. Tool 2: Understanding of a Project Task

The understanding tool helps to reveal the facts, not obvious when a designer is thinking out a solution for a software system, and to come to some new conclusions with the help of the knowledge already recorded in the project ontology, which the designer is unlikely to be aware of.

The current version of the tool lets that a designer enter a text description of a project task and shows him/her the definitions of all the concepts, presented in the text, and all the concepts related to them by any type of relation. This

Figure 14. Dictionary selecting interface form

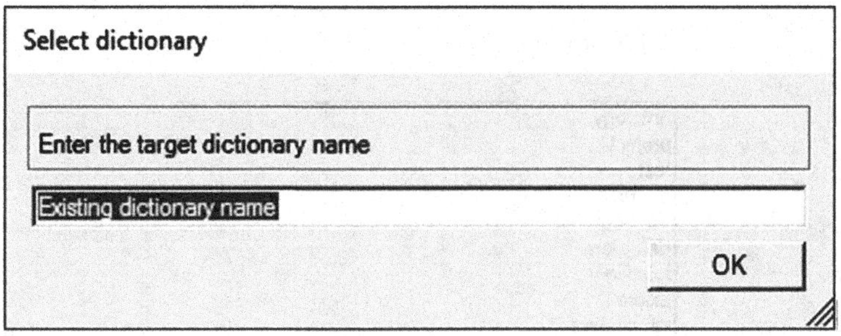

Figure15. Group selecting interface form

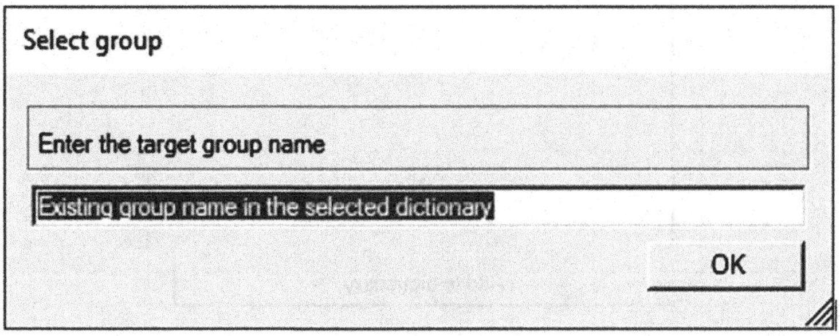

helps to gain more information about the task and, therefore, get a better understanding of what has to be done. Figure 17 shows the interface of the tool.

To demonstrate programmed access to the ontology in OwnWIQA, let us represent the procedure of extracting definitions of the concepts. For convenience, we wrote all these concepts to a separate text file.

```
PROCEDURE &ExtractDefinitions&
&dictName&:= INPUTSTRING("Select dictionary", "Enter the target
dictionary name", "Existing dictionary name") // set a working
dictionary
&groupName&:= INPUTSTRING("Select group", "Enter the target
group name", "Existing group name in the selected dictionary")
// set a working group
&dictID&:= Onto_GetDictId(&dictName&)
&groupID&:= Onto_GetGroupId(&dictID&, &groupName&)
&i&:= 0
&n&:= CountStringsInFile("C:\\WIQA\\concepts.txt")
// count the number of concept presented in a text
LABEL &lcycle&
IF &i& >= &n& THEN goto &lout&
```

Figure 16. Filling dictionary interface form

Figure17. Understanding tool interface

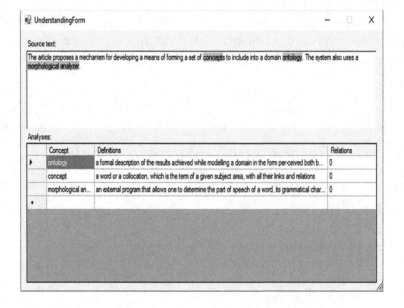

```
&concept&:= ReadFromFile(&i&, "C:\\WIQA\\concepts.txt") // read
concept from file with the current index
&conceptID&:= Onto_GetWordId(&dictID&, &groupID&, &concept&) //
get the identification number of the concept from the ontology
&definition&:= Onto_GetWordDefinitionText(&conceptID&)
// extract the definition of the current concept from the
ontology
&definedConcept&:= &concept&: &definition&
&write&:= AddStringToFile(&definedConcept&,
"C:\\WIQA\\definedconcepts.txt")
// write the concept with its definition to a separate file so
that we can work with it further
&i&:= &i& +1
GOTO &lcycle&
LABEL &lout&
ENDPROC &ExtractDefinitions&
```

4.3. Tool 3: Extracting Questions

In a reasoning modeling process, it is very important to have the opportunity to extract questions from a text description of a task in order to itemize it further. We attempted to automatize the question extraction process with the help of the following question indicators:

1. Interrogative sentences (question marks).
2. Ambiguity and modality markers, such as:
    a. **Adjectives and Adverbs:** Very, too, about, at least, much, probable, probably, possible, possibly, likely, unlikely, certain, certainly, clearly, clear, almost, really, perhaps, sure;
    b. **Nouns (Parts of Set Phrases, Such as "to Make an Assumption," "Point of View," etc.):** View, mind, assumption;
    c. **Unions:** whatever;
    d. **Verbs:** Think, believe, suggest, introduce, happen, seem, appear, promise, estimate, mind, assume, presume, guess, suppose, imagine, expect, suspect, surmise, imply, involve, presuppose, propose, conjecture, say, contemplate, fancy, understand, design, indicate, look, doubt, dare;
    e. **Modal Verbs:** May, can, must, ought, will, shall, need, might, could, would, should.
3. Cause and Effect Markers:

a. **Subordinating Conjunctions:** Because, as, since, since, now that, as long as, such ... that, so ... that;
b. **Prepositions:** Because of, due to, in order to;
c. **Conjunctive Adverbs and Transitions:** Therefore, consequently; - conjunctions: so.
4. Qualitative adjectives;
5. Words, not presented in the ontology, but that can potentially be included into the working dictionary.

Figure 18 demonstrates the work of the extracting questions tool.

To extract question we are going to use the following algorithm of lexical control:

1. Select a text (T) for analysis.
2. Check if there are any interrogative sentences {I} in a text:
   a. IF yes, THEN add the whole sentence (S) to the list of questions {Q};
   b. IF no, THEN go to 3.

Figure 18. Extracting questions process

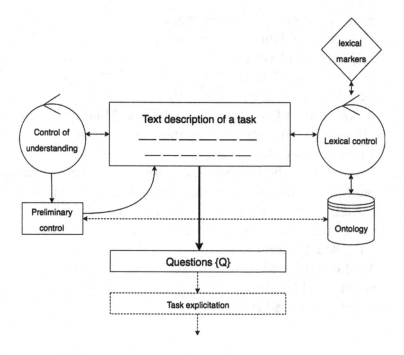

3. Check if there are any ambiguity and modality markers {AM} in a text:
   a. $N = 0$;
   b. Select the marker AM_N;
   c. IF there is no marker (AM) with the index N, THEN go to 4, ELSE
   d. IF the text contains the marker AM_N, THEN add all the words after each entry of the marker AM_N (without any punctuation marks) before a comma or a full stop to the list of questions {Q};
   e. ELSE go to 3.6;
   f. $N = N + 1$;
   g. GOTO 3.1.
4. Check if there are any cause and effect markers {CM} in a text:
   a. $N = 0$;
   b. Select the marker CM_N;
   c. IF there is no marker (CM) with the index N, THEN go to 5, ELSE
   d. IF the text contains the marker CM_N, THEN add all the words before (from the beginning of the sentence or a comma) and all the words before a comma or a full stop after each entry of the marker CM_N (without any punctuation marks) to the list of questions {Q};
   e. ELSE go to 4.6;
   f. $N = N + 1$;
   g. GOTO 4.1.
5. Check if there are any qualitative adjectives {AQ} in a text:
   a. $N = 0$;
   b. Select the qualitative adjective AQ_N;
   c. IF there is no qualitative adjective (AQ) with the index N, THEN go to 6, ELSE
   d. IF the text contains the qualitative adjective AQ_N, THEN add up to 3 words after each entry of the qualitative adjective AQ_N (without any punctuation marks) to the list of questions {Q};
   e. ELSE go to 5.6;
   f. $N = N + 1$;
   g. GOTO 3.1.
6. Check if the list of questions {Q}, contains any concepts {C} from the ontology (O):
   a. IF yes, THEN show to the user all the concepts that are linked to each entry {C_L};
   b. IF no, THEN goto 7.
7. Pick the words (word collocations), not presented in the ontology, but that can potentially be included into the working dictionary:

a. Split the text (T) into wordforms {WF};
b. Filter stopwords {SW} out of the wordforms {WF} and get a list of potential concepts {P};
c. Compose collocations with potential concepts {P} with the help of collocation rules (described in the previous section) and add them to the list of potential concepts {P};
d. Check if the ontology (O) contains any of the potential concepts {P}:
    i. $N = 0$;
    ii. Select a potential concept P_N;
    iii. IF there is no potential concept (P) with the index N, THEN go to 8, ELSE
    iv. IF the ontology (O) does not contain the potential concept, P_N THEN add the potential concept P_N to the list of questions {Q};
    v.   ELSE go to 7.4.6;
    vi. $N = N + 1$;
    vii. GOTO 7.4.1.
8. Show the list of questions {Q} to the user.

A screenshot of the extracting questions tool can be seen in Figure 8. It illustrates the questions that can be asked to the text in the large textbox. All the markers described above are highlighted in the text. The designer can see the analyses of each question by clicking the "See details" button – all the concepts that can be found in the text of the questions are also highlighted, and the right lower part of the screen shows the concepts that are related to them.

Thereby, the designer can learn more details about his/her general task and itemize it by formulating a set of more detailed tasks. These detailed tasks can also be analyzed with the help of this tool if they need further itemization.

For illustrative purposes, we provide here and an example of a pseudocode procedure that allows finding out which words in the text of a question are store in the ontology as concepts and writing them to a separate text file in order to use it the further data processing:

```
PROCEDURE &ExtractConcepts&
&dictName&:= INPUTSTRING("Select dictionary", "Enter the target
dictionary name", "Existing dictionary name")
&groupName&:= INPUTSTRING("Select group", "Enter the target
group name", "Existing group name in the selected dictionary")
&dictID&:= Onto_GetDictId(&dictName&)
```

232

Figure 19. Extracting questions tool

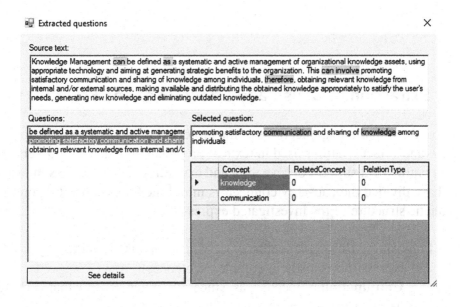

```
&groupID&:= Onto_GetGroupId(&dictID&, &groupName&)
&q&:= INPUTSTRING("Question", "Enter the question to extract
concepts from:", "")
// get the question to analyze (for demonstration purposes a
user enters a question via the input form but in reality it is
selected from the list of question extracted from the source
text &split&:= SplitStringToFile(&q&)
// split the question into wordforms and write them to a
separate file
&i&:= 0
&n&:= CountStringsInFile(&split&)
// count how many wordforms are there in the file
LABEL &lcycle&
IF &i& >= &n& THEN goto &lout&
&wordform&:= ReadFromFile(&i&, &split&) // select the current
wordform
&wordID&:= Onto_GetWordId(&dictID&, &groupID&, &wordform&) //
get the word identification number IF &wordID& == 0 THEN goto
&L1&
// if the word ID is equal to 0, that means that there is no
such concept in the ontology
&write&:= AddStringToFile(&wordform&, «C:\\WIQA\\
selectedconcepts.txt»)
// if there is such a concept in the ontology, add it to a
separate file so that we can use it further
LABEL &L1&
```

```
&i&:= &i& + 1
GOTO &lcycle&
LABEL &lout&
ENDPROC &ExtractConcepts
```

4.4. Extraction of Cause-and-Effect Relations From Text

One of the important applications of the project ontology is the extraction of cause-and-effect relations used in texts of project documents. In our version of an ontological support of revealing and extracting the causalities in texts, we have divided the causality connectors into three types depending on the syntactic structure of the investigated expression:

1.   Prepositions (in simple sentences), conjunctions and introductory words and expressions (mostly in complex sentences)^
      a.   **Conjunctions:** Because, as, since, inasmuch as, now that, as long as, such ... that, so ... that, so, for this reason, etc.
      b.   **Prepositions:** Because of, due to, owing to, on account of, in order to, etc.
      c.   **Introductory Words and Expressions:** Therefore, consequently, as a result, accordingly, for this reason, hence, thus, nevertheless, that's why, etc.
2.   Set phrases and expressions containing nouns and adjectives as well as nouns which may indicate cause and effect (mostly implicitly due to their ambiguity)^
      a.   **Explicit:** To be an influence on, to be the effect of, the result is, as a result of, to be the reason for, to be the cause of, to be the factor of, to have an impact on, to have an influence on, to be responsible for, etc.
      b.   **Implicit:** Antecedent, ground, justification, motivation, motive, necessity, occasion, start, etc.
3.   Causative verbs indicating cause and effect (in some cases implicitly):
      a.   **Explicit (Used Both in the Active and the Passive Voice):** To result in/from, to cause, to produce, to lead to, to affect, to contribute to, to determine, to influence, to bring about, to generate, to induce, to occasion, to secure, to set off, to stir up, to touch off, to trigger, to force, to produce, etc.

     b.   **Implicit:** Let, get, make, keep, put (in some values), order, ask, persuade, mean, etc.

This division was used for defining a set of tags based on the grammatical characteristics of a sentence containing the connectors described above. We also defined a set of rules for each type of connectors that help extract syntactic tokens (text fragments) indicating causality. These definitions are presented in Table 4.

Defined tags and rules were used in developing the program agent and a specialized procedure that are responsible for extracting the causality relations from investigated texts. The scheme of extracting is shown in Figure 20 in the context of creating a model of a precedent because this artifact has the causality nature.

After the agent finishes processing an investigated text, we will get N pairs of text fragments of the following type: (C, E) = ([cause], [effect]). Let us consider the fragment referring to the cause as F^C, and the fragment referring to the effect as F^E. Each fragment is a sequence of lexical tokens (words): $F = \{W\}$.

These tokens are processed with the following procedure:

1. Pick a $\mathbf{F}_i$ fragment from the $\{\mathbf{F}\}$ set
2. *If* the $\{\mathbf{F}\}$ set is not empty, *then* go to *(3)*, *else end*
3. Pick a $\mathbf{W}_i$ word from the $\{\mathbf{W}\}$ set
4. *If* the $\{\mathbf{W}\}$ set is not empty, *then* go to *(5)*, *else* go to *(11)*
5. *If* the $\mathbf{W}_i$ word belongs to the $\{\mathbf{C}\}$ set of ontology concepts, *then* go to *(6)*, *else* go to (11)
6. *If* the $\mathbf{W}_i$ word is linked to any ontology concept by a cause-and-effect relation $\mathbf{R}^{CE}(\mathbf{W}_i, \mathbf{C}^{CE})$, *then* go to *(7)*, *else* go to *(8)*
7. Show the $\mathbf{R}^{CE}(\mathbf{W}_i, \mathbf{C}^{CE})$ pair to the user
8. *If* the $\mathbf{W}_i$ word is linked to any ontology concept by a synonymic relation $\mathbf{R}^S(\mathbf{W}_i, \mathbf{C}^S)$, *then* go to *(9)*, *else* go to *(11)*
9. *If* the $\mathbf{W}_i$ word is linked to the $\mathbf{C}^S$ concept by a cause-and-effect relation $\mathbf{R}^{CE}(\mathbf{W}_i, \mathbf{C}^S)$ *and* $((\mathbf{F}_i = \mathbf{F}^C$ *and* the $\mathbf{W}_i$ word is the main one) *or* $(\mathbf{F}_i = \mathbf{F}^E$ *and* the $\mathbf{W}_i$ word is the subordinate one)), *then* go to *(11)*, *else* go to *(10)*
10. Add the $\mathbf{R}^{CE}(\mathbf{W}_i, \mathbf{C}^S)$ relation to the ontology
11. Go to *(3)*

Table 4. Tags and rules oriented on extracting the causality

#	Tag Type	Rules of Extracting Fragments	Tags
A	Indicates the cause	Often stands between the effect and the cause. We consider the cause to be the part of a sentence after the tag and up to the full stop (comma or any other punctuation mark). The effect is the beginning of a sentence up to the tag (if the tag stands in the middle of it) or the end of a sentence after a comma (if the tag stands in the beginning).	*because, as, since, inasmuch as, as long as, now that*
B		Often stands between the effect and the cause. We consider the cause to be the *noun phrase* after the tag. The effect is the beginning of a sentence up to the tag (if the tag stands in the middle of it) or the end of a sentence after a comma (if the tag stands in the beginning).	*because of, due to, owing to, on account of, as a result of*
C		Predicate referring to the cause. The subject is the cause, the noun phrase after the tag is the effect.	*be/have an influence on, be the reason for, be the cause of, be the factor of, have an impact on, be responsible for, result in*
D	Indicates the effect	Often stands in the beginning of a sentence and indicates the effect (up to any punctuation mark). The cause may stand in the previous sentence (if the sentence containing the tag is a simple one) or in the beginning of a sentence up to the tag (if the tag stands in the middle).	*for this reason, so, therefore, consequently, as a result, accordingly, for this reason, hence, thus, nevertheless, that's why*
E		More often than not stands between the cause and the effect. We consider the effect to be the *noun phrase* after the tag. The cause is the beginning of a sentence up to the tag (if the tag stands in the middle of it) or the end of a sentence after a comma (if the tag stands in the beginning).	*in order to*
F		Predicate referring to the effect. The subject is the effect, the noun phrase after the tag is the cause.	*be the effect of, result from,*
G		Indicates the effect, which is a noun phrase. The cause may stand in the previous sentence (if the sentence containing the tag is a simple one) or in the beginning of a sentence up to the tag (if the tag stands in the middle).	*the result is*
H	Indicates both the cause and the effect	Pair tags. The first one indicated the cause, the second one – the effect	*such ... that, so ... that*
I		Predicate referring to the cause (in the Active Voice) and to the effect (in the Passive Voice). In the Active Voice the subject is the cause and the noun phrase after the tag is the effect. In the Passive Voice – vice versa.	*cause, produce, lead to, affect, contribute to, determine, influence, bring about, generate, induce, occasion, secure, set off, stir up, touch off, trigger, force, produce*

Figure 20. Scheme of cause-and-effect analysis

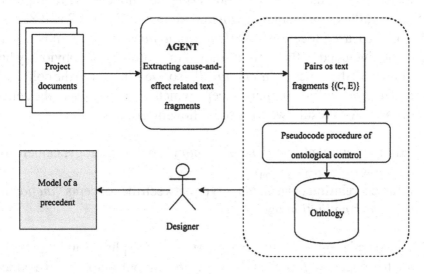

4.5. Example of Applying for the Ontological Support

Let us consider the main opportunities of our toolset on the example of our own project task.

We have selected two subtasks for the demonstration purposes:

Z1: To fetch out the ontology concept use-cases with the help of mature mechanisms of logic and linguistic text processing at the level of lexical items and groups of lexical items, such as filtering out stopwords, applying syntactic models and semantic tokens as well as using specific NLP tools, namely a POS-tagger.

Z2: To use the pseudocode functions allowing programmed access to the project ontology in its current state, as well as to its working dictionary, in order to exercise lexical control namely to specify or expand the concept meanings, to complement the ontology and to adjust it to the project task.

Agent C extracts the following list of the concepts from the two example texts: *ontology concept, concept use-case, filtering out stopwords, working dictionary, lexical control, concept meaning, project task, filtering out stopwords, pseudocode functions allowing programmed access to the project ontology in its current state.*

The first thing we have to do after analyzing the ambiance is to complement our ontology, the current state of which is shown in Figures 7 and 8.

We noticed a collocation *"working dictionary"* in the ambiance list, which is not included in the current state of the ontology but obviously has a connection with the concept *"dictionary"* – so, we considered the collocation *"working dictionary"* as another concept, which is an *instance* of the concept *"dictionary."* As a result, we took the following actions:

A1: Add a **new concept** *"working dictionary"* to the ontology, namely to its *"Ontology entities"* group.

A2: Add a **new relation** of an *instance* type between the concepts *"dictionary"* and *"working dictionary."*

When considering the *"filtering out stopwords"* phrase and the fact that there are to concepts *"filter"* and *"stopword"* in our ontology, we added a new relation of an instrument type:

A3: Add a **new relation** of an *instrument* type between the concepts *"filter"* and *"stopwords."*

The phrase *"pseudocode functions allowing programmed access to the project ontology in its current state"* in a list allows us to add a definition to the concept *"pseudocode function"* presented in our ontology:

A4: Add a **new definition** to the concept *"pseudocode function"* stated as follows: *"A function which allows programmed access to the project ontology in its current state."*

After taking actions to complement the ontology, let us consider if there are any changes that we have to make in the source text based on the analyses.

In the first text, there is a concept *"use case,"* which has a relation of a *part-and-whole* type with the concept *"documentation"* in our ontology. Thus, we have to **edit the text** a little and formulate it as follows (the changes are underlined):

Z1^E: To fetch out the ontology concept use-cases **from the documentation** with the help of mature mechanisms of logic and linguistic text processing at the level of lexical items and groups of lexical items, such as filtering out stopwords, applying syntactic models and semantic tokens as well as using specific NLP tools, namely a POS-tagger.

4.6. Ontological Support in Designing the Configured Templates

Offered means have been tested in the development of some projects the last of which is a system for designing of tooling. In the aircraft industry, for manufacturing the parts of a fuselage, wings, and aileron, including details of their covering, technological templates are widely used. Any template for the part is a kind of its machining attachment that supports definite technological operations, for example, manufacturing of the corresponding part. Described means of the ontological support was applied for designing of the template tooling that usually consists of tens of thousands of templates. The built ontology consists of the following sections:

1. The system of typical templates as concepts;
2. The visualized classification of templates;
3. Templates in manufacturing of aviation parts;
4. Templates in a production control of parts;
5. Templates as models of precedents.

In the section of concepts, the model of the template is described by its type and attributes some which are expressed through relations with other concepts. Items in this section are interactively accessible.

The used systematization of concepts and their classifier are shown in Figure 21 where relations are demonstrated on the example of one of the template. The classifier combines partof-relations that facilitate the search for appropriate templates.

In the built ontology, any template is defined in the form of the precedent model that has the structure shown in Figure 22. Since all interfaces in Russian, some fields are marked with labels.

It should be noted the specificity of the program components used in the precedent model. The life cycle of template manufacturing includes the stages that require the creative-intensive activity of workers that participate in designing of the templates. It is caused by the need to take account of future ways to move the laser beam on all lines that represent the template for its steel billet. Therefore, the template model includes two algorithmic

Figure 21. System relations in the ontology

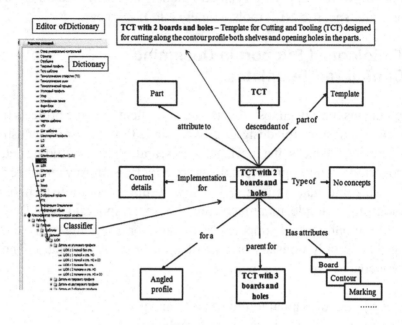

Figure 22. Structure of the template definition

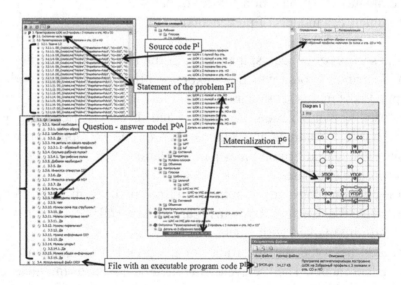

descriptions. The first description imitates the movement of the laser beam in tasks of searching the effective trajectories. The second description is a result of computer numerical control programming that provides the process of laser cutting.

5. SOME REMARKS TO THE CHAPTER 7

1. The success of conceptual designing the systems is based on a personal and mutual understanding of designers and other stakeholders when they operatively use accessible experience in collaborative work.

2. In order to understand something, for example, the designer needs to fulfill the certain work focusing own attention on the object of understanding in appropriate conditions. For this book, the central place occupies the objects of understanding that concern project tasks and processes of their conceptual solutions.

3. In our research and developments, we have developed a complex of means that provide a constructive achievement of understanding in work with tasks at the conceptual level. These means have embedded in the reifying of the precedent-oriented approach and QA approach. The intertwining use of these approaches includes an ontological support of works aimed at the achievement of sufficient understanding in interactions with tasks.

4. The suggested version of the ontology of a project helps to achieve the following positive effects: using the controlled vocabulary; systematizing the methods and means used in an occupational activity; specifying the conceptualization; checking the semantics of the built text and applied reasoning; operating with machine-readable and machine-understandable content.

5. It is necessary to note that the designer has the opportunity for appointing relations such as "is-a," "part-of," "attributive," "causative," "associative" (temporal, spatial, synonymous, opposite, following) and relations of pragmatic types. The designer has the opportunity for extending the list of relations.

6. There is two version of reifying the project ontologies the first of which fulfills its function in collaborative environment WIQA.Net. In this version, step by step filling the ontology by informational content requires sufficient linguistic competencies. Therefore, fulfilling this work is a responsibility that corresponds to a specialized role.

7. In this version, for the transition to simple sentences, the responsible member of the team uses the pseudo physical algorithm, in which a force field simulates a semantic net of a complex sentence.
8. In interactions with the ontology, designers apply the manual operations. The main function of the ontology is a systematization of the experience base.
9. The ontology in the OwnWIQA system can be accessed via the specific pseudocode functions that request the ontological database in the controlled pseudocode interpretation mode.
10. This possibility has led to creation pseudocode programs for a lexical control of textual units generated during designing, a support of understanding in the lexical analysis of sentences and for extracting questions from the text descriptions.

REFERENCES

Eden, A. H., & Turner, R. (2007). Problems in the Ontology of Computer Programs. Applied Ontology, 2(1), 13–36.

Garcia, A. C. B., Kunz, J., Ekstrom, M., & Kiviniemi, A. (2003). *Building a Project Ontology with Extreme Collaboration and Virtual Design & Construction*. CIFE Technical Report # 152, Stanford University.

Martins, A. F., & De Almeida, F. R. (2008). Models for Representing Task Ontologies. Proc. of the 3rd Workshops on Ontologies and their Application, 1-12.

Sosnin, P. (2010). Creation and Usage of Project Ontology in Development of Software Intensive Systems. *Polibits*, *42*, 51–58. doi:10.17562/PB-42-5

Sosnin, P. (2015). *An Ontological Support for Interactions with Experience in Designing the Software Intensive Systems. In LNCS 9158* (pp. 387–400). Heidelberg: Springer.

Sosnin, P. (2016). A place and role of an ontology in using a base of experience in designing the software intensive systems. *International Journal of Web Information Systems*, *12*(1), 62–82. doi:10.1108/IJWIS-10-2015-0035

ADDITIONAL READING

Bullinger, H.-J., Warschat, J., Schumacher, O., Slama, A., & Ohlhausen, P. (2005). Ontology-Based Project Management for Acceleration of Innovation Project. *Lecture Notes in Computer Science, 3379*, 280–288. doi:10.1007/978-3-540-31842-2_28

Fitsilis, P., Gerogiannis, V., & Anthopoulos, L. (2014). Ontologies for Software Project Management: A Review. *Journal of Software Engineering and Applications, 7*(13), 1096–1110. doi:10.4236/jsea.2014.713097

Gargouri, F. (2010). *Ontology Theory, Management and Design: Advanced Tools and Models* (1st ed.). Information Science Reference. doi:10.4018/978-1-61520-859-3

Gómez-Pérez, A., Fernández-López, M., & Corcho, O. (2004). *Ontological Engineering*. Springer-Verlag.

Guarino, N., Oberle, D., & Staab, S. (2009). What is an Ontology? In S. Staab and R. Studer (eds.), Handbook on Ontologies, Second Edition. International handbooks on information systems. Springer Verlag, 1-17. doi:10.1007/978-3-540-92673-3_0

Sosnin, P. (2016). Figuratively semantic support in precedent-oriented solving the Project Tasks. In *Proc. of the 10th International Conference on Application of Information and Communication Technologies*, pp.479-48

Wiel, W. M., Hasberg, M. P., Weima, I., & Huiskamp, W. (2010). Concept Maturity Levels Bringing structure to the CD&E process, In *Proc. of Interservice industry training, simulation and education conference*, pp. 2547-2555.

Chapter 8
Figuratively Semantic Support of Human– Computer Interactions

ABSTRACT

This chapter focuses on one more mental phenomenon – mental imagination that provides simulating the activity of human senses in conditions of interactions with a computerized environment. Constructive using of this phenomenon helps to represent possible situations discloses states of a life cycle of any new task that is important for study described in this book. Moreover, such possibility helps to predict the course of events in design process or in reality. For constructive work with mental imagery, we have developed a complex of means that provides figuratively semantic support of design thinking in work with a new task. A kernel of this complex is a set of interactive visual models of pictured, declarative and conceptually algorithmic types with a system of transformations defined on this set. Transformations help to build necessary (program) forms of visualization for any typical steps of design thinking based on conceptual experimenting.

DOI: 10.4018/978-1-5225-2987-3.ch008

1. PLACE AND ROLES OF FIGURATIVELY SEMANTIC MODELS IN SOLVING THE PROJECT TASKS

1.1. Nature of Mental Imagery

he main feature of human interactions with or in the physical world (natural interactions) is an explicit or implicit use of a human of the natural experience (EN), the becoming of which occurs in the intellectual processing of behavioral actions for the future reuse.

In the general case, any new item of EN begins its life cycle with mental processing the information flows coming from the senses. In cases, when informational input flows are absent or explicitly do not use, the becoming of a new item can begin with activating the phenomenon of mental imagery, and its activation can be unpredictable or deliberate. There are numerous definitions that are specified this phenomenon from different viewpoints but our research orients on following functions of the phenomenon:

1. "Allows us to simulate reality at will, and, because of this, allows us to predict what we would experience in a specific situation or after we perform a specific action;"
2. "Allow us to generate specific predictions based on experience."

It should be noted; the mental imagery is the part of the intelligence, which activates this phenomenon in common mental processes in accordance with the laws of mind. Usually, the semantics of signs or signals activates these phenomena, and this occurs both in human interactions as with the physical world so with a computerized environment.

In the described research, our attention focuses on an appearance of a new task in designing the SIS. There are varied situations that signalize about the necessity to bind with them the new task and include it to a set of tasks appointed to the designer.

Let us suppose, the similar situation is formed when the designer is working with one of the appointed tasks in the computerized environment, and in this time, some signal about the new task appears on the monitor of the computer, with which the designer interacts.

In interactions with a computer, human senses focus on a computerized medium, from which they can get audio and video information in forms that are created by programmers who used appropriate kinds of data and their materializations. By other words, programmers used appropriate solutions from the theory and practice of HCI. Consequently, the perception of audio and video artifacts will reflect results of computerized solutions, and interfaces built by designers will provide interactions of users with computer's applications.

It should be noted, perceiving such audio and video information via interfaces, the human mind will process it by using functions of intelligence, including functions of mental imagery. Such processing will continue the computer processing that created informational flows from the computer side. Thus, integral processing has two components of natural and artificial types correspondingly, and final results of interactions with the computer will essentially depend on a way, which uses for the coordination of these components.

One of such ways could be based on interfaces that provide a transition of the human (developer or user) to visual modeling aimed at support of the mental imagery be activating that concerns the new task. For the initial awareness of the new task, thinking tries to express it in an understandable form by conducting the actions (doing) with conceptual components that are appropriate and useful. Thus, thinking and doing with conceptual objects (in mind) lead to an initial statement of the task on the initial level of understanding. Such process can be interpreted as a mental experiment in which the understanding confirms that the formed statement (or its part) is adequate to the discovered new task.

1.2. Reaction on a New Task

For the new project task, its life cycle begins with discovering the definite signal perceived by the designer whose mind reacts on the semantics of the signal, first of all, by activating the mental imagery. The responsibility of this phenomenon is its participation in forming the initial presentation of the task by filtering the appropriate conceptual components extracted from experience E^N for their combining in a wholeness. In this process, that has iterative character, checking the wholeness W is the responsibility of understanding.

Such result of the reaction as W can be presented in pictorial or verbal forms or as their combinations. Any of these forms is better to place beyond the brain. In transition internal versions of forms to their external versions, they are materialized and accessible to their perception by senses of the designer. Any external version is a model M representing W, and this model can be used for the following purposes:

1. Attempts to activate W at any time even in cases when the designer forgot W.
2. Use of M for filtering the internal and external informational flows influencing on W.
3. Use of M for an investigation of W and any its components or their group.
4. Understanding of W due to understanding M.
5. Manipulation with M instead manipulations with W or its components (in mind).
6. Use of M for modification of W due to modification of M or creation of its new version.
7. Participation in management of mental processes by organizing the flow of interactions with M.

In practice, designers actively use enumerated functions of various M while solving the project tasks especially at the conceptual stage of designing. At this stage, the designer is solving the task Z_i by using an appropriate set $\{M^v_j\}$ of textual (verbal) descriptions (models) and graphical models $\{M^G_k\}$ thereby forming its conceptual view. Features of such type of decisions figuratively were presented in Figure 3 where it was also shown iterative developing the statement $St(Z_i, t)$ of task Z_i in the process of its conceptual solution.

As told above, the life cycle of the new task Z_i begins with a reaction on the semantics perceived by the designer. This semantics is better to register by a set of signs $\{w_q\}$ outside of the brain. The next step of actions is awareness of this set, in the result of which the designer formulates the initial statement of the task $St(Z_i, t_0)$. With this moment of time t_0 of the life cycle, the state of the task becomes observable in the form $St(Z_i, t)$. Further, step by step, with the use of conceptual actions described above and other needed actions, the designer solves the task, registering the states of the process in corresponding descriptions of $St(Z_i, t)$. Any state $St(Z_i, t_n)$ of this description is caused by verbal and graphical models that were chosen or created and used by the designer up to the moment of time t_n.

1.3. A Set of Visual Models Affected on Mental Imagery

The basic aims of conceptual solving the task are following:

1. To present the statement $St(Z_i, t)$ in the understandable form for which is verified achieving the algorithmic realizability of the task solution.
2. To develop and test a conceptually algorithmic solution in conditions corresponding the place of the task in the project of SIS.

For achieving the first aim, the designer includes the necessary textual and graphical models from $\{M^v_j\}$ and $\{M^G_k\}$ in the construct $St(Z_i, t)$, and embedded components will provide reuse of understanding in the process of which these models will repeatedly activate the mental imagery. Without such activation, the needed understanding is impossible. It should be noted, in a stimulation of the mental imagery, visual items of any text will participate as special graphics, but, in understanding, the use of models $\{M^G_k\}$ is more effective. The toolkit WIQA supports creating and transforming the visual models for types presented in Figure 1.

A set of types include:

1. Pictorial type M^P, models of which help to express the structure of the requested graphical construct as an interactive model I^P or not. For both versions of models, the used graphical editor automatically create programmatic versions, changing of which reflected on graphical models. Such opportunity is also realized for other types of models.

Figure 1. Normative types of visual models

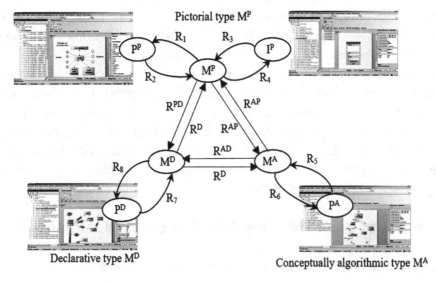

248

2. Declarative type M^D that is intended for visualizing the semantics of textual models $\{M^V\}$ that are important for the achievement of understanding. The main cause for using of this type is the check of $St(Z_i, t)$ and its verbal components via mechanisms of declarative programming. Therefore, the version P^D additionally has a Prolog-like description.

3. Conceptually algorithmic type M^A provides visual modeling of the algorithmic components of the task being solved. For this, the designer can use a pseudocode language L^{WIQA} that is built for the semantic memory of the toolkit WIQA. In the current state of WIQA, the type M^A supports the work with Use-Case diagrams, Activity diagrams, and diagrams of Classes. For the transition to the version P^A, it is applied the automatic mode based on the model-driven approach.

The scheme in Figure 1 includes not only types but also relations among them. The set of relations consist of pairs presenting the transitions between corresponding models of different types (transitions $[R^{PD}, R^{DP}]$, $[R^{PA}, R^{AP}]$, $[R^{DA}, R^{AD}]$) and between models and their programmatic versions $([R_1, R_2], [R_3, R_4], [R_5, R_6], [R_7, R_8])$. Each of these transitions is realized either automatically or automated, including behavioral actions. Any program version corresponds to the executed pseudocode program that could be changed by the designer, for instance, to correct errors or to reduce uncertainty in the created and used visual model.

1.4. Precedent-Oriented Solution of the New Task

Subsections 6.2.1 and 8.1.2 have been disclosed our version of the conceptual solution that suggests its development based on a model of a precedent for the corresponding task Z_i. It can be additionally said, that for the solution of the task, the designer also applies a model-driven approach based on a framework of the precedent. The scheme in Figure 2 demonstrates features of this approach.

At the scheme, the statement $St(Z_i, t)$ in the form of corresponding QA-tree fulfills the role of a source of verbal increments $\Delta T_{nu}^{mX}\left(Z_i, t_j\right)$ each of which (with index u) is formulated on mlevel and n-step of the stepwise refinement for creating the next increment $\Delta P_{nu}^{mX}\left(Z_i, t_k\right)$ for X- component of corresponding the precedent model P(t). Let us remind, in this work, the designer uses the framework [2] that presents such models as an aggregation of following Xcomponents: a textual description P^T of the precedent; its

Figure 2. Iterative creating and using the model of the precedent

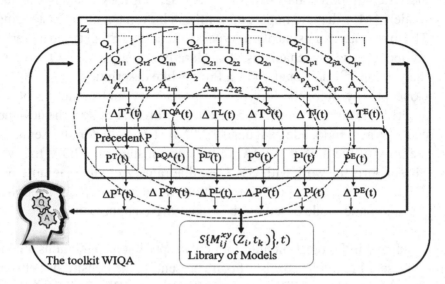

model P^{QA} in the form of the registered QA-reasoning; the logical formulae P^L of the precedent regularity; a graphical (diagram) representation P^G; pseudocode model P^I in a form of a pseudocode program; and a model which presents its executable code P^E. Our choice of these components was caused by the use of similarity between intellectual processing the solution of the task and intellectual processing the conditioned reflexes (Sosnin, 2013).

Suppose, that at time t_j the designer will prepare the next increment $\Delta T_{nr}^{mX}\left(Z_i, t_j\right)$. As it was told above, this verbal item used as the potential model of M^V-type that should be conceptually checked. In the described case, the first check should be fulfilled on understanding by the use of mental experimenting.

When the text $\Delta T_{nr}^{mX}\left(Z_i, t_j\right)$ is visually observable, the designer explicitly or implicitly activates the mental imagination that will lead to creation of the appropriate graphical model as the next increment $\Delta P_{nu}^{mG}\left(Z_i, t_k\right)$ of the component P^G. Formally, such causal transition can be represented by the expression

$$\Delta T_{nr}^{mG}\left(Z_i, t_j\right) \overset{R_1^G}{\to} \Delta P_{nu}^{mG}\left(Z_i, t_k\right) \tag{1}$$

where R_1^G is a reflection provided the transition "text-graphic", and "p" is the unique index of this transition. If the purpose of the transition is the achievement of understanding then

$$\Delta P_{np}^{mG}\left(Z_i, t_k\right) = M_v^{Gy}\left(Z_i, t_k\right) \qquad (2)$$

where $M_r^{Gy}\left(Z_i, t_k\right)$ is the graphical model with the unique index r and $<y>$ is the type of the subordinated model, with which the image $M_r^{Gy}\left(Z_i, t_k\right)$ should be bound. As a value for the reuse, this image should be embedded into the library $S\left\{M_v^{G}\left(Z_i, t_k\right)\right\}, t$.

In turns, it is possible the increment of graphics will lead to the following reflection

$$\Delta P_{np}^{mG}\left(Z_i, t_k\right) \xrightarrow{R_2^z} \Delta St_p^{G}\left(Z_i, t_r\right) \qquad (3)$$

the result of which will develop the current state of the statement of the task

$$St\left(Z_i, t_r\right) = St\left(Z_i, t\right) \cup \Delta St_p^{G}\left(Z_i, t_r\right). \qquad (4)$$

Let us note, transitions among other kinds of increments $\Delta T_{nr}^{mX}\left(Z_i, t_j\right)$ and $\Delta P_{nu}^{mG}\left(Z_i, t_k\right)$ also lead to similar results and effects. Thus, in the process of the stepwise refinement, with the use of feedback, the designer will create the model of the precedent and use it for constructing the solution of corresponding task.

1.5. Declarative Visual Modeling

Above, we have presented the place of the transition between the increment $\Delta T_{nr}^{mG}\left(Z_i, t_j\right)$ and model $M_v^{Gy}\left(Z_i, t_k\right)$ in the precedent-oriented solution of the project task. Both these increments are conceptual models that controllably activate the mental imagination in the real time. As told above any transition can be interpreted as mental experimentation during which the mental imagery helps to achieve the definite aim or aims. When the transition will be aimed at the graphical model of the declarative type (when y=D), the designer will

Figure 3. Iterative coordinating the textual item and its semantic scheme

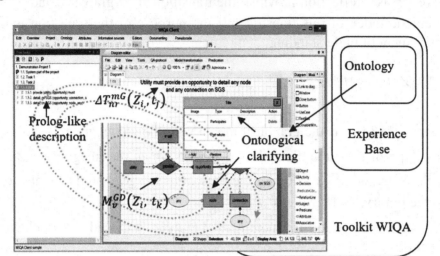

try to understand the item $\Delta T_{nr}^{mG}\left(Z_i, t_j\right)$ and correct it in parallel actions in the operational space shown in Figure 3.

Interacting with the text $\Delta T_{nr}^{mG}\left(Z_i, t_j\right)$, the designer builds the initial version of its semantic scheme $M_v^{Gy}\left(Z_i, t_{k0}\right)$ that automatically reflects on the corresponding Prolog-like description. Then this description is checked by the use of Prolog interpreter and if it has errors, they are corrected by the designer. All changing of the description is automatically reflected in the semantic scheme that can be switched to the ontology for possible corrections of the text and graphics. The designer repeats these actions up to the state when the changes will stop. The achieved state will signalizes that models $\Delta T_{nr}^{mG}\left(Z_i, t_j\right)$ and $M_v^{Gy}\left(Z_i, t_{k0}\right)$ are mutually consistent, errors are absent and the designer understand the text $\Delta T_{nr}^{mG}\left(Z_i, t_j\right)$. Achieving the necessary understanding is a fundamental goal of conceptual experimenting.

2. TRANSFORMATIONS OF FIGURATIVELY SEMANTIC MODELS

2.1. Transformations of Visualized Models

The choice of pointed out models is caused by our decision to support in conceptual activity not only a phenomenon of mental imagery but also model-driven transfer to declarative programming (declarative type) and imperative programming (conceptually algorithmic type).

Let us note, the scheme of types include a number of ways that provide transformations on a set of build and used models. The first way of transformations is reified on the base of the following description of a graph G:

$$G := (V, E), V - \text{a set of nodes}$$
$$E := (V_i, V_j), V_i, V_j \in G \tag{5}$$

where E is a set of relations that define the structure of the graph. In their turn, transformations consist of a number of certain rules that are described as a graph of the search and a graph of the replacement by the following expressions:

$$Rule := G_1, G_2 \text{ , где}$$
$$G_1 := V_1, E_1, V_{H1}, V_{K1} \text{ , } V_{H1}, V_{K1} \in V_1$$
$$G_2 := V_2, E_2 \text{ , } E_2 = \varnothing \tag{6}$$

In our case, as it is specified in the description, the graph of the replacement is degenerated (a set of relations E_2 of the graph G_2 is empty). This is necessary to ensure that every step of receiving a simple graph through a series of transformations to get a graph consisting of a single node (containing the corresponding line of the pseudocode). It should be noted additionally, here rules only given without clarifying a number of details.

The process of transformation can be represented as follows:

if $V_1 \subseteq V \wedge E_1 \subseteq E$, the $G := {}'(V', E')$, where

$$V' = V \cup V_2 \setminus \tag{7}$$

$$V_1, E' = E \cup E_{n2}' \cup E_{k2}' \setminus E_1 \setminus E_{n1}' \setminus E_{k1}, \text{ where :}$$

1. G '- the graph obtained after the application of the rule to the G graph.
2. En2 '- a lot of outgoing links from each node of the graph G and its member V2 (Vn1).
3. Ek2 '- a lot of links coming from V2 (Vk1) and members of each of the nodes G
4. En1 '- a lot of links coming from any node G and included in Vn1.
5. Ek1 '- a lot of links coming from Vk1 and members of each of the node G

In practice, the transformation rules contain additional information necessary for storing data on the semantic block after its convolution. Such information is the pseudocode obtained after applying the transformation. Box 1 shows a small part of the rules.xml file that represents the transformation rule for the IF block of the activity diagram.

Each rule is described by the following tags:

1. "Items" tag. Contains an array of all vertices of the semantic block with their types (in the palette) and unique identifiers (id attribute). The "id" attribute is used later to describe links, input and output vertices.
2. "In" tag. Contains the identifier of the input vertex, the vertex, which has inputs "outside".
3. "Out" tag. It contains the identifier of the output vertex, the vertex, which has an output "outward".

Box 1.

```
- <rule name="if 2 action">
   - <items>
       <item id="1">ActyvityDiagram_Pal.AD_Condition_Element</item>
       <item id="2">ActyvityDiagram_Pal.AD_Action_Element</item>
       <item id="3">ActyvityDiagram_Pal.AD_EndCondition_Element</item>
       <item id="4">ActyvityDiagram_Pal.AD_Action_Element</item>
   </items>
   <in>1</in>
   <out>3</out>
   - <connections>
       <connection id="1cn" note="" to="2" from="1"/>
       <connection id="" note="" to="3" from="2"/>
       <connection id="2cn" note="" to="4" from="1"/>
       <connection id="" note="" to="3" from="4"/>
   </connections>
   <code>IF (1cn.text) THEN\r\n\t2.text\r\nelse if(2cn.text) THEN\r\n\t4.text\r\nEND</code>
   <collapseElementType>ActyvityDiagram_Pal.AD_Action_Element</collapseElementType>
</rule>
```

4. "Connection" tags. Contains information about the relationships within the block. The connection leaves the "from" vertex, enters the vertex "to", has the identifier "id" (necessary for the formation of the pseudocode) and the signature "note". If the signature is not specified, then it is assumed that it can take any value. The id value is recommended to be of the form <number> cn, so that it was immediately clear that there is a call to communication

5. "Code" tag. Contains the rule for obtaining the vertex code. It can contain the <id> .text macro, instead of which the text value of the link or vertex will be substituted.

6. CollapseElementType" tag. Contains the type of the vertex that will be created after the transformation is applied. The vertex type is recommended to be selected within the palette used.

Rules can be combined into groups (convectors), specify synonyms for types of vertices, and combine transformations into chains. The latter is necessary in order to obtain a transformation from ("A" to "C") in the presence of rules for the transformation of models ("A" to "B") and ("B" to "C"). The format for the description of synonyms and the chain of transformations is presented below:

Graph transformation can be ambiguous if there are links that lead to the nodes of the corresponding sub-graph.

Box 2.

```xml
<?xml version="1.0"?>
- <convectors>
    + <convector text_regexp="([A-Яа-я]+[A-Яа-я0-9\ \t]+[\?]?)" name="diagram to code">
    + <convector text_regexp="([A-Яа-я]+[A-Яа-я0-9\ \t]+)" name="diagram to PROMELA">
    + <convector text_regexp="([A-Яа-я]+[A-Яа-я0-9\ \t]+)" name="oracle BPEL to diagram">
    - <groupConvector name="oracle BPEL to PROMELA">
        <convector name="oracle BPEL to diagram"/>
        <convector name="diagram to code"/>
      </groupConvector>
    - <synonyms>
        <synonym to="ActyvityDiagram_Pal.AD_Begin_Element" from="u_m_l_activity_shapes._begin"/>
        <synonym to="ActyvityDiagram_Pal.AD_End_Element" from="u_m_l_activity_shapes._end_element"/>
        <synonym to="ActyvityDiagram_Pal.AD_Condition_Element" from="u_m_l_activity_shapes._decision"/>
        <synonym to="ActyvityDiagram_Pal.AD_EndCondition_Element" from="u_m_l_activity_shapes._end_decision"/>
        <synonym to="ActyvityDiagram_Pal.AD_Action_Element" from="u_m_l_activity_shapes._activity"/>
      </synonyms>
  </convectors>
```

The base of the second way is a replacing the graphical primitives of the block-and-line scheme on the corresponding operator of the specialized pseudocode language (will be clarified below). The third way uses two steps transition from the semantic net of corresponding text to declarative program in the Prolog-like language (Box 2).

2.2. Pictorial Transformations

As told above, the basic feature of transformations for the pictorial type is an automatic reflection of drawn diagrams on their pseudocode descriptions that can be executed by the use of any of three regimes. It is possible to apply an automatic regime with the use of the compiler, the automated regime in the form of handy interpretation and the regime of compositions of compiling and interpreting for chosen parts of the program. The operational space of pictorial transformations is shown in Figure 4

In this case of transformations, the drown diagram corresponds to its program version that is automatically registered in the pseudocode form

Figure 4. Operational space of pictorial transformations

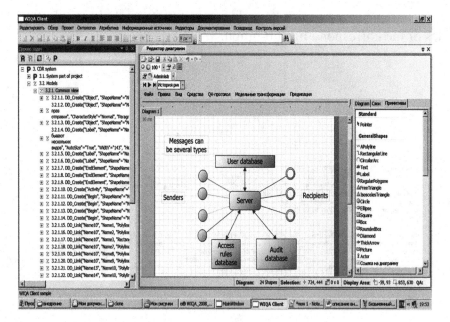

in the left area of the operational space. The basic operators are typical for programming the block-and-line schemes, for example:

1. DD_CREATE – creating the primitive with the use of the chosen panel.
2. DD_LINK - linking the two chosen primitives.
3. DD_UPDATE - modifying the previously created primitives or links.
4. DD_DELETE – removing the chosen primitive or link from the observed diagram.
5. DD_LINKDIAGRAM - linking diagrams together.
6. DD_OPENDIAGRAM - opening the diagram from the corresponding file.

A set of DD_X-operators is embedded into executed pseudocode language of the toolkit WIQA.

2.3. Conceptually Algorithmic Transformations

This kind of transformation uses technics with a graph of the search and graph of the replacement in a full volume. An example presented in Figure

Figure 5. Operational space of conceptually algorithmic transformations

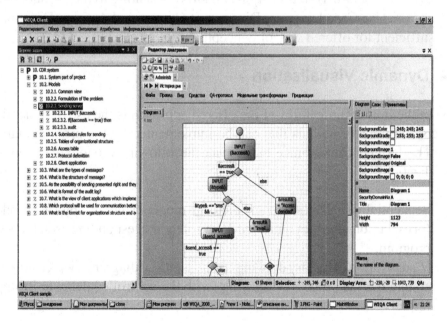

5 reflects the model-driven transition to the pseudocode description for the activity diagram (UML) that we use for creating the Prolog-like programs.

As in the case with the pictorial diagrams, a fragment of the pseudocode program demonstrates the view of transition:

```
& & Result = "";
& & Command = command is received ();
IF service commands? (Command & &) THEN

& Result & = Run command (command &);
ELSE IF commands for working with dictionaries of Ontology (command
      & &)
& Result & = Edit Dictionary command of Ontology (command & &); ELSE
& & Answer = execute command (Command & &);
IF & answer & == "error" THEN
& Result &: = Format error (& & answer);
ELSE
& Result &: = Format (& & answer);
END
END
The Print Console (& & result);
```

Now, the model-driven transition supports translating to the pseudocode only for the Use-Case Diagram, Diagram of Classes and Activity Diagram. It is sufficient for offered way of conceptual solving the project tasks.

2.4. Dynamic Visualization

One of the important features of the offered approach is the use of dynamic effects and transformations that can be implemented by the programmatic way. The designer can organize and activate the following versions of dynamic visualization:

1. Sequential visualization of any pictorial model in the step-by-step mode (or execution with the controlled delay) of the corresponding pseudocode program.
2. Visualization of history drawing for the pictorial diagrams, which allows simulating the process of drawing (with the controlled delay or in step mode).

3.   Use of different placement options. For example, when for distributing the nodes of the model it is convenient to take into account the number of input and output connections. The controlled replacement is available through a consistent application to the created diagram of different options of the placement.

4.   Use of the slide show mode for programmatic transitions from the diagram to diagram that were created, for example, in solving the task.

To realize the possibility of sequential visualization of the created graphic models (saved in the format of a specialized graphic editor) as a slide show, the pseudocode function DD_OpenDiagram was created, which takes as an argument the path to the diagram file. When this function is called in succession, the editor loads the indicated diagrams and simulates a slide show.

To do this, you need (for example, saved models to disks, and a slide show is also available for models stored in the protocol):

1.   Create a task in the project and fill it with the following units:
    ◦   DD_OpenDiagram ("C: // temp / Model calculating coordinates. nspj")
    ◦   DD_OpenDiagram ("C: // temp / Model of the task description. nspj")
    ◦   DD_OpenDiagram ("C: // temp / Test UseCase model.nspj")
2.   Go to the menu "Pseudocode" - "Start the interpreter"
3.   Consistently execute the commands and look at the result in a specialized editor, for example in a view shown in Figure 6.

Figure 6. Example of emulating the slide show

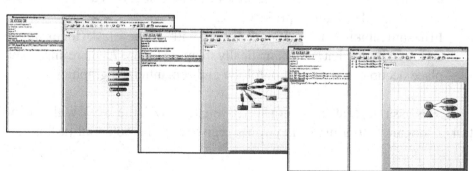

3. SOME DETAILS OF DESIGNER'S WORK WITH A NEW TASK

3.1. Design Thinking in Solving a New Task

Let us return to the role of the new task in our understanding of experience based HCI. This position has the following basic features:

1. In the process of conceptual designing the definite SIS, its developers create and apply the specialized artifact $TT(Z^*, t)$ that reflects the SIS-project from the viewpoint of project tasks.
2. This artifact is used for creating the project theory $Th^P(t)$ and developing the project documentation $P^D(t)$ that is interpreted as one of theory models.
3. In developing the artifacts $TT(Z^*, t)$, $Th^P(t)$ and $P^D(t)$, designers apply reflecting the activity space onto the semantic memory of the QA-type and processing the conceptual objects in this memory in manual, automated and automatic modes.
4. Processing the conceptual objects is based on the question-answer analysis in the context of stepwise refinement of tasks, model-driven development oriented on precedents, and design thinking approach in real-time using the interactions with the affordable experience. 5. Designers use the stepwise refinement when they work:
5. With project tasks $\{Z_i\}$ beginning with initial statement $S(Z^*, t_0)$ of the root task Z^* of the project;
6. With the initial statement $S(Z_i, t_{0i})$ of any project task Z_i the work with which can lead to generating the subordinated project tasks or to the corresponding artifact $TT(Z_i, t)$ and so on.
7. Thus artifact $TT(Z^*, t)$ can be presented as the system $S(\{TT(Z_i, t)\})$, and therefore, in this book, almost all that we suggest can be clarified on an example of a new project task.
8. In design thinking (DT), designers work with any new task (for example Z_i) in conditions that are schematically shown in Figure 7. where important place occupies the project ontology and semanticized graphics.

Let us assume, that in the constructive use of DT, the work with a new task Z_i begins with a list of keywords registering this potential task at the

Figure 7. Conditions of design thinking

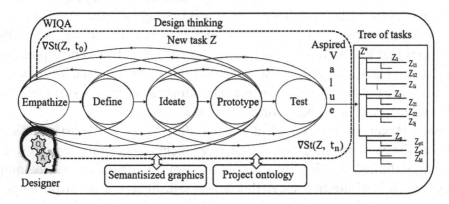

level of an initial uncertainty $\nabla U(Z, t_0)$. In accordance with subsection 3.3.2, this initial state of the task can be presented by an implication

$$?^U U\left(Z_i\right) \xrightarrow{?^W W\left(Z_i\right)} ?^V V\left(Z_i\right) \qquad (8)$$

where symbols $?^U, ?^V$ and $?^W$ indicates applying of QA- approach to the components of a condition U, value V and gap W of the task Z_i.

At the Empathize stage, initial keywords are used by the designer for generating some discourses (Dorst, 2010) that implicitly or explicitly describe future components of the implicative expression of the task Z_i. Wording the discourses, the designer checks them on compliance with the ontology. Additionally, interactions with the ontology help to the designer in extracting the useful questions. Indicated usages of the ontology that lead to reducing the initial uncertainty were described in the seventh section.

Moreover, any of such discourses should be tested on its understanding with the use of an appropriate conceptual experiment that will require expressing the conditions of experimenting and a result of this process. For achieving these goals, the designer can apply appropriate means of the semanticized graphics described above in this section.

At the Define stage, the designer must combine the generated discourses in an understood wholeness where discourses will be coordinated. Actions of this stage also require interacting with the ontology and creating the useful schemes that help the designer in continuous reducing the uncertainty in work with the task Z_i.

The basic feature of the Ideate stage is the search for appropriate ideas that help to solve the task. Therefore, for this stage, a principle role plays extracting the questions from texts created at the previous stage, especially questions that lead to formulating initial statements of tasks corresponding perspective ideas. In any of such statements, working with extracted questions, the designer (or designers) must include information that is sufficient for achieving the physical and algorithmic realizations.

At the Prototype stage, for any alternative idea, the designer must invent and conduct the corresponding conceptual experiment that not only demonstrates the way of the task solution but also discloses some its characteristics helping in comparisons of alternatives. At this stage, the designer can use all developed mechanisms of ontological and figuratively semantic support, including the following possibilities:

1. Discovering the cause-and-effects relations that are implicitly and explicitly expressed in the description of alternative (described in subsection 6.3.1).
2. Useful versions of conceptually algorithmic prototypes that can be built and tested in the WIQA-environment.

The second possibility has the following versions:

1. Pictured prototypes (P-prototypes) that have some similarities with *paper* prototypes [], but P-prototypes are a system of pictorial schemes created in the graphical editor described above. This version of prototypes includes a *drawn* interface that can be combined in an executable system.
2. In the second version of P-prototypes, they are programmed by designers in the pseudocode language L^{WIQA} with the use of drawn interfaces.

It should be noted; that pseudocode means can be applied for combining the pictorial schemes in a prototype system, for example, they can be combined into a slide show with automated or automatic switching among schemes.

Described versions of prototypes can be tested in some versions also. Differences among versions are caused by the following intentions:

1. Orientation on understanding with the use of combining the different architectural viewpoints on the prototype to be tested.
2. Orientation on an understanding the conceptually algorithmic structure of the executable prototype.

Figure 8. Conceptual experiments and mental imaginations in design thinking

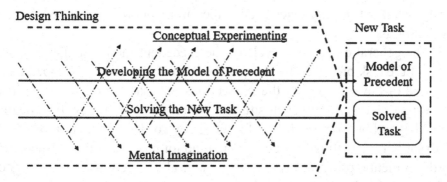

3. Intention to use the ways of testing applied in traditional programming.
4. Attempt to prepare and conduct a conceptual experiment that must demonstrate a model of a precedent for the task to be prototyped.

Told above discloses a number of positive effects that are caused by the use of design in thinking in reactions of designers on new tasks the main of which is the root task Z* of the SISproject. In our version of design thinking, features of its process are schematically shown in Figure 8.

The scheme demonstrates inclusions of conceptual experiments prepared and conducted with the constructive use of mental imaginations in design thinking for reactions on new project tasks.

In the general case of design thinking, in order to construct a solution to a new (unpredictable) task, a set of interrelated conceptual experiments may be required, the results of which will led not only to the task solution on a set of alternatives, but also to the precedent model for this task. As told above, in this process, the designer will interact with natural experience and accessible models of experience for automated imagination, reasoning and conceptual experimenting, and such interactions will be occurred in conditions that are created by designer in conceptual space. By other words, in the real time, the designer creates conditions for the work with the arisen task and develop means of interactions for their using in a task space. Such version of interactions has features that we bound with HCI of experience-based type.

3.2. Space of Precedent-Oriented Activity

The scheme (Figure 2) of the iterative creating and using the model of the precedent has the certain similarity with the scheme of design thinking presented in Figure 7. Analogies with steps of design thinking help us to clarify details of our approaches described in this book. Let us begin these clarifications.

In the general case, a life cycle of the precedent model begins with the intent of the task provoked by the question that is unpredictably appeared in the mind of the designer. In the subsections 5.3.3 and 8.1.2, we described the designer's reaction to such situation when the similar new task begins its life beyond brain in the form of a set of keywords, the function of which are to support activating the question in mind for its reuse. Such influence of words on mental processes is a result of natural interactions of the designer with observable language signs.

Thus, the life cycle of the new task (and a life cycle of the corresponding precedent) begins with the (first) step of registering the observable state of the task containing the list of registered keywords. The basic function of this list is fulfilling the role of a mediator between mental processes and the process of formulating the corresponding question. Even at this step of the life cycle of the task, processes inside and beyond brains are intertwined, and iterative incite the dialogical activity of consciousness and mental imagination or

Figure 9. Space of precedent-oriented solving the project task

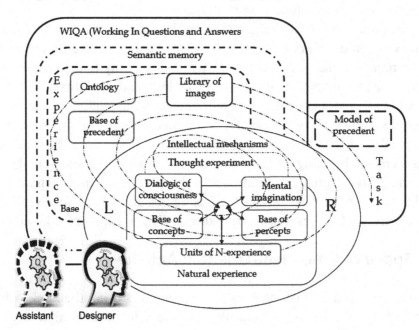

more widely intellectual mechanisms in left (L) and right (R) hemispheres that are schematically shown in Figure 9.

The scheme is also figuratively express that in such processes the designer interacts with a personal intellectual assistant (intellectual processor) in conditions when both of which interacts with natural experience and models of experience correspondingly. The first of them activate access to a base of concept and a base of percept while the second uses a base of precedent and a library of figuratively semantic schemes. At the first step, the greater part of these activities is not activated. The involved activities occur implicitly. Explicitly, the designer can get the help from the use of the ontology.

At the second step of the life cycle, the designer creates a verbal model of the question written in the language of the project. Let us remind, that in our research, we understand a question as the naturally artificial phenomenon that is incited by an attempt of a human to use own natural experience. Therefore, after discovering a question, the designer should identify the type and features of a question, and also build its adequate model, test, and use in accordance with a certain goal.

Actions of the second step are very responsible, and their implementation needs to automate and control. At this step, the use of QA-approach and its means leads to positive effects. For example, regular perceiving the keywords stimulates phenomenon of mental imagery on the search appropriate percepts in their "base." Additionally, keywords repeatedly activate the perception of the question for which they have been registered and this perception as a specific filter influence on the search percepts. Such a way the designer tries graphically expressing the appropriate results of mental imaginations, one of which will be chosen as for writing the verbal model of the question so for its verifying. Described work is better to implement as the conducting of the corresponded conceptual experiment. For this experiment, mental imaginations help to build the condition of its conducting (or precondition of the corresponding question).

It should be noted, that any model is created for certain goals. Therefore, the model of the question must implicitly or explicitly express the question appointment that will help in creating an answer. In the general case, a question corresponds to a task and creating the answer requires developing a way for solving the task. Additionally, we note, the question model should take into account the users of a future answer. In design thinking, it is achieved by an empathizing activated by the designer. Therefore, all told about the question model points out the wide area for conceptual experimenting in creating this model.

The goal of the third step of the life cycle is to find a way to creating an appropriate answer (let us suppose for the question of the task type). In the process of design thinking, this step corresponds to a generation of useful hypothesis or promising idea. For the support of generating, in the use of our approaches, the designer can apply QA-analysis and mental imaginations incited by the figuratively semantic schemes.

At the fourth step, the design thinking scheme suggests using appropriate prototyping. The typical version of prototyping is visualizing the alternatives for their comparing. In the WIQA toolkit, such version of prototyping is accessible, but this toolkit allows building the prototypes in forms of executed QA-programs and, therefore, programmed prototypes are more effective. Moreover, they are more suitable for their testing at the fifth step of the life cycle. In the design thinking, this step has name "Test."

Moreover, for the task and the corresponding precedent model, described steps of their life cycles are fulfilled with the use of precedent-oriented approach, features, and effects of which were described above. Thus, question-answer approach and precedent-oriented approach can find their applications not only in designing the system but, for example, in the subject area of "Design thinking" also.

4. SOME NOTES TO THE CHAPTER 8

1. One of the main intellectual phenomena of a person is a mental imagination that helps to simulate perception in conditions when, for various reasons, the streams of information coming from the senses of a person in real time can be implicitly or explicitly disconnected.
2. Without a mental imagination, it is impossible the meaningful understanding of the perceived situations even in cases of active using the sense organs, and also forecasting the situations in the future.
3. One of the especially useful functions of imagination is a support of a mental experimenting in different conditions and for different purposes.
4. When a designer interacts with a computer screen natural and artificial lines of interactions are intertwined, and in this intertwining processes, natural components of integrated imaginations play the role of filters that help to construct an integrated result in any situation perceived with the screen.

5. Therefore, it is useful to model an artificial line of imagination, for example, with the help of visualized images that are aimed at activating the necessary line of natural imagination for managing of this line and increasing the positive effect from this phenomenon.

6. That is why in interactions with computerized technologies of developing the systems, designers actively apply various method and means of visualization, for example, UML diagrams.

7. In our approaches to the conceptual design, we could not pass by this phenomenon and paid special attention to automating the mental imagination, especially in the context of working with new tasks.

8. With orienting on design thinking, we have developed a complex of means that provide constructive using of three types of visualization each of which has graphical and corresponding program forms.

9. These forms correspond graphical (pictorial), declarative and conceptually algorithmic versions of (pseudocode) programming that help to build the corresponding versions of prototypes in design thinking.

10. In any version of visualization, the designer has the possibility to use the ontological support in the work with the image and its program form.

11. Having the program forms of images opens the possibility for the use of pseudocode programming for achieving the effects of dynamic visualization.

12. Automated mental imagination and interactions with the project ontology are intensively used in conceptual experimenting that, in design thinking, provides achieving the understanding in creating the textual units and checking the regularities expressed in verbal forms.

13. Additionally, conceptual experimenting helps to build and test prototypes developing during design thinking in work with a new task as for the searching its solution so for developing the corresponding model of the precedent.

14. In the line of creating the project theory, each application of design thinking to a new task is a source of new and tested theoretical constructs and also play the role of generating the next rule of inference in this theory.

15. In described version of design thinking, the designer interacts with natural experience and accessible models of experience for automated imagination, reasoning, and conceptual experimenting, and such interactions will occur in conditions that are created by a designer in conceptual space.

16. Moreover, the designer creates necessary conditions for the work with any new task and develop means of interactions for their use in the space of this task. Taking into account the features of such interactions of a human with a computerized environment, they were named as CHI of the experience-based type.

5. CONCLUSION

Our research and developments described in this book were targeted for the search of innovations in interactions of people with computerized environments in forms which are similar to (natural) interactions of the human with a natural environment (with the physical world). This goal was caused by the fact that existing forms of human-computer interactions are far from the naturalness, and such the state of affairs is a source of different problems one of which is an incredibly low level of the success (about 40%) in designing the systems that intensive use of the software. In our deep opinion, one of the promising area for the search of innovations is bound with a type of human-computer interactions that facilitate the increasing of the success in designing this class of systems. All in this book implicitly or explicitly concern these systems.

The main our innovations are question-answer approach and precedent-oriented approach, combining of which in conceptual designing the systems facilitate achieving some positive effects that were described above. The central place in these approaches occupies experience-based human-computer interaction that has following features:

1. Demonstrates own existence trough question-answering that activated by the designer in interactions with the accessible experience in conceptual solutions of project tasks in designing the systems with the software;
2. Involves in its processes of natural interactions of the designer with operational space in monitor screen and artificially natural interactions implemented by the same designer who fulfills the role of the intellectual processor. Both of these lines of interactions are intertwined for achieving the target;
3. Supports the real-time interactions with accessible experience as in predictable so in unpredictable situations perceived on a monitor screen of a computer;

4. Focuses on interactions with conceptual objects and scenes with their compositions that are observable in conceptual space reified in the semantic memory (in our version this space is formed in the semantic memory of the WIQA);
5. Provides controlled influences on mental processes in the designer's mind, at least on mental imaginations and experimentation.

Indicated features define the essence of experience-based HCI described in this book. This kind of interactions helped us (and will help to designers of SISs) to define and develop (for the effective use in designing) following useful artifacts:

1. Tree of tasks, states of which register results of question-answer analysis of the conceptual view on the project from the viewpoint of tasks to be solved. This artifact fulfills the role of a collections of models of tasks, and it is also an informational source for creating the project theory and the system of project documents.
2. Substantially evolutionary kind of project theory, the kernel of which includes the description phase that is visualized in the form of the semantic net that includes, for example, nodes expressing principles, assertions, settings, requirements, restrictions, motives, goals, factors, conditions, consequences, effects, arguments, cautions, advice, remarks and others that unite in the useful wholeness.
3. Framework intended for creation models of precedents for corresponding tasks. By another word, this framework is coordinated with reflecting any project task on the theory of the project, and this reflection for the certain task is its precedent model that integrate a set of theoretical constructs and models.
4. A set of kinds of conceptual representations for basic essences used in designing the systems, for example, tasks, workflows designers, groups of designers, teams, units of experience, models of precedents, ontology, base od precedents and other essences.

With orientation on the experience-based HCI we developed:

1. Question-answer approach as a system of methods and corresponding artifacts that provide creative work of designers at the conceptual stage of designing the systems;

2. Precedent-oriented approach that provides conceptual solutions of project tasks and in parallel help to build models of precedents for corresponding tasks;
3. Instrumental system that provides conceptually algorithmic programming of tasks, objects of which are placed in the semantic memory
4. Methods and means that provide conducting the conceptual experiments.
5. Methods and means that provide ontological and figuratively semantic support in the conceptual solution of project tasks and other actions of conceptual designing.

All told above in this subsection was a source of reasons and requirements for the development the WIQA toolkits in the several version, the use of which provide the corresponding system of workflows. Potential of the WIQA toolkits was used as for self-development and for developing a number of systems based on the WIQA.

REFERENCES

Dorst, K. (2010). *The Nature of Design Thinking, in DTRS8 Interpreting Design Thinking: Design Thinking Research Symposium Proceedings*. Available at http://epress.lib.uts.edu.au/research/handle/10453/16590

Moulton, S. T., & Kosslyn, St. M. (2009). Imagining predictions: Mental imagery as mental emulation Phil. *Trans. R. Soc. B, 364*(1521), 1273–1280. doi:10.1098/rstb.2008.0314 PMID:19528008

Petre, M. (2010). Mental imagery and software visualization in high-performance software development teams. *Journal of Visual Languages and Computing, 21*(3), 171–183. doi:10.1016/j.jvlc.2009.11.001

Pylyshyn, Z. (2002). Mental Imagery: In Search of a Theory. *Behavioral and Brain Sciences, 25*(2), 157–237. doi:10.1017/S0140525X02000043 PMID:12744144

Sosnin, P. (2016) Figuratively semantic support in precedent-oriented solving the Project Tasks. *Proc. of the 10th International Conference on Application of Information and Communication Technologies*, 479-481.

Sosnin, P., Galochkin, M., & Luneckas, A. (2016). *Figuratively Semantic Support in Interactions of a Designer with a Statement of a Project Task. In Advances in Intelligent Systems and Computing* (Vol. 451, pp. 257–267). Springer International Publishing.

Wiel, W. M., Hasberg, M. P., Weima, I., & Huiskamp, W. (2010). Concept Maturity Levels Bringing structure to the CD&E process. *Proc. of Interservice industry training, simulation and education conference*, 2547-2555.

ADDITIONAL READING

Alberts, D. S., & Hayes, R. E. (2005). *Campaigns of Experimentation.* Washington, DC: CCRP.

Alberts, D. S., & Hayes, R. E. (2006). *Understanding Command and Control.* Washington, DC: CCRP.

Brown, T. (2009). *Change by Design: How Design Thinking Transforms Organizations and Inspires Innovation.* HarperBusiness.

Henninger, S. (2003). Tool Support for Experience-based Software Development Methodologies. *Advances in Computers, 59,* 29–82. doi:10.1016/S0065-2458(03)59002-7

Lengler, R., & Eppler, M. J. (2007). Towards A Periodic Table of Visualization Methods for Management. In *Proceedings of the IASTED International Conference on Graphics and Visualization in Engineering (GVE '07)*, Mohammad Alam (Ed.). ACTA Press, Anaheim, CA, USA, pp. 83-88.

MCM-0056-2010, (2010). NATO Concept Development and Experimentation (CD&E) Process. Brussels: NATO HQ.

Sosnin, P. (2012). Question-Answer Approach to Human-Computer Interaction in Collaborative Designing. Chapter in the book Cognitively Informed Intelligent Interfaces: Systems Design and Development Published IGI Global, pp. 157-176 doi:10.4018/978-1-4666-1628-8.ch010

Sosnin, P. (2012). Experiential Human-Computer Interaction in Collaborative Designing of Software Intensive Systems, In *Proc. of 11th International conference on Software Methodology and Techniques*, pp. 180-197.

16. Sosnin, P. (2013). A Scientifically Experimental Approach to the Simulation of Designer Activity in The Conceptual Designing of Software Intensive Systems. *IEEE ACCESS*, *1*, 488–504. doi:10.1109/ACCESS.2013.2274896

Sosnin, P. (2013). Role Intellectual Processor in Conceptual Designing Of Software Intensive Systems. In proc. of the 11-th International Conference on Computational Science and Applications, Part III, LNCS 7973 Springer, Heidelberg, pp. 1-16. doi:10.1007/978-3-642-39646-5_1

Sosnin, P. (2016). Processing of a New Task in Conditions of the Agile Management with Using of Programmable Queues. *LNCS*, *9789*, 554–569.

Sosnin, P. (2016). Precedent-Oriented Approach to Conceptually Experimental Activity in Designing the Software Intensive Systems. *International Journal of Ambient Computing and Intelligence*, *7*(1), 69–93. doi:10.4018/IJACI.2016010104

Sosnin, P., "A place and role of an ontology in using a base of experience in designing the software intensive systems", International Journal of Web Information Systems, Vol. 12 (1), pp.62 – 82

Related Readings

To continue IGI Global's long-standing tradition of advancing innovation through emerging research, please find below a compiled list of recommended IGI Global book chapters and journal articles in the areas of human-computer interaction, artificial intelligence, and smart environments. These related readings will provide additional information and guidance to further enrich your knowledge and assist you with your own research.

Abdulrahman, M. D., Subramanian, N., Chan, H. K., & Ning, K. (2017). Big Data Analytics: Academic Perspectives. In H. Chan, N. Subramanian, & M. Abdulrahman (Eds.), *Supply Chain Management in the Big Data Era* (pp. 1–12). Hershey, PA: IGI Global. doi:10.4018/978-1-5225-0956-1.ch001

Al-Aiad, A., Alkhatib, K., Al-Ayyad, M., & Hmeidi, I. (2016). A Conceptual Framework of Smart Home Context: An Empirical Investigation. *International Journal of Healthcare Information Systems and Informatics*, *11*(3), 42–56. doi:10.4018/IJHISI.2016070103

Almajano, P., Lopez-Sanchez, M., Rodriguez, I., Puig, A., Llorente, M. S., & Ribera, M. (2016). Training Infrastructure to Participate in Real Life Institutions: Learning through Virtual Worlds. In F. Neto, R. de Souza, & A. Gomes (Eds.), *Handbook of Research on 3-D Virtual Environments and Hypermedia for Ubiquitous Learning* (pp. 192–219). Hershey, PA: IGI Global. doi:10.4018/978-1-5225-0125-1.ch008

Ammari, H. M., Shaout, A., & Mustapha, F. (2017). Sensing Coverage in Three-Dimensional Space: A Survey. In N. Ray & A. Turuk (Eds.), *Handbook of Research on Advanced Wireless Sensor Network Applications, Protocols, and Architectures* (pp. 1–28). Hershey, PA: IGI Global. doi:10.4018/978-1-5225-0486-3.ch001

Ang, L., Seng, K. P., & Heng, T. Z. (2016). Information Communication Assistive Technologies for Visually Impaired People. *International Journal of Ambient Computing and Intelligence*, *7*(1), 45–68. doi:10.4018/IJACI.2016010103

Ang, R. P., Tan, J. L., Goh, D. H., Huan, V. S., Ooi, Y. P., Boon, J. S., & Fung, D. S. (2017). A Game-Based Approach to Teaching Social Problem-Solving Skills. In R. Zheng & M. Gardner (Eds.), *Handbook of Research on Serious Games for Educational Applications* (pp. 168–195). Hershey, PA: IGI Global. doi:10.4018/978-1-5225-0513-6.ch008

Anthopoulos, L., Janssen, M., & Weerakkody, V. (2016). A Unified Smart City Model (USCM) for Smart City Conceptualization and Benchmarking. *International Journal of Electronic Government Research*, *12*(2), 77–93. doi:10.4018/IJEGR.2016040105

Antonova, A. (2017). Preparing for the Forthcoming Industrial Revolution: Beyond Virtual Worlds Technologies for Competence Development and Learning. *International Journal of Virtual and Augmented Reality*, *1*(1), 16–28. doi:10.4018/IJVAR.2017010102

Applin, S. A., & Fischer, M. D. (2017). Thing Theory: Connecting Humans to Smart Healthcare. In C. Reis & M. Maximiano (Eds.), *Internet of Things and Advanced Application in Healthcare* (pp. 249–265). Hershey, PA: IGI Global. doi:10.4018/978-1-5225-1820-4.ch009

Armstrong, S., & Yampolskiy, R. V. (2017). Security Solutions for Intelligent and Complex Systems. In M. Dawson, M. Eltayeb, & M. Omar (Eds.), *Security Solutions for Hyperconnectivity and the Internet of Things* (pp. 37–88). Hershey, PA: IGI Global. doi:10.4018/978-1-5225-0741-3.ch003

Auza, J. M., & de Marca, J. R. (2017). A Mobility Model for Crowd Sensing Simulation. *International Journal of Interdisciplinary Telecommunications and Networking*, *9*(1), 14–25. doi:10.4018/IJITN.2017010102

Ayesh, A., Arevalillo-Herráez, M., & Ferri, F. J. (2016). Towards Psychologically based Personalised Modelling of Emotions Using Associative Classifiers. *International Journal of Cognitive Informatics and Natural Intelligence*, *10*(2), 52–64. doi:10.4018/IJCINI.2016040103

Badilla, G. L., & Gaynor, J. M. (2017). Analysis of New Opotoelectronic Device for Detection of Heavy Metals in Corroded Soils: Design a Novel Optoelectronic Devices. In O. Sergiyenko & J. Rodriguez-Quiñonez (Eds.), *Developing and Applying Optoelectronics in Machine Vision* (pp. 273–302). Hershey, PA: IGI Global. doi:10.4018/978-1-5225-0632-4.ch009

Balas, C. E. (2016). An Artificial Neural Network Model as the Decision Support System of Ports. In E. Ocalir-Akunal (Ed.), *Using Decision Support Systems for Transportation Planning Efficiency* (pp. 36–60). Hershey, PA: IGI Global. doi:10.4018/978-1-4666-8648-9.ch002

Barbeito, A., Painho, M., Cabral, P., & ONeill, J. G. (2017). Beyond Digital Human Body Atlases: Segmenting an Integrated 3D Topological Model of the Human Body. *International Journal of E-Health and Medical Communications*, 8(1), 19–36. doi:10.4018/IJEHMC.2017010102

Berrahal, S., & Boudriga, N. (2017). The Risks of Wearable Technologies to Individuals and Organizations. In A. Marrington, D. Kerr, & J. Gammack (Eds.), *Managing Security Issues and the Hidden Dangers of Wearable Technologies* (pp. 18–46). Hershey, PA: IGI Global. doi:10.4018/978-1-5225-1016-1.ch002

Bhargavi, P., Jyothi, S., & Mamatha, D. M. (2017). A Study on Hybridization of Intelligent Techniques in Bioinformatics. In S. Bhattacharyya, S. De, I. Pan, & P. Dutta (Eds.), *Intelligent Multidimensional Data Clustering and Analysis* (pp. 358–379). Hershey, PA: IGI Global. doi:10.4018/978-1-5225-1776-4.ch014

Bhattacharya, S. (2017). A Predictive Linear Regression Model for Affective State Detection of Mobile Touch Screen Users. *International Journal of Mobile Human Computer Interaction*, 9(1), 30–44. doi:10.4018/IJMHCI.2017010103

Biagi, L., Comai, S., Mangiarotti, R., Matteucci, M., Negretti, M., & Yavuz, S. U. (2017). Enriching Geographic Maps with Accessible Paths Derived from Implicit Mobile Device Data Collection. In S. Konomi & G. Roussos (Eds.), *Enriching Urban Spaces with Ambient Computing, the Internet of Things, and Smart City Design* (pp. 89–113). Hershey, PA: IGI Global. doi:10.4018/978-1-5225-0827-4.ch005

Bogatinov, D. S., Bogdanoski, M., & Angelevski, S. (2016). AI-Based Cyber Defense for More Secure Cyberspace. In M. Hadji-Janev & M. Bogdanoski (Eds.), *Handbook of Research on Civil Society and National Security in the Era of Cyber Warfare* (pp. 220–237). Hershey, PA: IGI Global. doi:10.4018/978-1-4666-8793-6.ch011

Bottrighi, A., Leonardi, G., Piovesan, L., & Terenziani, P. (2016). Knowledge-Based Support to the Treatment of Exceptions in Computer Interpretable Clinical Guidelines. *International Journal of Knowledge-Based Organizations*, *6*(3), 1–27. doi:10.4018/IJKBO.2016070101

Bureš, V., Tučník, P., Mikulecký, P., Mls, K., & Blecha, P. (2016). Application of Ambient Intelligence in Educational Institutions: Visions and Architectures. *International Journal of Ambient Computing and Intelligence*, *7*(1), 94–120. doi:10.4018/IJACI.2016010105

Castellet, A. (2016). What If Devices Take Command: Content Innovation Perspectives for Smart Wearables in the Mobile Ecosystem. *International Journal of Handheld Computing Research*, *7*(2), 16–33. doi:10.4018/IJHCR.2016040102

Champaty, B., Ray, S. S., Mohapatra, B., & Pal, K. (2017). Voluntary Blink Controlled Communication Protocol for Bed-Ridden Patients. In N. Kamila (Ed.), *Handbook of Research on Wireless Sensor Network Trends, Technologies, and Applications* (pp. 162–195). Hershey, PA: IGI Global. doi:10.4018/978-1-5225-0501-3.ch008

Chawla, S. (2017). Multi-Agent-Based Information Retrieval System Using Information Scent in Query Log Mining for Effective Web Search. In G. Sreedhar (Ed.), *Web Data Mining and the Development of Knowledge-Based Decision Support Systems* (pp. 131–156). Hershey, PA: IGI Global. doi:10.4018/978-1-5225-1877-8.ch008

Chen, G., Wang, E., Sun, X., & Lu, Y. (2016). An Intelligent Approval System for City Construction based on Cloud Computing and Big Data. *International Journal of Grid and High Performance Computing*, *8*(3), 57–69. doi:10.4018/IJGHPC.2016070104

Cointault, F., Han, S., Rabatel, G., Jay, S., Rousseau, D., Billiot, B., & Salon, C. et al. (2017). 3D Imaging Systems for Agricultural Applications: Characterization of Crop and Root Phenotyping. In O. Sergiyenko & J. Rodriguez-Quiñonez (Eds.), *Developing and Applying Optoelectronics in Machine Vision* (pp. 236–272). Hershey, PA: IGI Global. doi:10.4018/978-1-5225-0632-4.ch008

Connor, A. M. (2016). A Historical Review of Creative Technologies. In A. Connor & S. Marks (Eds.), *Creative Technologies for Multidisciplinary Applications* (pp. 1–24). Hershey, PA: IGI Global. doi:10.4018/978-1-5225-0016-2.ch001

Connor, A. M., Sosa, R., Karmokar, S., Marks, S., Buxton, M., Gribble, A. M., & Foottit, J. et al. (2016). Exposing Core Competencies for Future Creative Technologists. In A. Connor & S. Marks (Eds.), *Creative Technologies for Multidisciplinary Applications* (pp. 377–397). Hershey, PA: IGI Global. doi:10.4018/978-1-5225-0016-2.ch015

Cook, A. E., & Wei, W. (2017). Using Eye Movements to Study Reading Processes: Methodological Considerations. In C. Was, F. Sansosti, & B. Morris (Eds.), *Eye-Tracking Technology Applications in Educational Research* (pp. 27–47). Hershey, PA: IGI Global. doi:10.4018/978-1-5225-1005-5.ch002

Corradini, A., & Mehta, M. (2016). A Graphical Tool for the Creation of Behaviors in Virtual Worlds. In J. Turner, M. Nixon, U. Bernardet, & S. DiPaola (Eds.), *Integrating Cognitive Architectures into Virtual Character Design* (pp. 65–93). Hershey, PA: IGI Global. doi:10.4018/978-1-5225-0454-2.ch003

Corrêa, L. D., & Dorn, M. (2017). Multi-Agent Systems in Three-Dimensional Protein Structure Prediction. In D. Adamatti (Ed.), *Multi-Agent-Based Simulations Applied to Biological and Environmental Systems* (pp. 241–278). Hershey, PA: IGI Global. doi:10.4018/978-1-5225-1756-6.ch011

Croatti, A., Ricci, A., & Viroli, M. (2017). Towards a Mobile Augmented Reality System for Emergency Management: The Case of SAFE. *International Journal of Distributed Systems and Technologies*, 8(1), 46–58. doi:10.4018/IJDST.2017010104

Dafer, M., & El-Abed, M. (2017). Evaluation of Keystroke Dynamics Authentication Systems: Analysis of Physical and Touch Screen Keyboards. In M. Dawson, D. Kisku, P. Gupta, J. Sing, & W. Li (Eds.), *Developing Next-Generation Countermeasures for Homeland Security Threat Prevention* (pp. 306–329). Hershey, PA: IGI Global. doi:10.4018/978-1-5225-0703-1.ch014

Das, P. K., Ghosh, D., Jagtap, P., Joshi, A., & Finin, T. (2017). Preserving User Privacy and Security in Context-Aware Mobile Platforms. In S. Mukherjea (Ed.), *Mobile Application Development, Usability, and Security* (pp. 166–193). Hershey, PA: IGI Global. doi:10.4018/978-1-5225-0945-5.ch008

De Filippi, F., Coscia, C., & Guido, R. (2017). How Technologies Can Enhance Open Policy Making and Citizen-Responsive Urban Planning: MiraMap - A Governing Tool for the Mirafiori Sud District in Turin (Italy). *International Journal of E-Planning Research, 6*(1), 23–42. doi:10.4018/IJEPR.2017010102

De Pasquale, D., Wood, E., Gottardo, A., Jones, J. A., Kaplan, R., & DeMarco, A. (2017). Tracking Children's Interactions with Traditional Text and Computer-Based Early Literacy Media. In C. Was, F. Sansosti, & B. Morris (Eds.), *Eye-Tracking Technology Applications in Educational Research* (pp. 107–121). Hershey, PA: IGI Global. doi:10.4018/978-1-5225-1005-5.ch006

Del Fiore, G., Mainetti, L., Mighali, V., Patrono, L., Alletto, S., Cucchiara, R., & Serra, G. (2016). A Location-Aware Architecture for an IoT-Based Smart Museum. *International Journal of Electronic Government Research, 12*(2), 39–55. doi:10.4018/IJEGR.2016040103

Desjarlais, M. (2017). The Use of Eye-gaze to Understand Multimedia Learning. In C. Was, F. Sansosti, & B. Morris (Eds.), *Eye-Tracking Technology Applications in Educational Research* (pp. 122–142). Hershey, PA: IGI Global. doi:10.4018/978-1-5225-1005-5.ch007

Diviacco, P., & Leadbetter, A. (2017). Balancing Formalization and Representation in Cross-Domain Data Management for Sustainable Development. In P. Diviacco, A. Leadbetter, & H. Glaves (Eds.), *Oceanographic and Marine Cross-Domain Data Management for Sustainable Development* (pp. 23–46). Hershey, PA: IGI Global. doi:10.4018/978-1-5225-0700-0.ch002

Dragoicea, M., Falcao e Cunha, J., Alexandru, M. V., & Constantinescu, D. A. (2017). Modelling and Simulation Perspective in Service Design: Experience in Transport Information Service Development. In S. Rozenes & Y. Cohen (Eds.), *Handbook of Research on Strategic Alliances and Value Co-Creation in the Service Industry* (pp. 374–399). Hershey, PA: IGI Global. doi:10.4018/978-1-5225-2084-9.ch019

El Khayat, G. A., & Fashal, N. A. (2017). Inter and Intra Cities Smartness: A Survey on Location Problems and GIS Tools. In S. Faiz & K. Mahmoudi (Eds.), *Handbook of Research on Geographic Information Systems Applications and Advancements* (pp. 296–320). Hershey, PA: IGI Global. doi:10.4018/978-1-5225-0937-0.ch011

Eteme, A. A., & Ngossaha, J. M. (2017). Urban Master Data Management: Case of the YUSIIP Platform. In S. Faiz & K. Mahmoudi (Eds.), *Handbook of Research on Geographic Information Systems Applications and Advancements* (pp. 441–465). Hershey, PA: IGI Global. doi:10.4018/978-1-5225-0937-0.ch018

Fisher, K. J., Nichols, T., Isbister, K., & Fuller, T. (2017). Quantifying "Magic": Creating Good Player Experiences on Xbox Kinect. In B. Dubbels (Ed.), *Transforming Gaming and Computer Simulation Technologies across Industries* (pp. 1–16). Hershey, PA: IGI Global. doi:10.4018/978-1-5225-1817-4.ch001

Flores-Fuentes, W., Rivas-Lopez, M., Hernandez-Balbuena, D., Sergiyenko, O., Rodríguez-Quiñonez, J. C., Rivera-Castillo, J., & Basaca-Preciado, L. C. et al. (2017). Applying Optoelectronic Devices Fusion in Machine Vision: Spatial Coordinate Measurement. In O. Sergiyenko & J. Rodriguez-Quiñonez (Eds.), *Developing and Applying Optoelectronics in Machine Vision* (pp. 1–37). Hershey, PA: IGI Global. doi:10.4018/978-1-5225-0632-4.ch001

Forti, I. (2017). A Cross Reading of Landscape through Digital Landscape Models: The Case of Southern Garda. In A. Ippolito (Ed.), *Handbook of Research on Emerging Technologies for Architectural and Archaeological Heritage* (pp. 532–561). Hershey, PA: IGI Global. doi:10.4018/978-1-5225-0675-1.ch018

Gammack, J., & Marrington, A. (2017). The Promise and Perils of Wearable Technologies. In A. Marrington, D. Kerr, & J. Gammack (Eds.), *Managing Security Issues and the Hidden Dangers of Wearable Technologies* (pp. 1–17). Hershey, PA: IGI Global. doi:10.4018/978-1-5225-1016-1.ch001

Ghaffarianhoseini, A., Ghaffarianhoseini, A., Tookey, J., Omrany, H., Fleury, A., Naismith, N., & Ghaffarianhoseini, M. (2016). The Essence of Smart Homes: Application of Intelligent Technologies towards Smarter Urban Future. In A. Connor & S. Marks (Eds.), *Creative Technologies for Multidisciplinary Applications* (pp. 334–376). Hershey, PA: IGI Global. doi:10.4018/978-1-5225-0016-2.ch014

Gharbi, A., De Runz, C., & Akdag, H. (2017). Urban Development Modelling: A Survey. In S. Faiz & K. Mahmoudi (Eds.), *Handbook of Research on Geographic Information Systems Applications and Advancements* (pp. 96–124). Hershey, PA: IGI Global. doi:10.4018/978-1-5225-0937-0.ch004

Ghosh, S., Mitra, S., Ghosh, S., & Chakraborty, S. (2017). Seismic Reliability Analysis in the Framework of Metamodelling Based Monte Carlo Simulation. In P. Samui, S. Chakraborty, & D. Kim (Eds.), *Modeling and Simulation Techniques in Structural Engineering* (pp. 192–208). Hershey, PA: IGI Global. doi:10.4018/978-1-5225-0588-4.ch006

Guesgen, H. W., & Marsland, S. (2016). Using Contextual Information for Recognising Human Behaviour. *International Journal of Ambient Computing and Intelligence*, 7(1), 27–44. doi:10.4018/IJACI.2016010102

Hameur Laine, A., & Brahimi, S. (2017). Background on Context-Aware Computing Systems. In C. Reis & M. Maximiano (Eds.), *Internet of Things and Advanced Application in Healthcare* (pp. 1–31). Hershey, PA: IGI Global. doi:10.4018/978-1-5225-1820-4.ch001

Harrati, N., Bouchrika, I., Mahfouf, Z., & Ladjailia, A. (2017). Evaluation Methods for E-Learning Applications in Terms of User Satisfaction and Interface Usability. In P. Vu, S. Fredrickson, & C. Moore (Eds.), *Handbook of Research on Innovative Pedagogies and Technologies for Online Learning in Higher Education* (pp. 427–448). Hershey, PA: IGI Global. doi:10.4018/978-1-5225-1851-8.ch018

Harwood, T. (2016). Machinima: A Meme of Our Time. In A. Connor & S. Marks (Eds.), *Creative Technologies for Multidisciplinary Applications* (pp. 149–181). Hershey, PA: IGI Global. doi:10.4018/978-1-5225-0016-2.ch007

Hassani, K., & Lee, W. (2016). A Universal Architecture for Migrating Cognitive Agents: A Case Study on Automatic Animation Generation. In J. Turner, M. Nixon, U. Bernardet, & S. DiPaola (Eds.), *Integrating Cognitive Architectures into Virtual Character Design* (pp. 238–265). Hershey, PA: IGI Global. doi:10.4018/978-1-5225-0454-2.ch009

Herpich, F., Nunes, F. B., Voss, G. B., & Medina, R. D. (2016). Three-Dimensional Virtual Environment and NPC: A Perspective about Intelligent Agents Ubiquitous. In F. Neto, R. de Souza, & A. Gomes (Eds.), *Handbook of Research on 3-D Virtual Environments and Hypermedia for Ubiquitous Learning* (pp. 510–536). Hershey, PA: IGI Global. doi:10.4018/978-1-5225-0125-1.ch021

Higgins, C., Kearns, Á., Ryan, C., & Fernstrom, M. (2016). The Role of Gamification and Evolutionary Computation in the Provision of Self-Guided Speech Therapy. In D. Novák, B. Tulu, & H. Brendryen (Eds.), *Handbook of Research on Holistic Perspectives in Gamification for Clinical Practice* (pp. 158–182). Hershey, PA: IGI Global. doi:10.4018/978-1-4666-9522-1.ch008

Honarvar, A. R., & Sami, A. (2016). Extracting Usage Patterns from Power Usage Data of Homes Appliances in Smart Home using Big Data Platform. *International Journal of Information Technology and Web Engineering*, *11*(2), 39–50. doi:10.4018/IJITWE.2016040103

Hulsey, N. (2016). Between Games and Simulation: Gamification and Convergence in Creative Computing. In A. Connor & S. Marks (Eds.), *Creative Technologies for Multidisciplinary Applications* (pp. 130–148). Hershey, PA: IGI Global. doi:10.4018/978-1-5225-0016-2.ch006

Ion, A., & Patrascu, M. (2017). Agent Based Modelling of Smart Structures: The Challenges of a New Research Domain. In P. Samui, S. Chakraborty, & D. Kim (Eds.), *Modeling and Simulation Techniques in Structural Engineering* (pp. 38–60). Hershey, PA: IGI Global. doi:10.4018/978-1-5225-0588-4.ch002

Iyawe, B. I. (2017). User Performance Testing Indicator: User Performance Indicator Tool (UPIT). In S. Saeed, Y. Bamarouf, T. Ramayah, & S. Iqbal (Eds.), *Design Solutions for User-Centric Information Systems* (pp. 205–229). Hershey, PA: IGI Global. doi:10.4018/978-1-5225-1944-7.ch012

Izumi, S., Hata, M., Takahira, H., Soylu, M., Edo, A., Abe, T., & Suganuma, T. (2017). A Proposal of SDN Based Disaster-Aware Smart Routing for Highly-Available Information Storage Systems and Its Evaluation. *International Journal of Software Science and Computational Intelligence*, 9(1), 68–82. doi:10.4018/IJSSCI.2017010105

Jarušek, R., & Kocian, V. (2017). Artificial Intelligence Algorithms for Classification and Pattern Recognition. In E. Volna, M. Kotyrba, & M. Janosek (Eds.), *Pattern Recognition and Classification in Time Series Data* (pp. 53–85). Hershey, PA: IGI Global. doi:10.4018/978-1-5225-0565-5.ch003

Jayabalan, J., Yildirim, D., Kim, D., & Samui, P. (2017). Design Optimization of a Wind Turbine Using Artificial Intelligence. In M. Ram & J. Davim (Eds.), *Mathematical Concepts and Applications in Mechanical Engineering and Mechatronics* (pp. 38–66). Hershey, PA: IGI Global. doi:10.4018/978-1-5225-1639-2.ch003

Jena, G. C. (2017). Multi-Sensor Data Fusion (MSDF). In N. Ray & A. Turuk (Eds.), *Handbook of Research on Advanced Wireless Sensor Network Applications, Protocols, and Architectures* (pp. 29–61). Hershey, PA: IGI Global. doi:10.4018/978-1-5225-0486-3.ch002

Kale, G. V., & Patil, V. H. (2016). A Study of Vision based Human Motion Recognition and Analysis. *International Journal of Ambient Computing and Intelligence*, 7(2), 75–92. doi:10.4018/IJACI.2016070104

Kasemsap, K. (2017). Mastering Intelligent Decision Support Systems in Enterprise Information Management. In G. Sreedhar (Ed.), *Web Data Mining and the Development of Knowledge-Based Decision Support Systems* (pp. 35–56). Hershey, PA: IGI Global. doi:10.4018/978-1-5225-1877-8.ch004

Kim, S. (2017). New Game Paradigm for IoT Systems. In *Game Theory Solutions for the Internet of Things: Emerging Research and Opportunities* (pp. 101–147). Hershey, PA: IGI Global. doi:10.4018/978-1-5225-1952-2.ch004

Ladjailia, A., Bouchrika, I., Harrati, N., & Mahfouf, Z. (2017). Encoding Human Motion for Automated Activity Recognition in Surveillance Applications. In N. Dey, A. Ashour, & S. Acharjee (Eds.), *Applied Video Processing in Surveillance and Monitoring Systems* (pp. 170–192). Hershey, PA: IGI Global. doi:10.4018/978-1-5225-1022-2.ch008

Lanza, J., Sotres, P., Sánchez, L., Galache, J. A., Santana, J. R., Gutiérrez, V., & Muñoz, L. (2016). Managing Large Amounts of Data Generated by a Smart City Internet of Things Deployment. *International Journal on Semantic Web and Information Systems*, *12*(4), 22–42. doi:10.4018/IJSWIS.2016100102

Lee, H. (2017). The Internet of Things and Assistive Technologies for People with Disabilities: Applications, Trends, and Issues. In C. Reis & M. Maximiano (Eds.), *Internet of Things and Advanced Application in Healthcare* (pp. 32–65). Hershey, PA: IGI Global. doi:10.4018/978-1-5225-1820-4.ch002

Li, W. H., Zhu, K., & Fu, H. (2017). Exploring the Design Space of Bezel-Initiated Gestures for Mobile Interaction. *International Journal of Mobile Human Computer Interaction*, *9*(1), 16–29. doi:10.4018/IJMHCI.2017010102

Ludwig, T., Kotthaus, C., & Pipek, V. (2015). Should I Try Turning It Off and On Again?: Outlining HCI Challenges for Cyber-Physical Production Systems. *International Journal of Information Systems for Crisis Response and Management*, *7*(3), 55–68. doi:10.4018/ijiscram.2015070104

Luo, L., Kiewra, K. A., Peteranetz, M. S., & Flanigan, A. E. (2017). Using Eye-Tracking Technology to Understand How Graphic Organizers Aid Student Learning. In C. Was, F. Sansosti, & B. Morris (Eds.), *Eye-Tracking Technology Applications in Educational Research* (pp. 220–238). Hershey, PA: IGI Global. doi:10.4018/978-1-5225-1005-5.ch011

Mahanty, R., & Mahanti, P. K. (2016). Unleashing Artificial Intelligence onto Big Data: A Review. In S. Dash & B. Subudhi (Eds.), *Handbook of Research on Computational Intelligence Applications in Bioinformatics* (pp. 1–16). Hershey, PA: IGI Global. doi:10.4018/978-1-5225-0427-6.ch001

Marzuki, A. (2017). CMOS Image Sensor: Analog and Mixed-Signal Circuits. In O. Sergiyenko & J. Rodriguez-Quiñonez (Eds.), *Developing and Applying Optoelectronics in Machine Vision* (pp. 38–78). Hershey, PA: IGI Global. doi:10.4018/978-1-5225-0632-4.ch002

McKenna, H. P. (2017). Urbanizing the Ambient: Why People Matter So Much in Smart Cities. In S. Konomi & G. Roussos (Eds.), *Enriching Urban Spaces with Ambient Computing, the Internet of Things, and Smart City Design* (pp. 209–231). Hershey, PA: IGI Global. doi:10.4018/978-1-5225-0827-4.ch011

Meghanathan, N. (2017). Diameter-Aggregation Delay Tradeoff for Data Gathering Trees in Wireless Sensor Networks. In N. Kamila (Ed.), *Handbook of Research on Wireless Sensor Network Trends, Technologies, and Applications* (pp. 237–253). Hershey, PA: IGI Global. doi:10.4018/978-1-5225-0501-3.ch010

Moein, S. (2014). Artificial Intelligence in Medical Science. In *Medical Diagnosis Using Artificial Neural Networks* (pp. 11–23). Hershey, PA: IGI Global. doi:10.4018/978-1-4666-6146-2.ch002

Moein, S. (2014). Artificial Neural Network for Medical Diagnosis. In *Medical Diagnosis Using Artificial Neural Networks* (pp. 85–94). Hershey, PA: IGI Global. doi:10.4018/978-1-4666-6146-2.ch007

Moein, S. (2014). Types of Artificial Neural Network. In *Medical Diagnosis Using Artificial Neural Networks* (pp. 58–67). Hershey, PA: IGI Global. doi:10.4018/978-1-4666-6146-2.ch005

Moser, S. (2017). Linking Virtual and Real-life Environments: Scrutinizing Ubiquitous Learning Scenarios. In S. Şad & M. Ebner (Eds.), *Digital Tools for Seamless Learning* (pp. 214–239). Hershey, PA: IGI Global. doi:10.4018/978-1-5225-1692-7.ch011

Mumini, O. O., Adebisi, F. M., Edward, O. O., & Abidemi, A. S. (2016). Simulation of Stock Prediction System using Artificial Neural Networks. *International Journal of Business Analytics*, *3*(3), 25–44. doi:10.4018/IJBAN.2016070102

Muñoz, M. C., & Moh, M. (2017). Authentication of Smart Grid: The Case for Using Merkle Trees. In M. Ferrag & A. Ahmim (Eds.), *Security Solutions and Applied Cryptography in Smart Grid Communications* (pp. 117–136). Hershey, PA: IGI Global. doi:10.4018/978-1-5225-1829-7.ch007

Mushcab, H., Kernohan, W. G., Wallace, J., Harper, R., & Martin, S. (2017). Self-Management of Diabetes Mellitus with Remote Monitoring: A Retrospective Review of 214 Cases. *International Journal of E-Health and Medical Communications*, *8*(1), 52–61. doi:10.4018/IJEHMC.2017010104

Mutlu-Bayraktar, D. (2017). Usability Evaluation of Social Media Web Sites and Applications via Eye-Tracking Method. In S. Hai-Jew (Ed.), *Social Media Data Extraction and Content Analysis* (pp. 85–112). Hershey, PA: IGI Global. doi:10.4018/978-1-5225-0648-5.ch004

Nadler, S. (2017). Mobile Location Tracking: Indoor and Outdoor Location Tracking. In S. Mukherjea (Ed.), *Mobile Application Development, Usability, and Security* (pp. 194–209). Hershey, PA: IGI Global. doi:10.4018/978-1-5225-0945-5.ch009

Nagpal, R., Mehrotra, D., & Bhatia, P. K. (2017). The State of Art in Website Usability Evaluation Methods. In S. Saeed, Y. Bamarouf, T. Ramayah, & S. Iqbal (Eds.), *Design Solutions for User-Centric Information Systems* (pp. 275–296). Hershey, PA: IGI Global. doi:10.4018/978-1-5225-1944-7.ch015

Nava, J., & Osorio, A. (2016). A Hybrid Intelligent Risk Identification Model for Configuration Management in Aerospace Systems. In A. Ochoa-Zezzatti, J. Sánchez, M. Cedillo-Campos, & M. de Lourdes (Eds.), *Handbook of Research on Military, Aeronautical, and Maritime Logistics and Operations* (pp. 319–345). Hershey, PA: IGI Global. doi:10.4018/978-1-4666-9779-9.ch017

Nazareth, A., Odean, R., & Pruden, S. M. (2017). The Use of Eye-Tracking in Spatial Thinking Research. In C. Was, F. Sansosti, & B. Morris (Eds.), *Eye-Tracking Technology Applications in Educational Research* (pp. 239–260). Hershey, PA: IGI Global. doi:10.4018/978-1-5225-1005-5.ch012

Neves, J., Zeleznikow, J., & Vicente, H. (2016). Quality of Judgment Assessment. In P. Novais & D. Carneiro (Eds.), *Interdisciplinary Perspectives on Contemporary Conflict Resolution* (pp. 96–110). Hershey, PA: IGI Global. doi:10.4018/978-1-5225-0245-6.ch006

Niewiadomski, R., & Anderson, D. (2017). The Rise of Artificial Intelligence: Its Impact on Labor Market and Beyond. In R. Batko & A. Szopa (Eds.), *Strategic Imperatives and Core Competencies in the Era of Robotics and Artificial Intelligence* (pp. 29–49). Hershey, PA: IGI Global. doi:10.4018/978-1-5225-1656-9.ch003

Nishani, L., & Biba, M. (2017). Statistical Relational Learning for Collaborative Filtering a State-of-the-Art Review. In V. Bhatnagar (Ed.), *Collaborative Filtering Using Data Mining and Analysis* (pp. 250–269). Hershey, PA: IGI Global. doi:10.4018/978-1-5225-0489-4.ch014

Ogata, T. (2016). Computational and Cognitive Approaches to Narratology from the Perspective of Narrative Generation. In T. Ogata & T. Akimoto (Eds.), *Computational and Cognitive Approaches to Narratology* (pp. 1–74). Hershey, PA: IGI Global. doi:10.4018/978-1-5225-0432-0.ch001

Ozpinar, A., & Kucukasci, E. S. (2016). Use of Chaotic Randomness Numbers: Metaheuristic and Artificial Intelligence Algorithms. In N. Celebi (Ed.), *Intelligent Techniques for Data Analysis in Diverse Settings* (pp. 207–227). Hershey, PA: IGI Global. doi:10.4018/978-1-5225-0075-9.ch010

Ozpinar, A., & Ozil, E. (2016). Smart Grid and Demand Side Management: Application of Metaheuristic and Artificial Intelligence Algorithms. In A. Ahmad & N. Hassan (Eds.), *Smart Grid as a Solution for Renewable and Efficient Energy* (pp. 49–68). Hershey, PA: IGI Global. doi:10.4018/978-1-5225-0072-8.ch003

Papadopoulos, H. (2016). Designing Smart Home Environments for Unobtrusive Monitoring for Independent Living: The Use Case of USEFIL. *International Journal of E-Services and Mobile Applications*, 8(1), 47–63. doi:10.4018/IJESMA.2016010104

Papadopoulos, H. (2016). Modeling Place: Usage of Mobile Data Services and Applications within Different Places. *International Journal of E-Services and Mobile Applications*, 8(2), 1–20. doi:10.4018/IJESMA.2016040101

Parey, A., & Ahuja, A. S. (2016). Application of Artificial Intelligence to Gearbox Fault Diagnosis: A Review. In S. John (Ed.), *Handbook of Research on Generalized and Hybrid Set Structures and Applications for Soft Computing* (pp. 536–562). Hershey, PA: IGI Global. doi:10.4018/978-1-4666-9798-0.ch024

Parikh, C. (2017). Eye-Tracking Technology: A Closer Look at Eye-Tracking Paradigms with High-Risk Populations. In C. Was, F. Sansosti, & B. Morris (Eds.), *Eye-Tracking Technology Applications in Educational Research* (pp. 283–302). Hershey, PA: IGI Global. doi:10.4018/978-1-5225-1005-5.ch014

Peng, M., Qin, Y., Tang, C., & Deng, X. (2016). An E-Commerce Customer Service Robot Based on Intention Recognition Model. *Journal of Electronic Commerce in Organizations*, 14(1), 34–44. doi:10.4018/JECO.2016010104

Pessoa, C. R., & Júnior, M. D. (2017). A Telecommunications Approach in Systems for Effective Logistics and Supply Chains. In G. Jamil, A. Soares, & C. Pessoa (Eds.), *Handbook of Research on Information Management for Effective Logistics and Supply Chains* (pp. 437–452). Hershey, PA: IGI Global. doi:10.4018/978-1-5225-0973-8.ch023

Pineda, R. G. (2016). Where the Interaction Is Not: Reflections on the Philosophy of Human-Computer Interaction. *International Journal of Art, Culture and Design Technologies*, 5(1), 1–12. doi:10.4018/IJACDT.2016010101

Poitras, E. G., Harley, J. M., Compeau, T., Kee, K., & Lajoie, S. P. (2017). Augmented Reality in Informal Learning Settings: Leveraging Technology for the Love of History. In R. Zheng & M. Gardner (Eds.), *Handbook of Research on Serious Games for Educational Applications* (pp. 272–293). Hershey, PA: IGI Global. doi:10.4018/978-1-5225-0513-6.ch013

Powell, W. A., Corbett, N., & Powell, V. (2016). The Rise of the Virtual Human. In A. Connor & S. Marks (Eds.), *Creative Technologies for Multidisciplinary Applications* (pp. 99–129). Hershey, PA: IGI Global. doi:10.4018/978-1-5225-0016-2.ch005

Prakash, L. S., & Saini, D. K. (2017). Instructional Design Technology in Higher Education System: Role and Impact on Developing Creative Learning Environments. In C. Zhou (Ed.), *Handbook of Research on Creative Problem-Solving Skill Development in Higher Education* (pp. 378–406). Hershey, PA: IGI Global. doi:10.4018/978-1-5225-0643-0.ch017

Rahmani, M. E., Amine, A., & Hamou, R. M. (2016). Supervised Machine Learning for Plants Identification Based on Images of Their Leaves. *International Journal of Agricultural and Environmental Information Systems*, 7(4), 17–31. doi:10.4018/IJAEIS.2016100102

Ramanathan, U. (2017). How Smart Operations Help Better Planning and Replenishment?: Empirical Study – Supply Chain Collaboration for Smart Operations. In H. Chan, N. Subramanian, & M. Abdulrahman (Eds.), *Supply Chain Management in the Big Data Era* (pp. 25–49). Hershey, PA: IGI Global. doi:10.4018/978-1-5225-0956-1.ch003

Rao, M., & Kamila, N. K. (2017). Target Tracking in Wireless Sensor Network: The Current State of Art. In N. Kamila (Ed.), *Handbook of Research on Wireless Sensor Network Trends, Technologies, and Applications* (pp. 413–437). Hershey, PA: IGI Global. doi:10.4018/978-1-5225-0501-3.ch017

Rappaport, J. M., Richter, S. B., & Kennedy, D. T. (2016). A Strategic Perspective on Using Symbolic Transformation in STEM Education: Robotics and Automation. *International Journal of Strategic Decision Sciences*, 7(1), 39–75. doi:10.4018/IJSDS.2016010103

Rashid, E. (2016). R4 Model for Case-Based Reasoning and Its Application for Software Fault Prediction. *International Journal of Software Science and Computational Intelligence*, 8(3), 19–38. doi:10.4018/IJSSCI.2016070102

Rathore, M. M., Paul, A., Ahmad, A., & Jeon, G. (2017). IoT-Based Big Data: From Smart City towards Next Generation Super City Planning. *International Journal on Semantic Web and Information Systems*, *13*(1), 28–47. doi:10.4018/IJSWIS.2017010103

Reeberg de Mello, A., & Stemmer, M. R. (2017). Automated Visual Inspection System for Printed Circuit Boards for Small Series Production: A Multiagent Context Approach. In O. Sergiyenko & J. Rodriguez-Quiñonez (Eds.), *Developing and Applying Optoelectronics in Machine Vision* (pp. 79–107). Hershey, PA: IGI Global. doi:10.4018/978-1-5225-0632-4.ch003

Rodrigues, P., & Rosa, P. J. (2017). Eye-Tracking as a Research Methodology in Educational Context: A Spanning Framework. In C. Was, F. Sansosti, & B. Morris (Eds.), *Eye-Tracking Technology Applications in Educational Research* (pp. 1–26). Hershey, PA: IGI Global. doi:10.4018/978-1-5225-1005-5.ch001

Rosen, Y., & Mosharraf, M. (2016). Computer Agent Technologies in Collaborative Assessments. In Y. Rosen, S. Ferrara, & M. Mosharraf (Eds.), *Handbook of Research on Technology Tools for Real-World Skill Development* (pp. 319–343). Hershey, PA: IGI Global. doi:10.4018/978-1-4666-9441-5.ch012

Rosenzweig, E. D., & Bendoly, E. (2017). An Investigation of Competitor Networks in Manufacturing Strategy and Implications for Performance. In A. Vlachvei, O. Notta, K. Karantininis, & N. Tsounis (Eds.), *Factors Affecting Firm Competitiveness and Performance in the Modern Business World* (pp. 43–82). Hershey, PA: IGI Global. doi:10.4018/978-1-5225-0843-4.ch002

S., J. R., & Omman, B. (2017). A Technical Assessment on License Plate Detection System. In M. S., & V. V. (Eds.), *Multi-Core Computer Vision and Image Processing for Intelligent Applications* (pp. 234-258). Hershey, PA: IGI Global. doi:10.4018/978-1-5225-0889-2.ch009

Saiz-Alvarez, J. M., & Leal, G. C. (2017). Cybersecurity Best Practices and Cultural Change in Global Business: Some Perspectives from the European Union. In G. Afolayan & A. Akinwale (Eds.), *Global Perspectives on Development Administration and Cultural Change* (pp. 48–73). Hershey, PA: IGI Global. doi:10.4018/978-1-5225-0629-4.ch003

Sang, Y., Zhu, Y., Zhao, H., & Tang, M. (2016). Study on an Interactive Truck Crane Simulation Platform Based on Virtual Reality Technology. *International Journal of Distance Education Technologies, 14*(2), 64–78. doi:10.4018/IJDET.2016040105

Sarkar, D., & Roy, J. K. (2016). Artificial Neural Network (ANN) in Network Reconfiguration for Improvement of Voltage Stability. In S. Shandilya, S. Shandilya, T. Thakur, & A. Nagar (Eds.), *Handbook of Research on Emerging Technologies for Electrical Power Planning, Analysis, and Optimization* (pp. 184–206). Hershey, PA: IGI Global. doi:10.4018/978-1-4666-9911-3.ch010

Schafer, S. B. (2016). The Media-Sphere as Dream: Researching the Contextual Unconscious of Collectives. In S. Schafer (Ed.), *Exploring the Collective Unconscious in the Age of Digital Media* (pp. 232–260). Hershey, PA: IGI Global. doi:10.4018/978-1-4666-9891-8.ch010

Scheiter, K., & Eitel, A. (2017). The Use of Eye Tracking as a Research and Instructional Tool in Multimedia Learning. In C. Was, F. Sansosti, & B. Morris (Eds.), *Eye-Tracking Technology Applications in Educational Research* (pp. 143–164). Hershey, PA: IGI Global. doi:10.4018/978-1-5225-1005-5.ch008

Schneegass, S., Olsson, T., Mayer, S., & van Laerhoven, K. (2016). Mobile Interactions Augmented by Wearable Computing: A Design Space and Vision. *International Journal of Mobile Human Computer Interaction, 8*(4), 104–114. doi:10.4018/IJMHCI.2016100106

Shah, Z., & Kolhe, A. (2017). Throughput Analysis of IEEE 802.11ac and IEEE 802.11n in a Residential Home Environment. *International Journal of Interdisciplinary Telecommunications and Networking, 9*(1), 1–13. doi:10.4018/IJITN.2017010101

Shaqrah, A. A. (2016). Future of Smart Cities in the Knowledge-based Urban Development and the Role of Award Competitions. *International Journal of Knowledge-Based Organizations, 6*(1), 49–59. doi:10.4018/IJKBO.2016010104

Shayan, S., Abrahamson, D., Bakker, A., Duijzer, C. A., & van der Schaaf, M. (2017). Eye-Tracking the Emergence of Attentional Anchors in a Mathematics Learning Tablet Activity. In C. Was, F. Sansosti, & B. Morris (Eds.), *Eye-Tracking Technology Applications in Educational Research* (pp. 166–194). Hershey, PA: IGI Global. doi:10.4018/978-1-5225-1005-5.ch009

Sosnin, P. I. (2017). Conceptual Experiments in Automated Designing. In R. Zuanon (Ed.), *Projective Processes and Neuroscience in Art and Design* (pp. 155–181). Hershey, PA: IGI Global. doi:10.4018/978-1-5225-0510-5.ch010

Starostenko, O., Cruz-Perez, C., Alarcon-Aquino, V., Melnik, V. I., & Tyrsa, V. (2017). Machine Vision Application on Science and Industry: Real-Time Face Sensing and Recognition in Machine Vision – Trends and New Advances. In O. Sergiyenko & J. Rodriguez-Quiñonez (Eds.), *Developing and Applying Optoelectronics in Machine Vision* (pp. 146–179). Hershey, PA: IGI Global. doi:10.4018/978-1-5225-0632-4.ch005

Stasolla, F., Boccasini, A., & Perilli, V. (2017). Assistive Technology-Based Programs to Support Adaptive Behaviors by Children with Autism Spectrum Disorders: A Literature Overview. In Y. Kats (Ed.), *Supporting the Education of Children with Autism Spectrum Disorders* (pp. 140–159). Hershey, PA: IGI Global. doi:10.4018/978-1-5225-0816-8.ch008

Stratigea, A., Leka, A., & Panagiotopoulou, M. (2017). In Search of Indicators for Assessing Smart and Sustainable Cities and Communities Performance. *International Journal of E-Planning Research*, 6(1), 43–73. doi:10.4018/IJEPR.2017010103

Su, S., Lin, H. K., Wang, C., & Huang, Z. (2016). Multi-Modal Affective Computing Technology Design the Interaction between Computers and Human of Intelligent Tutoring Systems. *International Journal of Online Pedagogy and Course Design*, 6(1), 13–28. doi:10.4018/IJOPCD.2016010102

Sun, X., May, A., & Wang, Q. (2017). Investigation of the Role of Mobile Personalisation at Large Sports Events. *International Journal of Mobile Human Computer Interaction*, 9(1), 1–15. doi:10.4018/IJMHCI.2017010101

Szopa, A. (2017). The Influence of Crowdsourcing Business Model into Artificial Intelligence. In R. Batko & A. Szopa (Eds.), *Strategic Imperatives and Core Competencies in the Era of Robotics and Artificial Intelligence* (pp. 15–28). Hershey, PA: IGI Global. doi:10.4018/978-1-5225-1656-9.ch002

Tokunaga, S., Tamamizu, K., Saiki, S., Nakamura, M., & Yasuda, K. (2017). VirtualCareGiver: Personalized Smart Elderly Care. *International Journal of Software Innovation*, 5(1), 30–43. doi:10.4018/IJSI.2017010103

Trabelsi, I., & Bouhlel, M. S. (2016). Comparison of Several Acoustic Modeling Techniques for Speech Emotion Recognition. *International Journal of Synthetic Emotions*, 7(1), 58–68. doi:10.4018/IJSE.2016010105

Truman, B. (2017). New Constructions for Understanding using Virtual Learning- Towards Transdisciplinarity. In A. Stricker, C. Calongne, B. Truman, & F. Arenas (Eds.), *Integrating an Awareness of Selfhood and Society into Virtual Learning* (pp. 316–334). Hershey, PA: IGI Global. doi:10.4018/978-1-5225-2182-2.ch019

Turner, J. O. (2016). Virtual Soar-Agent Implementations: Examples, Issues, and Speculations. In J. Turner, M. Nixon, U. Bernardet, & S. DiPaola (Eds.), *Integrating Cognitive Architectures into Virtual Character Design* (pp. 181–212). Hershey, PA: IGI Global. doi:10.4018/978-1-5225-0454-2.ch007

Urrea, C., & Uren, V. (2017). Technical Evaluation, Development, and Implementation of a Remote Monitoring System for a Golf Cart. In N. Dey, A. Ashour, & S. Acharjee (Eds.), *Applied Video Processing in Surveillance and Monitoring Systems* (pp. 220–243). Hershey, PA: IGI Global. doi:10.4018/978-1-5225-1022-2.ch010

Veerapathiran, N., & Anand, S. (2017). Reducing False Alarms in Vision-Based Fire Detection. In N. Dey, A. Ashour, & S. Acharjee (Eds.), *Applied Video Processing in Surveillance and Monitoring Systems* (pp. 263–290). Hershey, PA: IGI Global. doi:10.4018/978-1-5225-1022-2.ch012

Vorraber, W., Lichtenegger, G., Brugger, J., Gojmerac, I., Egly, M., Panzenböck, K., & Voessner, S. et al. (2016). Designing Information Systems to Facilitate Civil-Military Cooperation in Disaster Management. *International Journal of Distributed Systems and Technologies*, 7(4), 22–40. doi:10.4018/IJDST.2016100102

Vyas, D., Kröner, A., & Nijholt, A. (2016). From Mundane to Smart: Exploring Interactions with Smart Design Objects. *International Journal of Mobile Human Computer Interaction*, 8(1), 59–82. doi:10.4018/IJMHCI.2016010103

Wang, L., Li, C., & Wu, J. (2017). The Status of Research into Intention Recognition. In J. Wu (Ed.), *Improving the Quality of Life for Dementia Patients through Progressive Detection, Treatment, and Care* (pp. 201–221). Hershey, PA: IGI Global. doi:10.4018/978-1-5225-0925-7.ch010

Wang, Y., Valipour, M., & Zatarain, O. A. (2016). Quantitative Semantic Analysis and Comprehension by Cognitive Machine Learning. *International Journal of Cognitive Informatics and Natural Intelligence*, 10(3), 13–28. doi:10.4018/IJCINI.2016070102

Xie, L., Zheng, L., & Yang, G. (2017). Hybrid Integration Technology for Wearable Sensor Systems. In C. Reis & M. Maximiano (Eds.), *Internet of Things and Advanced Application in Healthcare* (pp. 98–137). Hershey, PA: IGI Global. doi:10.4018/978-1-5225-1820-4.ch004

Xing, B., & Gao, W. (2014). Overview of Computational Intelligence. In *Computational Intelligence in Remanufacturing* (pp. 18–36). Hershey, PA: IGI Global. doi:10.4018/978-1-4666-4908-8.ch002

Xu, R., Li, Z., Cui, P., Zhu, S., & Gao, A. (2016). A Geometric Dynamic Temporal Reasoning Method with Tags for Cognitive Systems. *International Journal of Software Science and Computational Intelligence*, 8(4), 43–59. doi:10.4018/IJSSCI.2016100103

Yamaguchi, T., Nishimura, T., & Takadama, K. (2016). Awareness Based Recommendation: Passively Interactive Learning System. *International Journal of Robotics Applications and Technologies*, 4(1), 83–99. doi:10.4018/ IJRAT.2016010105

Zentall, S. R., & Junglen, A. G. (2017). Investigating Mindsets and Motivation through Eye Tracking and Other Physiological Measures. In C. Was, F. Sansosti, & B. Morris (Eds.), *Eye-Tracking Technology Applications in Educational Research* (pp. 48–64). Hershey, PA: IGI Global. doi:10.4018/978-1-5225-1005-5.ch003

Zielinska, T. (2016). Professional and Personal Service Robots. *International Journal of Robotics Applications and Technologies*, 4(1), 63–82. doi:10.4018/ IJRAT.2016010104

Zohora, S. E., Khan, A. M., Srivastava, A. K., Nguyen, N. G., & Dey, N. (2016). A Study of the State of the Art in Synthetic Emotional Intelligence in Affective Computing. *International Journal of Synthetic Emotions*, 7(1), 1–12. doi:10.4018/IJSE.2016010101

Index

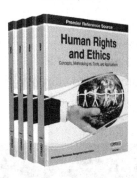
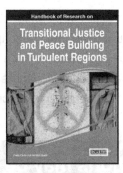
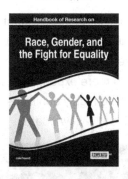

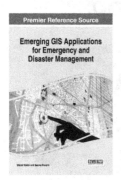
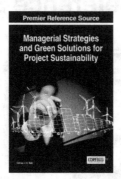

Become an IRMA Member

Members of the **Information Resources Management Association (IRMA)** understand the importance of community within their field of study. The Information Resources Management Association is an ideal venue through which professionals, students, and academicians can convene and share the latest industry innovations and scholarly research that is changing the field of information science and technology. Become a member today and enjoy the benefits of membership as well as the opportunity to collaborate and network with fellow experts in the field.

IRMA Membership Benefits:

- **One FREE Journal Subscription**
- **30% Off Additional Journal Subscriptions**
- **20% Off Book Purchases**
- Updates on the latest events and research on Information Resources Management through the IRMA-L listserv.
- Updates on new open access and downloadable content added to Research IRM.
- A copy of the Information Technology Management Newsletter twice a year.
- A certificate of membership.

IRMA Membership $195

Scan code or visit **irma-international.org** and begin by selecting your free journal subscription.

Membership is good for one full year.

Printed in the United States
By Bookmasters